Investing in
Income Properties

Investing in Income Properties

THE BIG SIX FORMULA FOR ACHIEVING WEALTH IN REAL ESTATE

Kenneth D. Rosen

WILEY

John Wiley & Sons, Inc.

Published by John Wiley & Sons, Inc., Hoboken, New Jersey.
Published simultaneously in Canada.

For general information on our other products and services or for technical support, please contact our Customer Care Department within the United States at (800) 762–2974, outside the United States at (317) 572–3993 or fax (317) 572–4002.

Wiley also publishes its books in a variety of electronic formats. Some content that appears in print may not be available in electronic books. For more information about Wiley products, visit our web site at www.wiley.com.

Library of Congress Cataloging-in-Publication Data:

Rosen, Kenneth D.
   Investing in income properties : the big six formula for achieving wealth in real estate / Kenneth D. Rosen.
     p. cm.
   Includes index.
   ISBN 978-0-470-19083-8 (cloth)
     1. Commercial real estate—United States. 2. Real estate investment— United States. I. Title.
HD1393.58.U6R67   2008
332.63'24—dc22

                                               2008004972

Printed in the United States of America

10 9 8 7 6 5 4 3 2 1

To Ellen with love,
for her abiding faith and confidence in me

Contents

Acknowledgments

As you read this book, you'll understand how important it is to assemble the right team to help you with your real estate investments. The right team was also crucial in the writing of this book, and I am most grateful to all those who shared their expertise, advice, and inspiration as this project unfolded.

I am especially grateful to my personal editor, Mary Dempsey, who worked tirelessly day and night. Without her, this book would not have been possible. Mitch Chefitz planted the seed for the book, and Bill Falloon at John Wiley & Sons made sure it saw water and sunshine. Many thanks to Taylor Larimore for recommending me to Bill, and to Emilie Herman, Laura Walsh, and Christina Verigan at John Wiley & Sons for their editing and excellent follow-up work.

I regret that two friends, my mentor David Probinsky, who always was an inspiration, and Philip A. Thomas, who shared a depth of knowledge and wisdom with me, did not live to see this book's publication. Their impact on my career was considerable.

Dick Weiner, who recommended Mary Dempsey to me, also served as my sounding board, coach, and confidant, and he kept me on track. Jason Krieger, a skilled wordsmith and my technology connection, burned the midnight oil with me on more than one occasion. My longtime attorney Joe Reisman has offered his wise counsel throughout my career.

I would be remiss if I did not acknowledge the many other colleagues and friends who helped me bring this book to fruition. They include: Chris Amarger, Gina Anderhub, Alicia Baro, Steve Bernstein, Jorge Cantero, Jeff Cohen, David Dabby, Rosie DeRosa, Tony DeRosa, Anthony Dilweg, Tom Dixon, Bob Gallaher, Jose Gaviria, Bobby Glick, Julian Goldstein, Sandra Goldstein, Phil Leitman, Hal Lewis, Joe Martinez, Ed Mazzei, Ted Pappas, Jim Pollack, Andy Roberts, Britt Rosen, Ritchie Lucas, Al Sherman, Saul Silverman, Scott Sime, Herbert Lee Simon, Ashley Socarras, Debra Spadafora, Cliff Suchman, Bob Valledor, Martin Waas, Paul White, and Ana Vega-Garcia.

Investing in
Income Properties

Introduction

The country is in an economic crisis, primarily because of the collapse of the housing market. This has caused tremendous financial losses in the stock market and the banking industry. In mid-March 2008, Standard & Poor's issued a statement estimating that write-downs for large financial institutions on subprime debt would hit $285 billion ("Subprime Write-Downs Could Reach $285 Billion, But Are Likely Past The Halfway Mark," March 13, 2008, on S&P's Web-based data service Ratings Direct). But this does not represent the end of the housing market in this country. It will eventually come back, and when it does, it may be stronger than ever.

Good quality income properties in top locations remain vibrant and healthy – and these are the kinds of properties that I spotlight in this book. They comprise apartment buildings, small shopping centers, office buildings, and industrial properties.

As far back as I can remember, the demand for top-grade properties has always exceeded the supply – and it is no different today than it has been in the past. These types of properties are hard to find because only a small percentage of owners will sell them. However, buying one of these top-grade properties does not guarantee that you will make money. That will come from those properties among them that meet the Big Six criteria, which is the focus of this book. The Big Six is a formula that I developed many years ago. Using it will virtually ensure your success and bring you great wealth, just as it has done for me.

I started my own career with nothing, and over the past 30 years I have bought and sold $300 million in income-producing real estate. It was because of my drive and adherence to the Big Six formula that I eventually became financially independent. I am going to share with you the strategies and techniques that brought me success throughout my career. And I will also tell you about my setbacks. By the time you finish reading this book you will have the tools to achieve your own success—most likely in a shorter period of time than it took me.

I realize that this book will be read by a wide spectrum of people, including investors and potential investors, some with a small amount of cash to invest and others with substantial financial resources. I will be principally dealing with income properties in the price range of $500,000 to $5 million. Additionally, I will be using the terms *income properties* and *commercial properties*. They are synonymous, as are *net operating income* and *net income.*

The public and the media think of real estate as homes and condominiums, but real estate is much more than that. The best kept secret in America is that fortunes are being made every day in income-producing real estate—not just by the rich, but by people who started off buying little apartment buildings, neighborhood shopping centers, small office buildings, and clusters of small warehouses. They started investing in a single $500,000 building, with as little as $50,000 to $100,000 in cash, and then began to buy more and more buildings.

Ride up and down any street in the country and observe the small commercial buildings that dot the American landscape. These buildings are not owned by real estate moguls but by entrepreneurial people who got the bug to become owners of income-producing real estate. They knew that commercial properties would give them far more impressive returns—and with less risk—than any other type of investment. Their goal? To become wealthy enough to live the lives of their dreams without having to work.

The book is divided into three parts. The first part reviews the basics and how to get started. It explores how income-producing real estate is superior to other investments. Most people have fears of investing in the commercial real estate market because it is unknown territory for them. I outline how to overcome those fears. And it is in this part of the book that we explore how to assemble the cash resources you'll need and where you can find the most effective educational resources as you work to become a savvy investor.

Also in the first part of the book, you will learn how to bring together a first-rate team of professionals to provide needed expertise and counsel regarding your real estate investments. Among them are the right real estate broker, attorney, and accountant. Each will prove invaluable in helping you build a portfolio of wise investments.

New investors, as well as those unhappy with the results of their past investments, should spend time soaking up the lessons provided in the opening pages. Experienced investors may know a lot about the basics, but a review can reveal new insight. As with a good golfer or tennis player, it pays to revisit the fundamentals.

In the second section of the book, I detail the criteria for identifying the right buildings to buy. These chapters contain the most important advice you'll ever receive, including how to finance deals with the most leverage and the best rates of return. Adherence to the Big Six formula will build your equity, cut your income taxes, and help you escalate the return on your investment. My play-by-play examples of Big Six transactions demonstrate the fine points of negotiating price and revenue considerations. They will help you understand exactly how each element of the Big Six meshes with the other components for a no-fail deal.

The third part of the book focuses on moving forward with your investment after you have closed the deal. There are many people who have never invested in commercial real estate because they say that they don't want to become landlords. They don't have to! Most successful investors do not personally manage their own properties. What most investors do is to hire a professional management and leasing company that handles everything for them. The cost of hiring such a firm usually pays for itself. Professional managers know the market inside and out and can, in many cases, increase income and reduce expenses.

The conversions of large rental apartment complexes to condominiums were the craze from 2003 until 2007. Hundreds of thousands of units were converted to condos. This came to a virtual dead end in 2007. However, when one door closes, another door opens. In the next-to-last chapter of the book, you will learn about the incredible amounts of money that can be made—with virtually no risk—via condo conversions of small apartment buildings.

"One Good Investment Is Worth a Lifetime of Labor," is the title of the closing chapter of the book. This is where you will read the personal stories of six investors, each of whom became a multimillionaire from just one investment. They all started with very little money of their own.

Throughout this book I will refer to the fact that you make your money in buying—and I'll tell you why. I will also emphasize that, if you adhere to the Big Six formula, you can, within a relatively short period of time, continually increase your rate of return—to 10 percent, 20 percent, 50 percent, 100 percent, 1,000 percent, and eventually to an infinity return, which is the ultimate goal of any investor. An infinity return is so great that it is immeasurable and incalculable.

This book is designed so that you will understand what it takes to become a successful real estate investor. You won't do it overnight or by being lucky. But you will be successful if you put into action the principles and strategies of the Big Six, which will give you the tools you need. The road to riches is open to you. Seize the moment—and enjoy the journey.

PART

I

THE BASICS

A notable portion of the population has been through at least one real estate negotiation—buying a home—and many have changed their residences more than once. Despite that, too often people don't understand the nuts and bolts of a real estate deal. That's not entirely their fault. Real estate is not taught on a regular basis in high schools or many universities. And, in recent years, financing tools have changed dramatically. Now there are many different kinds of mortgages and a long laundry list of mortgage terms. On top of that, there is an abundance of real estate advice floating around, much of it misleading or just plain incorrect.

In the case of commercial real estate investment, the old adage is wrong, because what you don't know *can* hurt you. Fortunately it's not hard to learn the fundamental principles of how real estate transactions take place and the terms used within the industry. (The glossary at the end of this book can help.) Easy as it may be to learn, however, you won't pick up the essentials when you're already in the middle of a deal. It is imperative that you have a grasp of real estate basics *before* you get going on your own investment portfolio.

The most important part of this book is the Big Six formula, the core concepts that will put you on the path to riches. However, before we jump into that formula for success, we're going to review the nitty–gritty of buying properties, the terminology you'll need to understand, and other essential workings within the world of real estate investment. Chapters 1 through 4 tackle these, starting with an explanation of why real estate offers greater wealth-building opportunities—with much less risk—than stocks and other investment vehicles. We'll also look at the sequence of steps in a real estate deal, the expert professionals you'll need on your real estate team, and, finally, how you can access enough money to get started.

Certain investment elements—such as zoning laws, contractual agreements, and construction standards—will vary from state to state and even city to city. But the basics remain the same everywhere in the country. Before you risk your investment, take some time to clearly understand what you're doing. If you do, you've set your stage for success.

CHAPTER 1

Why Commercial Real Estate?

Americans work, work, and work. A study by the Economic Policy Institute shows that worker productivity in the United States has risen 33 percent over the past decade ("The State of Working America 2006/2007" by Lawrence Mishel, Jared Bernstein, and Sylvia Allegretto). Yet many Americans have little to show for it. Only a small percentage of people achieve financial independence by the time they retire. The rest spend their retirement years surviving on pensions and Social Security benefits. For younger Americans, even those often-inadequate safety nets are becoming precarious. Increasing numbers of companies are abandoning pension plans as an employee benefit, and the beleaguered Social Security system faces an uncertain future. Because of those realities, people must shift the way they think about the future. They must take the initiative to invest now in order to live the way they want later. Instead of working for their money, their money should be working for them.

Commercial real estate investment is a powerful way to make that happen. And it is easier than you think. In fact, if you can master just half a dozen important keystones to property investment—the Big Six formula—you can put yourself on the road to real estate success.

What you really need as you enter the world of commercial real estate is an understanding of how to make wise investments. This book will help you comprehend the ins and outs of a real estate deal, why finding the right property to buy is the most crucial part of your investment, what the Big Six formula is, and how you can

7

master its steps. Why real estate is the way to go and why too few people pursue this option is the focus of this chapter.

Real Value, Real Ownership, Real Estate

The goal of real estate investment is to increase your net worth, strengthen your income, and achieve financial independence so that, if you eventually choose, you can stop working and begin living the life of your dreams. Different people have different financial goals. You could aspire to a net worth of several million dollars with a very substantial annual cash flow. Your cash flow is the money remaining in your pocket after deducting operating expenses and mortgage payments from gross rental income. Or your goal may be to achieve a $1 million net worth with a more modest cash flow. It depends on your particular needs, wants, and circumstances. That said, all investors—regardless of their financial objectives—need to learn the same strategies for identifying and taking advantage of opportunities.

You may already be saying: "I don't have enough money to invest." This is a misconception. It's true that the majority of salaried workers or professionals, whether they make $50,000 or $1 million per year, spend most of it. Then-Federal Reserve Chairman Alan Greenspan created a stir when he told Congress that U.S. residents in 2004 saved only about 1 percent of their annual income ("Testimony of the Chairman Alan Greenspan at the Federal Reserve Board's Semiannual Monetary Policy Report to the Congress" before the Committee on Banking, Housing and Urban Affairs, U.S. Senate, Feb. 16, 2005). Since then, the statistics have become even more alarming. The personal savings rate has fallen below zero. This is the lowest rate since the Great Depression and one of the lowest of any country in the world. (By contrast, the personal savings rate in China is about 30 percent.) The upshot is that Americans live from paycheck to paycheck and borrow—usually with credit cards—to get through tight times.

That may not sound promising for would-be investors seeking to enter the real estate market. But those statistics hide something important: Although savings rates are falling, the net worth of many Americans has been rising, in part because their homes have increased in value and, in some cases, because stock market investments have stabilized. This means that even without savings, most people have assets that can be turned into cash to get them started investing in real estate. You may have money available without realizing it.

Real estate is not the only place to invest, but it holds advantages over other investments. The stock market is volatile. But the volatility of the market is what brings the biggest return on investment. The higher the volatility, the higher the rewards may be, although the risks are also higher (as is the potential for crushing losses). Many factors come into play in the stock market other than the performance of a corporation. World events can affect the market. Just think of what happened on Wall Street after the 9/11 terrorist attacks or how the market fluctuated wildly during the so-called Asian Crisis of 1987; also consider the more recent turmoil in the Mideast caused by the war in Iraq. One bit of news in one single day, either in this country or anywhere else in the world, can cause havoc in the stock market and horrendous losses. Not so with real estate.

Mutual funds may be promoted as a way to diversify investments and establish a "safe" portfolio. A lone mutual fund may hold securities in hundreds of companies, meaning it is less susceptible to a single company's problems. The funds may also allow people to begin their investment with as little as $500. But the value of a mutual fund fluctuates and it has no guaranteed return. Furthermore, because a mutual fund is tied to the performance of the stocks in the fund, it could depreciate in value. At the same time, the fees, sales commissions, and administrative costs for the funds can offset some potential returns.

Bonds, meanwhile, tend to rise and fall less dramatically than stocks. That means they are more stable and carry lower risk, but they also carry a low rate of return. When you invest your money in bonds, it is tied up for a period of time. If you sell a bond before it matures, you may find that it's worth only what you invested or even less. These disadvantages are not normally associated with commercial real estate investments.

There are other investment vehicles, such as money market funds. They are solid and secure, but they are best used to help investors preserve what they already have, not to grow wealth. Inflation may sometimes even outpace these investments. So that brings us to commercial real estate. It is not without its risks, but if you're knowledgeable about investing in income properties, you can maximize your return while minimizing your risk. And your real estate investments, particularly well-researched investments in income-producing properties, can prove impervious to other economic ups and downs.

The Control Factor

One of the strongest arguments in favor of commercial real estate over other investments is that you're able to *control* your own financial destiny. People who invest in stocks think nothing of turning their money over to someone else, then hoping for the best. Mutual funds are also managed by professional portfolio counselors. But with real estate, *you* remain in the driver's seat.

Your control over your investment manifests itself in many ways. For starters, you get to see exactly where your money is going. You can do a physical inspection of the property you're buying—see it, touch it, feel it. You can also judge on your own the value of your investment, negotiating the price of your property both when you buy and when you sell. And you make the important decisions about financing and refinancing, including the terms under which each deal is structured.

Beyond that, you decide who will manage your properties. That's an important advantage over the stock market, where you must trust corporate executives and board members to make decisions in your best interest. And just as you oversee the management of your real estate investment, you're also able to maintain your own books on the investment. As a stockholder, you can see a corporation's quarterly earnings or read through its annual reports, but you won't have open access to the books. With real estate, the books are in your hands.

With this level of control, you can maximize efficiencies. You have the freedom to decide whether, when, and even how improvements and renovations are made. You negotiate the leases to your properties based on your wishes and priorities. And you use your discretion to decide when the time is appropriate to make changes, including rent increases or decreases. This flexibility is important. This is your investment. You should have a say over how it is handled.

Financing Options

When it comes to the array of financing options available, real estate has no competition. Banks, insurance companies, pension funds, and other entities that finance real estate investments offer a wide range of terms and conditions on their loans. As a result, the opportunities to find something that matches your financial situation are numerous. You don't need volumes of ready cash. There are mortgage loans available that allow you to borrow 80 percent (and in some cases, 90 percent) of the value of a commercial property based on amortization periods of 25—and sometimes 30—years.

Once you begin shopping for loans and comparing the terms offered, you'll see that the differences can be quite amazing. In Chapter 9, we'll explore in depth the strategic importance of how you finance your income-property purchases.

The Leverage Edge

Leverage, one of the most significant advantages of investing in real estate, refers to the practice of using a minimal amount of cash to buy a property while financing the balance for the longest term possible at the lowest available interest rate. Leverage is one of the most important tools in building wealth through investment real estate. For starters, it makes real estate affordable. Most investors couldn't make such a significant investment if they had to come up with all the cash at once. Wealthy real estate moguls know the power of leverage.

And leverage, which is, of course, intrinsically linked to the ability to borrow—or access money that is not your own—carries another important advantage. While interest rates on home mortgages have been low, homebuyers generally have no room to negotiate the amount or the terms of the mortgage. In commercial real estate, negotiating the right loan is part of the deal. Commercial financing is discussed in detail in Chapter 9.

Leverage is an extraordinary tool that exists because lenders believe in the stability of choice income properties. They recognize these properties as solid investments. For investors with a strong credit rating, they are happy to make loans for up to 90 percent of a commercial property's value, provided it is a choice property in a top location. I know of no other investment where you can put in as little cash and get as high a rate of return.

Tax Benefits

Income-producing properties carry special tax advantages. Land is not depreciable, but the buildings that sit on it are. Under the concept of depreciation, the Internal Revenue Service assigns a useful life to buildings, 39 years for commercial property and 27.5 years for residential property, including apartment buildings. The assumption is that as buildings get older, they decrease in value each year. But when properly maintained, most buildings actually *increase* in value over time. Depreciation is a bookkeeping expense and not an out-of-pocket expense. Therefore, if you have a net income from a building of $100,000 and the depreciation is $30,000, the net income now becomes $70,000. If you are in the 25 percent tax bracket, you will save $7,500 in income taxes ($30,000 × 25 percent = $7,500).

In the foregoing example, you may be able to substantially reduce your taxes on the net income by using a method known as segregated cost depreciation. Under this method, the IRS will permit you, based on a qualified engineering report, to divide the cost of the building into four components. One component would be the building itself (the real estate), based on either a 39-year or a 27.5-year useful life. The other three components can be classified as personal property based on a 6-year life, a 7-year life, or a 15-year life.

Because of the faster tax write-off under the preceding formula, your depreciation reduction would be significantly higher during the initial seven years of ownership using segregated cost depreciation. And that would reduce your income tax obligations dramatically. If you have already invested in real estate and haven't used this method of depreciation, you can go as far back as 1986 and calculate the additional depreciation you could have taken under segregated cost depreciation. You can state it as a deduction on your current income tax return without amending any previous returns. If you are a real estate professional (not necessarily a broker or agent) and active in the operation of the building, you can take any losses generated by depreciation as a deduction against your ordinary income—which lowers the amount of income tax that you pay. The resulting income tax savings would, in effect, increase your cash flow and, accordingly, your cash-on-cash return.

Paul White, a prominent real estate broker and educator in South Florida, states, "One of my clients who acquired 10 properties over the last 12 years was able to reclassify approximately 23 percent of their depreciable value of $25 million and realize an income tax reduction of over $1.5 million on their most recent tax return."

Meanwhile, exchanging one investment property for another investment property defers capital gains taxes until a subsequent property is resold (1031 Exchange). Those are just examples of the many tax benefits that are available on real estate investments. Later, as we explain different financing options and property sales approaches, we'll also discuss their tax advantages.

Access to Information

Real estate is an investment characterized by openness and quick access to information. Real estate sales are part of the public record, so it's easy to track sales histories and the financing details of a particular property. Local and national property listings, sales of tax liens, details on sheriff sales, and foreclosures are among the volumes of information available on the Internet. There are public records on how neighborhoods are zoned, and Census Bureau information details the demographics of different locations. There are simple formulas as well as statistics in trade publications that help determine the annual costs and expenses of a building.

Easy Troubleshooting

One of the other pluses of real estate investment is that when a downturn takes place and some real estate is at a standstill or declining in value, there are still opportunities to make money. For example, you can invest in properties (e.g., medical buildings) that remain profitable despite market forces. Or you can do condo conversions of small apartment buildings in response to market demands. (The process for converting small apartment buildings into condominiums is explained in detail in Chapter 13.) When owners sell properties, for whatever reason, during down markets, they will often agree to deals that they wouldn't otherwise consider. For example, if an owner was selling you a building for $500,000 but you thought the building was really worth $525,000, you could ask for a one-year option with an option fee of, let's say, $5,000. If within six months you then found a buyer willing to pay $525,000, you could exercise your option and make a $25,000 profit—on an investment that cost you only $5,000. In addition, the $5,000 option money would be credited to the purchase price. In effect, you've engineered a deal that brought you a whopping 500 percent return based on a six-month holding period and an annualized rate of return of 1,000 percent.

There is a risk, of course. But that risk would be that, if you didn't find a buyer within the prescribed period of time, you would forfeit the $5,000.

Another opportunity in such a market would be to persuade the seller to finance the deal with 20 percent cash down and to hold an 80 percent mortgage. The chances of the seller doing this in a down market would be much greater than if the market were on the ascent. In obtaining seller financing, you would save a barrel of money because you wouldn't have to pay a bank any points or closing costs.

The lesson here is that real estate is not an either-or investment arena. There are easy formulas and fixes for weathering its ups and downs.

Overcoming Fear

If real estate is such a great investment, why aren't more people investing in it? The answer is simple: Fear gets in their way. Of course, it is normal, particularly for a first-time investor, to be wary. In fact, no investor, whether inexperienced or experienced, is completely immune. Some of these fears may be self-imposed, while others come from external influences. But there's a single antidote for all of them: knowledge. The better you understand the "fear factors," the less intimidated you'll be. Let's explore the principal "fear factors."

No-Money-to-Invest Fear

This may be the biggest obstacle for many would-be investors, but it's also the easiest to overcome. That's because it's an ungrounded fear. Although people may look at their bank account balances and immediately assume they don't have enough to get started in real estate, they're wrong. You don't need a lot of ready cash. That's the joy of income-producing real estate. Besides, you likely have assets that you didn't realize could be turned into the seed money you need to get going. Chapter 4 will help you identify your hidden assets and show how to make them work for you.

Fear of Inexperience

Every real estate investor was inexperienced at some point. That's no reason not to take the first step. One of the best ways to handle this fear is by seeking out a trusted person who has been successful investing in, say, small apartment buildings. Ask whether he or she would consider letting you become a partner in the next investment. That way you learn the steps involved and get your feet wet while under the guidance of someone who knows the ropes. Once you have a successful deal under your belt, you'll have the confidence—and peace of mind—necessary to invest on your own.

Price Tag Fear

All investors have a moment where they wonder: "Is the price too high?" But you have to step back and ask yourself: "Too high compared to what?"

Price is all relative to the market at the time. There are people who bought their own home 20 years ago for $20,000 and then sold it for $350,000. Just because they made a big profit doesn't mean the price had peaked. The new owner might resell the home a year later for $425,000. The price paid for a property many years ago (even if it was $100) has no bearing on its value today, even if it sells for $2 million. If you can buy a property at (or below) market value, then certainly you are not paying too much.

The world is full of people who lament: "I could have bought that property 10 years ago for $50,000. It's now selling for $750,000. I could have made a killing if I'd bought it back then." These are the people who, because of price tag fears, pass up every opportunity. Don't let the same apprehension make you a "coulda', shoulda', woulda'" person. It's not only the price that matters but how smart a deal you make. I'm going to walk you through the steps of how to find investment real estate with the best moneymaking potential and then negotiate the best deal possible. You'll soon realize how unnecessary price tag fear can be.

Fear of Management and Leasing

The thought of managing property scares away some would-be investors. But property management doesn't have to be a headache. In fact, one of the best ways to increase the value of your building is with good management—by structuring the right leases, maximizing income, keeping operating expenses under control, and establishing harmonious relationships with tenants.

Owners often choose to self-manage small buildings. With big buildings, your best bet is to rely on a professional management firm.

A management company has an incentive to obtain the highest rent possible and keep the building at full occupancy, because the company usually works on a percentage of the gross rental income as well as on a percentage of new leases and renewals. In Chapter 12, we will discuss management and leasing and show how good management can substantially increase your bottom line and free you from the day-to-day operation of your building. In most cases, the cost of using a good management firm will be more than offset by the money the firm saves you.

Fear of an Economic Recession

No one can predict for sure when an up cycle will end and a down cycle will begin. When I refinanced my Kendar Office Building in 1998 for $3.75 million, the bank got nervous before closing the deal. The senior vice president of the bank said, "You know, Ken, we're making you this loan with some concern because we believe that prices have peaked." Since that time, my building has tripled in value and my loan is now only 26.2 percent of today's value of the property—one of the most conservative loans the bank is carrying on its books.

Smart investors know that there are ways to weather the ups and downs. Even more, there are ways to capitalize if a recession hits. It is a good time to pick up properties at lower prices. When it comes to real estate, it's easy to ameliorate the effects of a recession. "Good quality income properties in top locations are virtually recession proof," says David Dabby, a well-known South Florida real estate analyst and consultant.

Fear of Risk

Most people resist change because of the risk they associate with it. They prefer to stay where they're comfortable. Change brings anxiety. But life is filled with change. When people are familiar with a situation or routine, they do not think about it as risky even if the risk remains. For example, if you work and pay your bills, there's no risk. Right? But what happens if you lose your job? Risk is always there. Sometimes it's major, other times it's minor, but it's rarely absent.

What you need to recognize is that risk is one thing, but the *fear* of risk is quite another. Letting fear get in the way will cut your financial rewards. As you move forward with your investment strategy, pay attention to those who have been successful and avoid the naysayers who create false anxieties with tales of doom and gloom. Our goal is to strike a balance between risk and reward.

Lack-of-Information Fear

Some people steer clear of commercial real estate because they think they just don't know enough about it. This book is designed to demystify the property-investment landscape. But there are also other ways to become well informed. If you are just starting out on your investment career, one of the best strategies is to build a relationship with a good mentor. You would be surprised at the number of successful investors willing to share the techniques that have made them wealthy. All you have to do is ask. During my own investment career, only a handful of people have asked how I mastered real estate investment. Yet I would have been happy to talk shop with anyone interested.

Novice investors can also get valuable, unbiased advice from a Counselor of Real Estate (CRE). A CRE is a professional who has an overview of the dynamics of a given marketplace. He or she knows what types of properties and what locations represent a good investment with minimal risk. A CRE is a professional who understands the ins and outs of a successful investment. A CRE will charge a fee for the service, but it will be the best money you've ever spent. Furthermore, there are educational courses and seminars offered by professional real estate associations to provide the remaining nuts and bolts that you need to become a successful investor. In Chapter 2, we'll discuss how and where to find the most valuable courses.

Among investment choices, real estate affords the greatest opportunities for wealth. Financial independence is important. It provides a safety net during personal and business catastrophes, and it means that you can stop working for a salary at the time you determine. Probably the most important reason for financial independence was summarized by Oprah Winfrey: "The real beauty of having material wealth is that you don't have to worry about paying the bills, and you have more energy to be concerned about the things that matter" ("Leadership for the 21st Century," *Newsweek*, Oct. 24, 2005).

Keep in mind, however, that investing in real estate requires research and study. You shouldn't buy a property, even in a top location, unless you know what you are doing. You must be familiar with the market and make comparisons of rents, sales prices, and vacancy factors. You must check out zoning regulations as well as distances to shopping centers, houses of worship, restaurants, and entertainment venues. You have to understand mortgage financing and other factors. You'll also need common sense, persistence, and self-discipline. But once you master those and begin to make real estate investments, your money will be working for you.

The Bottom Line

Since the beginning of recorded history, wealth has almost always been measured by the amount of land a person owns. It defined classes—between royalty and commoners, "the haves" and "the have-nots," the rich and everyone else. There was even a term for people with investment real estate. They were the "landed class." Today, things haven't changed all that much. The difference is that in our free market society, by knowing what the rich know, you can apply the same principles to create your own wealth.

No investment is risk free. But real estate holds key advantages over other investment opportunities, including the stock market. One of the most important of these advantages is the ability to make a lot with just a little. If you put 10 percent down on a property and then sell it in a year for 10 percent more than you paid, the math shows that your return is a dramatic 100 percent! No other investment comes with this kind of leverage.

Even investors without piles of ready cash will find a welcome mat when it comes to real estate. The players in the financing game—banks, mortgage companies, and insurance companies—compete for your business. As a result, not only can the terms of a deal be exceptionally attractive, but they can be matched to your financial circumstances and abilities. Think back to what we've just said: You can make a real estate investment with as little as 10 percent down. You won't find options like that when it comes to stocks or bonds. On top of it, you'll enjoy tax benefits.

Some people are scared away from investments because they over-analyze or worry. "Over-analysis can lead to paralysis," says Sandra Goldstein, past chairperson of the Real Estate Commercial

Alliance of Greater Miami. But commercial real estate is not like other investments. There are numerous—and simple—strategies that can help you ride out the storms. Even more, you can make money in bad times as well as good. As for the other fears that hold back would-be investors, most are unfounded. The trick is to balance risk with reward. If you prepare properly, you'll know how to do that.

Most people dream of living with a financial safety net, of having the money they need to live the way they want. But few realize how close they could be to making that happen. Now that you know it's possible, it's time to walk through the basic steps of real estate investment. That is the focus of Chapter 2.

CHAPTER 2

Real Estate 101

When I started out in the real estate business many years ago, I knew practically nothing about what was involved. I was lucky to have a mentor, David Probinsky, who sat me down and took me through the basics. He explained that while each deal may be different, the overall elements in the buying and selling of property were usually the same. This chapter gives a simplified overview of the basics involved in the world of investment real estate. I will also cover the educational opportunities available.

What Is Real Estate?

Real estate consists of improved property. That means land with a building on it. Unimproved property refers to vacant land. Real estate is property that can't be picked up and moved, and this is what differentiates it from personal property. Think of a building as real estate and the furnishings in it as personal property.

Types of Income Properties

When you enter the commercial real estate arena, you'll find several types of income-producing properties from which to choose. You should examine your financial and family situation and think about the following: What kind of property investment will fulfill your needs? Do you have the money to invest? If not, do you know how to get it? (You will find out in Chapter 4 how easy it is to get the money.) Most income properties fall into the categories described in the following list.

Apartment complexes: Apartment buildings with five units or more are classified as commercial property. This type of property runs the range from small buildings with a few units to large complexes with hundreds of units.

Office buildings: Suburban office buildings are relatively small compared with large office buildings in downtown areas. Since the mid-1990s, a number of condominium office buildings have been constructed, and some rental office buildings have been converted to office condos.

Shopping centers: This refers to a collection of retail stores, either in an enclosed complex or side by side in a shopping mall. Many shopping centers have national chain tenants such as department stores, restaurants, electronics firms, sporting goods outlets, and supermarkets.

Retail strip stores: These are stores that sit among a lineup of other retail outlets, usually on a busy front street in a neighborhood or a downtown. A retail strip store is a space that may be used as a beauty salon, a florist shop, a luncheonette, or a shoe repair store, to name only a few possible options. Small shopping centers can also be considered retail strip stores.

Industrial properties: This real estate category includes flex space, which is a combination of office and warehouse facilities, and small bay warehouses. Factories and large distribution warehouses are also industrial properties.

Parking garages: Although municipalities and counties own some parking facilities, others are built and owned by private developers who recognize the need for parking in bustling areas.

Mobile home parks: These combine real estate and personal property. The land is real estate, but the mobile homes are personal property. Operating a mobile home park is a business, so, overall, it's a hybrid property.

Hotels and motels: These are hybrid types of properties because they combine real estate together with running a business.

What Real Estate Can Do for You

Individual investors approach real estate from different perspectives. What's good for one person may not be good for the next person. Some investors buy rental homes or small income properties to fix up and resell for a quick profit. Others want to invest in multiunit rental properties, with a plan to pay off the mortgages as soon as possible and then have substantial income flowing in for many years. Still others are interested in investing small amounts of cash and taking on big, long-term mortgages in order to leverage and maximize their cash flow. There are those who seek to buy freestanding buildings occupied by creditworthy national tenants—perhaps on a long-term triple net lease where the tenants pay every expense. And there are the flippers interested buying properties then quickly reselling them.

There are investors who don't need steady income and don't want the responsibility of management. They invest in vacant land that they believe will increase in value. Even investors who have a clear idea of what is best for them now may change their minds as their needs and objectives shift. That means that the type of property they invest in now might not be the type of property that they acquire in the future. However, as you'll learn later when we explore the Big Six in detail, the buy side of your real estate strategy—in other words, the property you choose to purchase—is the most crucial element that determines how successful your investment will become. A constant theme throughout this book is how you make your money in buying.

The Search Begins

Once you have decided which investment matches your objectives, it's time to begin searching for the right property. Bear in mind that "right" includes the right location and right price. Start by checking the real estate section of your local newspaper and local real estate publications. You can also search the Internet. This will give you an idea of what properties are for sale and the price ranges in locations that interest you. Although these steps will give you a better sense of the real estate marketplace, most investors use the services of a broker. You should do likewise. Chapter 3 will explain how and why.

It may take months to find the right property. Even with a broker working on your behalf, you should be actively involved in the buying process. You should look at each building with the broker and ask questions. You will want to see the records for income and expenses, a list of the tenants, how much rent the tenants are paying, the square footage of the rental spaces, the expiration dates of their leases, and whether the tenants have options to renew their leases.

You also need to know about neighborhood trends and proposed projects for the area, both governmental and private, that will affect real estate values. You will want to talk with nearby building owners to get their take on the history and future of the area. Eventually you will hit on the right property. I can't emphasize how crucial the property selection is. There is no other decision that has more impact on your success strategy than what property you buy. When I delve into the elements that make up the Big Six later in the book, I'll explain exactly how that decision affects everything that follows.

Purchase and Sale Contracts

In many states, the bar associations and real estate associations have approved a standard contract form. Each contract clause—and there are many—has been agreed upon by lawyers and brokers and revised over the years. Before the existence of these standard contracts, we had myriad contracts carrying numerous clauses that each required costly and time-consuming review by brokers, attorneys, buyers, and sellers. These new form contracts did away with that; they are used by brokers and attorneys because of their standard nomenclature. The form has been simplified into a fill-in-the-blank format that, among other things, includes blank spaces for the following:

- Date of contract
- Names of buyer and seller
- Address of property
- Legal description of property
- Purchase price
- Personal property included in sale
- Initial deposit
- Additional deposits

- Who holds the deposits (broker, attorney, or title company)
- Deadline for seller to accept the offer
- Financing amount
- Cash necessary to close the transaction
- Intended use of the property
- Time period for seller to deliver title commitment
- Time period for buyer to examine title commitment
- Time period for seller to resolve any defects in title
- Who pays for the survey
- Time period to conduct due diligence and inspection of the property
- Names of brokers
- Commission to be paid to brokers
- Closing date
- Place of closing

Although these standard contracts carry common clauses easily understood by investors, brokers, and attorneys, they also contain addenda with additional terms and contingencies specific to the particulars of each real estate deal. For large and complex transactions, most investors eschew standard contracts and have their attorneys prepare sales contracts from scratch.

Virtually all sales contracts provide an ample period of time for the buyer to inspect the physical condition of the property and conduct a due diligence, which is an examination of its soundness and the factors affecting the economic viability of the property. Prior to the end of this period, the buyer may, for any reason, cancel the contract. Another contingency relates to financing. If the buyer does not receive a mortgage loan with the terms and conditions desired, the buyer also has the right to cancel the contract. There are other contingencies besides these that an investor may wish to insert in the contract depending on the circumstances of a particular deal.

Closing

A closing consummates a real estate deal in accordance with the terms and conditions of the sales contract. The buyer, seller, broker, and attorneys attend the closing, at which time the seller and the buyer sign all documents. A deed conveying the property to the buyer, together with the mortgage and certain other legal documents, is recorded in the municipality or county where the property is located. In some states, "settlement" is used in place of "closing" to describe the process, but both words refer to the same procedure. Standard closing costs are usually spelled out in a sales contract, as well as clarification of whether they are the obligation of the buyer or the seller. Financing costs are paid by the buyer (borrower). The financing costs include the appraisal fee, points to obtain the loan, bank attorney's fee, and other loan expenses.

Points confuse many buyers. Points are fees paid to the lender to make a mortgage loan and, in effect, are additional interest that the lender charges. Each point equals 1 percent of the loan amount. The points should be negotiated with the lender during the initial negotiations between the borrower and the lender.

Education

Whether you are a beginner or experienced investor, mastering real estate is a lifetime endeavor. This is a dynamic arena that changes constantly. Several years ago, investors could take ownership of a property and assume the existing mortgage, meaning that they would have the same payment and at the same interest rate as the previous owner, and then pay off the mortgage without a prepayment penalty. Most mortgages today are not assumable, and most of them carry a prepayment penalty.

Today the mortgage landscape is far more complex. There are adjustable-rate mortgages (ARMs) for which the interest rate fluctuates. There are interest-only mortgages where no principal payments are made. In a negative amortization mortgage, you pay only a portion of the interest and the remainder of the interest is tagged on to the mortgage. Under this loan, your mortgage balance increases each month. In recent years, there have been a number of federal regulations covering depreciation changes, environmental issues, banking procedures, revisions in the tax laws, and closing requirements—for local as well as foreign investors. Educational courses and seminars can help you keep abreast of what's going on.

There are a number of places you can turn to help you expand your knowledge of real estate. They include:

Universities and community colleges: Extension courses—at a reasonable cost—are offered in the evenings and on weekends.

You can also arrange to sit in during day courses directed toward students majoring in real estate. Some of the classes address principles and practices of real estate, investment analysis, property development, as well as real estate appraisal, management, and financing.

Real estate associations: The National Association of Realtors (NAR) conducts intensive courses and seminars involving commercial and investment real estate. Brokers, investors, and developers teach these. The courses, which may last up to a week, lead to professional certification. You do not have to be a member of the NAR to take these courses.

Institutional seminars: Banks, mortgage companies, real estate publications, title insurance companies, and numerous real estate societies organize educational conferences on a variety of real estate-related issues.

Books, CDs, and tapes: There is a bounty of supplemental educational material available to complement courses that you have taken. These materials give you a perspective from the point of view of real estate pros, many of whom have been successful investors, brokers, and developers.

Investor contacts: You probably have a relative, a friend, or a friend of a friend who has become wealthy through real estate investments. Let several of them know that you're interested in how they became so successful. You will be surprised at how willing successful people are to share their stories and other information with you. Despite my willingness to share my experiences, only a handful of people have ever asked. One of them, my college-student grandson Adam, recently became my partner in a 120-acre transaction.

Real estate licensing courses: You may become enthusiastic enough about real estate to want to pursue it as a full- or part-time career. One of the great benefits to you is that you can pick up good deals before they are offered to the general public. A firefighter who used to work for me part time made substantial money investing in income properties. To become a real estate agent, you must pass a state licensing examination. State-approved courses are available at universities and through private firms. There are also courses offered online. The exams have become more difficult to pass in recent years, and the courses and tests may require a commitment of several months. Even if you aren't interested in working as a real estate agent, you can get a non-active license and activate it any time. Although these courses are designed for real estate professionals, they provide a good overview of the industry—including investment.

Real Estate Lingo

Real estate is a dynamic field where new concepts, techniques, and phraseology regularly surface. A few years ago, who would have known about conduit loans, mezzanine financing, infinity returns, and segregated cost depreciation? It took some time for these fairly sophisticated techniques to be understood by those well versed in real estate investments.

A sampling of some key terms includes the following:

- **Bottom fisherman:** An investor who tries to buy below a bargain price
- **Bumps:** Periodic increases in rent
- **Ceiling:** The maximum interest rate on an adjustable-rate mortgage
- **Condo reversion:** A condo conversion building that reverts to rental status
- **Debt service:** Mortgage payments that include principal and interest
- **Deal killer:** A proposal that keeps a sales contract from being consummated
- **Dog:** A worthless building
- **Evergreen loan:** A loan that is repeatedly renewed so that it remains on the books indefinitely
- **Firm price/firm offer:** A sales price or a sales offer that is nonnegotiable
- **Flex space:** A property containing a combination of warehouses and offices
- **Floor:** The minimum interest rate on an adjustable-rate mortgage
- **Going north:** Ascending values and/or ascending interest rates
- **Going south:** Declining values and/or declining interest rates
- **Grandfathered:** Describing a property out of conformance with current zoning

- **Growth rate:** The annual percentage increase in the value of a property
- **Hard costs:** Actual costs involved in the construction of a building
- **Hard money:** A nonrefundable deposit
- **Infinity return:** A cash flow with no cash investment
- **Knockdown:** A building with little or no value that can be razed to make room for a new building
- **Segregated cost depreciation:** Valuation of the different components of a building
- **Sleeper:** A good deal about which most people are unaware
- **Soft costs:** All other costs apart from hard costs
- **Steal:** A bargain buy
- **Sweetheart lease:** A special deal extended to a tenant
- **Turnaround:** When a nonperforming property is transformed into a successful one
- **Turnover:** The percentage of tenants that vacate a building annually
- **Wiggle room:** The negotiating space for a price when there is leeway on a deal

The Bottom Line

When people search for a new home, much is made of the house's foundation. A foundation may be constructed of concrete or stone. But there's one key commonality: A poorly built foundation can negatively affect the entire home's stability and durability. The same is true of real estate investment. You must start with a good foundation, a foundation that will serve you for many years. And that foundation is knowledge.

There's no magic secret to making money in real estate. It's all about good preparation and smart decision making. You must understand the types of investment real estate, the steps involved in a deal, and the terminology used in a purchase or sale. You must acquire the knowledge about what makes a deal successful. And part of that knowledge you assemble yourself. That is the part where you identify your needs and objectives. Once you're clear on those points, you're ready to begin searching for the right property, in the right location, and at the right price.

Knowing the basic elements of a sales contract and taking educational seminars—as well as talking to successful investors—will lay the groundwork before you find a good broker and kick off the property search. Avoid the temptation to delegate all tasks to others. You should consciously jump into the process so that you can deepen your understanding of real estate investing. What you expect the property to do for you will determine which type of property makes the most investment sense. When I entered real estate, I jumped into deals with little idea of what I was doing. They were small deals—but they were big for me at the time—and I often overpaid. Fortunately at that time, inflation took care of my mistakes. Eventually, I understood what to look for and could recognize a good deal from a bad one. I went from having nothing to eventually buying and selling more than $300 million-worth of real estate over a period of 30 years.

This book is designed to help you avoid mistakes and put you on the road to prosperity. This journey toward wealth is a step-by-step process. You begin by establishing a strong foundation of knowledge, through learning the basics. Then you assemble the right team of experts, the focus of the next chapter.

CHAPTER 3

Assembling the Team

Smart investors know that to be successful they must surround themselves with professionals who have expertise in each element of an investment deal. Real estate is no exception. In my own case, I have always relied on the services of experts who know a lot more than I do. Without them, I could not have become successful.

Besides your primary team—a broker, an attorney, and an accountant—you'll need to work with other professionals from time to time. For example, appraisers can help with financing or refinancing a property, and contractors and engineers can be crucial to successful renovations and repairs.

The Broker

A real estate broker is a middleman licensed by the state. He or she negotiates for buyers and sellers the sale or leasing of property; a broker also negotiates deals between landlords and tenants. Depending on state regulations, a broker may also perform duties such as property management, evaluations, and investment consulting. Many people think that anyone who works in real estate is a Realtor. They are unaware that the term Realtor is a patented trade name (spelled with a capital R) that can be used only by brokers who are members of the National Association of Realtors (NAR). Real estate agent is a term interchangeably used to refer to a broker, salesperson, or Realtor.

The majority of sellers list their properties with a broker known as the listing broker. The broker who sells the property is the selling broker. He or she works in conjunction with the listing broker. The commission, normally paid by the seller, is divided in accord with an agreement between the listing and selling brokers. The advantages of using the services of a broker include the following:

- Access to properties listed on local Multiple Listing Services (MLS)
- Access to properties listed on national MLS
- Access to properties not listed on MLS
- Access to properties that owners might wish to sell but haven't made their minds up about or listed yet
- Access to confidential listings
- Access to properties that have been repossessed by lenders
- Access to government-owned properties
- Access to real estate auctioneers
- Access to properties available through attorney's estates, divorces, and bankruptcies

A good broker is an expert negotiator. That is important, given that negotiation is one of the keys to real estate success. Once you've identified a property that seems right for you, your broker will encourage you to make an offer. Except in boom times when buyers may make offers above the asking price, I have seen few real estate deals that end with a buyer paying the listed price. If a property has been on the market for any length of time and if there have been offers and counteroffers, the broker will have a good sense of the price the seller will accept. A broker also has access to the price paid by buyers for properties comparable to yours. If there are no comparable deals, the broker has contacts among appraisers who can furnish information that may not be available in public records. Listen to your broker's advice, and remember that negotiation doesn't stop at the sales price. There is also bargaining over fees and other costs.

Because the broker does business with mortgage lenders all the time, he or she knows which lender can offer you the lowest interest rates and the best loan terms at the most economical costs. A lender who knows your broker will also take more personal interest and steer you around the red tape and hassles. The lender wants to protect his or her relationship with the broker so that additional business is directed the lender's way. Because of this, a good lender will work hard to meet your needs.

Brokers can also recommend real estate attorneys, accountants, land surveyors, architects, contractors, appraisers, inspection firms, title insurance companies, casualty insurance companies, and other professionals whose expertise you need.

Value of the Broker

For many years, I had my eye on an office building just a stone's throw from the building that I own and where my real estate firm is located. Every time I passed this office building, I said to myself, "What a gorgeous building. I would love to own it." It was a two-story, 25,000-square-foot structure that had won an architectural award from the city when it was built. I checked the tax records and found out that it was owned by an entity, but the names of the people involved were not listed. The address was a post office box in a small town in Massachusetts.

I sent numerous letters to the address over a period of a several months but never received a reply. I even did some detective work in an effort to identify the people behind this entity, but I had no success.

One jaw-dropping day I received a call from a broker whose office was just a few minutes from mine. He had an exclusive right of sale listing on this very building. I cannot describe my astonishment— the coincidence that he would call me about the exact building I'd been coveting for so long! He said it was a confidential listing, and the owner had given strict instructions not to place it on the open market. The broker, a resourceful young man, had no idea I was interested in the building. He simply knew that I had owned an office nearby for more than 20 years, and he thought I might be a logical buyer.

The sale price on the building was on the high side at $3.3 million. I negotiated and settled on a price of $2.925 million (or $117 per square foot). I brought Jim Pollack, an investor-attorney who had participated in many other deals with me, into the transaction, and we became 50/50 partners. Because the rents were substantially under the going market rate and the leases would expire in two years without any options to renew, we knew that we could increase the rents by at least 25 percent—thus greatly increasing the value of the property.

Fifteen months after we bought the property, Sonia Blair, one of Miami's savviest brokers, brought us a prospective buyer who could pay all cash. We did not want to sell, but Sonia persuaded us to let her show the building to her prospect. We set a firm price (which we never expected to get). To our surprise, Sonia delivered a signed contract for $4.375 million—exactly what we said we'd accept.

The man who bought the building has been able to increase the rents by about 50 percent and, after a five-year holding period, could easily sell it on today's market for $7.5 million. The broker who sold us the building made a six-figure commission, and Sonia, who resold it for us, made a six-figure commission. We would never have been able to acquire the property if it weren't for the first broker, nor could we have resold it at such a good profit if it weren't for the persistence of Sonia. Everyone came out well on this deal—but the brokers' role was the key to it all.

From Beginning to End

Often a buyer approaches a seller directly and makes a verbal offer. If a seller feels insulted by the offer—finding it unreasonable—an argument and angry responses can erupt. This won't happen if a broker is involved. A broker will obtain a deposit and a written offer from the buyer before submitting it to the seller.

And just as a broker can smooth the process at the beginning of a deal, he or she can ease the way once a sales contract has been signed by the parties. A broker can take responsibility for myriad details—everything from arranging for property inspections to obtaining documents to facilitate the due diligence period. A broker will coordinate with attorneys, accountants, and other professionals; check open building permits; assist in putting together the mortgage application and lender-required paperwork; and tackle unanticipated problems.

A broker can represent the seller or the buyer, but in the majority of deals the seller pays the broker's commission. A broker doesn't earn a penny until a deal is closed. This is different from the seller's relationship with other professionals, who get paid whether or not a deal closes. In the circumstances under which a buyer signs an agreement giving the broker the exclusive right to represent him or her, there will be an agreed-on fee. Even in this situation many sellers pay the broker's commission, in which case the buyer pays no fee to the broker.

Should You Use Only One Broker?

If you have already worked with a broker who helped you buy a great property, you might want to deal exclusively with that broker again. A one-broker relationship helps build mutual trust and respect, leaving the broker more motivated to find you the right deal—including properties not yet on the market.

However, there may be times when it is wiser to use more than one broker. Let's say you wish to buy an income property in the $1 million range, but you do not want to limit your choices to one type of property. You'd like to look at apartment buildings, retail strip stores, and small office buildings. The smart approach is to contact brokers specializing in each of the property types to guarantee that you have the widest choice of properties in the market place.

Going It on Your Own

Some owners don't wish to list their properties with any broker or deal with a broker. In the industry, this is known as a FSBO (pronounced fizzbo), or a property for sale by owner. These properties are advertised in newspapers, on the Internet, and via "by owner" signs on homes and land. Buyers assume they will get a lower price with this kind of deal because the owner doesn't have to pay a broker's commission. However, you'll rarely see this kind of sign on the exterior of an income-producing property.

Sometimes dealing directly can work. But more often, a FSBO is risky and frustrating. Many times you will end up paying a higher price than if you had used the services of a broker. After the contract is signed, you will be saddled with a number of details—some of them stressful—normally handled by a broker. Even though I am a broker myself, I generally use the services of other brokers. Since I am buying and selling as a principal, I don't receive any portion of the commission. This gives the broker a great incentive to deal with me.

Bear in mind that you can eliminate the broker, but you cannot eliminate the work the broker does.

The Attorney

A person who passes the state bar exam and is licensed by the state is referred to as an attorney, lawyer, or counselor at law. You should only use an attorney with real estate expertise. How do you find the right attorney? Ask for recommendations from successful investors, then interview the lawyers they mention. You'll want an attorney who

- Is held in high esteem by professionals and clients
- Maintains a high standard of excellence
- Is creative
- Pays attention to detail
- Has strong communication skills
- Is amiable
- Is known as an effective negotiator
- Follows through
- Works well with brokers

Investment property may be the biggest single purchase of your life. You owe it to yourself to be in the best hands.

The attorney should be on board *before* the sales contract is signed. Tasks that an attorney performs include preparation of complex sales contracts, issuance of a title insurance policy, preparation of legal documents, and review of documents prepared by the seller's attorney. Your attorney will examine mortgage loan documents to make certain they comply with the written mortgage commitment. In addition, your attorney will work with the lender's attorney to resolve any differences or concerns and ensure a smooth closing.

If you are purchasing an apartment building with a number of tenants, for example, your attorney will examine all the leases to make sure that they conform to the seller's representations. In addition, he or she will do numerous other tasks, including going over complex financing with a fine-tooth comb and tackling any zoning issues and environmental problems.

Value of the Attorney

Several years back I bought a 54-unit apartment building on the ocean in a prestigious area of greater Miami known as Bal Harbour. The executor of a Midwesterner's estate owned the property, and an old-time broker had brought it to my attention. It was an exceptional investment, but there were 70 years remaining on a 99-year ground lease on the land underneath the building. This made it difficult to get financing for the purchase (although later I was able to buy the land from the elderly widow who owned it). I managed to get the president of a bank to approve my loan, but it was through an informal letter and not a firm commitment. However, about a week before the closing, the bank reneged. I was in a panic: The executor of the estate was flying in with his attorney for the closing, and there was no way that I was going to call and say we couldn't close the deal. Not only would I be highly embarrassed, but I would have to forfeit a $50,000 deposit I had made on the property.

I had one of Miami's great attorneys, Morris Rosenberg, representing me, a veteran held in high esteem by his colleagues in the city as well as by top bankers and real estate investors. Among his credentials he had a degree from the Wharton School of Business at the University of Pennsylvania, and he was an astute businessman. He said he would try to persuade the seller to give me a 30-day extension.

When we assembled at my attorney's office for what the seller thought was the closing, Morris was brilliant. He explained that I was legitimately ready to close the deal, but the bank had not honored its commitment. His sincere, professional, and convincing argument won me the extension. In fact, we executed all the paperwork and kept everything in escrow so that the executor and his attorney would not be inconvenienced by having to travel all the way back to Miami again.

After everyone left the building, Morris chewed me out and told me how important it was to lock up a mortgage deal by getting a firm commitment in writing so that a bank could not renege on it. He referred me to a well-established banker who gave me the loan. Thirty days later, I closed on the purchase of the property. It was the most dramatic business situation I had ever been in, and the successful ending would not have been possible without Morris. I could never thank him adequately for what he did.

The Attorney's Fee

Usually, the bigger the deal, the bigger the fee. Your best bet is to sit down with your attorney and negotiate a fee to cover the entire transaction, including the issuance of a title insurance policy. In some areas of the country, title companies charge a substantial premium for the policy, in great part because they pay your attorney a hefty commission and that payment is folded into your charge. Some attorneys will only work for an hourly fee, rather than a set fee. In such instance, you should try and negotiate a ceiling on the fee.

The Certified Public Accountant

A Certified Public Accountant, or CPA, has an accounting degree and has passed a rigid state examination. As in law, there are numerous accounting specialties, but you want a CPA with experience in real estate matters. The CPA should come aboard early in the process to advise you on the type of entity you should take title in and how to minimize the tax obligations on your investment. Other real estate portfolio issues that may require the services of a CPA are estate planning, inheritances, gift giving, and charitable contributions in the form of real estate. Mortgage lenders will often accept your personal financial statements with your application, but they'll want two or three years' worth of CPA-prepared tax returns to approve a loan.

As you set out to find a CPA, you should look for someone who

- Has integrity
- Knows the ins and outs of tax regulations and how they can benefit you
- Saves you money on taxes
- Is effective in dealing with the IRS if you are audited
- Is highly regarded by colleagues
- Can establish an effective accounting system for you
- Works well with your attorney
- Is aggressive rather than conservative in preparing your income tax return
- Quotes estimated fees in advance

IRS tax code provisions and regulations have changed numerous times since the early 1900s, and these revisions have affected real estate investments. At one time, investors could avail themselves of quick tax write-offs and depreciate properties fast enough that paper losses could be deducted against regular income.

That meant a wealthy investor could wind up paying little or no income taxes. The capital gains holding periods and tax rates have changed many times since then, and there are now complex regulations. A good CPA will make life easier for you and save you money.

In a straightforward purchase of an apartment building, for example, there is no mystery to calculating net income. But that doesn't mean a seller's breakdown of expenses is the one you should use. Many sellers don't allow for management costs; as a result, their estimates reflect unrealistic expenses for maintenance and repairs. If you have had some experience, you can easily do your own financial projections together with the broker. You would first determine the rents for each apartment and then allow a 3 to 5 percent vacancy factor. After that, you would deduct the operating expenses, generally about 35 percent of the gross income depending on the number of units in the building. You can also come up with an estimate by comparing the expenses with those of comparable buildings. However, if you are buying your first property, you should have your CPA look over the numbers before signing a contract. Numbers are a CPA's bread and butter.

If you are investing in a hybrid property, you absolutely need a CPA on board. A hybrid property is real estate combined with the operation of a business. Examples are hotels, motels, parking garages, mobile home parks, groves, and recreational land that generates income. Analyzing the numbers on these properties can be complex. With a hybrid you more than likely will be using the replacement costs of the real estate, although the net income that the business generates will be the main factor in purchasing the property.

An accountant would likely begin by asking a seller for income tax returns for the past three years. Some owners will claim that they don't declare all their income; this should be a signal that other illegal techniques may be involved. To investigate a potential deal, your CPA should have a consulting agreement, most likely with the fee calculated on an hourly basis.

Setting Up Your Accounting System

When you invest in an income property, you need an accounting system for managing your building. If you are just starting out you can, with the advice of your CPA, set up a computerized system, then have your accountant review your books at intervals. A CPA will also prepare your income tax return in consultation with you. You may want to enroll in courses covering the basic principles of accounting, especially those that relate to real estate. As time goes on and you increase your investment portfolio, you may need the services of a full-time bookkeeper.

Value of the CPA

A few years ago I was chatting with my son-in-law Robert Glick, who is a CPA and a partner in the firm of Kaufman, Rossin & Co. We got on the subject of taxation. On my buildings, I had been employing the conventional method of depreciation, using 27.5 years or 39 years, depending on the classification of each building. Robert explained that there was a method known as segregated cost depreciation that allowed the depreciation of various components of a building over a much shorter life span. In effect, by using this method I could have substantially more depreciation. Depreciation is only a bookkeeping entry, but it can be expensed as a cash expenditure. I was able to save a great deal in income taxes, and it was only because of the knowledge and expertise of a CPA such as Robert Glick.

Accounting Fees

Your accounting fees depend, of course, on what you want the accountant to do. On a small property, you can arrive at a reasonable fixed fee to handle your annual tax return. As you get into bigger and more complex deals, you'll be consulting with your accountant more often on various issues. When this happens, the fees will be greater and more than likely on an hourly basis

Involvement of Other Professionals

Depending on your deal, there are other professionals you may need to add to your team. If you're buying a property to fix up and resell for a quick return on your investment, you may need to find architects and/or licensed contractors or engineers to help with the process. There are times when I have hired appraisers to revalue properties that I thought were appraised too low. Not long ago, I hired a roofing consultant who had to fly in from Chicago. His fee was \$3,500, including the plane fare and out-of-pocket expenses, but it was well worth it. He saved us \$50,000 in correcting a roof problem.

Your team for some deals may be small. For others, it may include as many as five or six professionals. But it's not about the number of people, it's about their knowledge. These are the people who will help you at the most critical points of the investment, the Big Six moments that you'll see in action when we walk through the details of a Big Six deal in Chapter 11.

The Bottom Line

If you were to have major surgery, you would want to employ a surgeon who specializes in the type of operation you need. After carefully checking the credentials of several doctors, you would choose the one who has the best track record and reputation. You'd also want that surgeon to be working with a good medical support team.

First-rate teamwork is also important in real estate investment. Buying a building will probably be one of the biggest investments (possibly *the* biggest) of your lifetime. In buying an income property, you should put together a professional team made up of specialists who bring the right expertise to your deal. You wouldn't want to select a broker who specializes in the leasing of homes, an attorney who does divorce work, or an accountant who focuses on probate and estate work. You will be only as successful as the professionals working on your behalf.

According to popular legend, industrialist Andrew Carnegie, who embodied a rags-to-riches life, once referred to teamwork as "the fuel that allows common people to attain uncommon results." Although he was referring to his experiences more than a century ago, the reflection remains true today. The most important members of your team will be your broker, your attorney, and your accountant. Research candidates carefully, choose them wisely, then tap their expertise as much as you need to put together the elements of a successful real estate transaction. Rely on their insider knowledge and trust their advice, but keep a hands-on approach to your investment. Remember: Control is one of the advantages of a real estate investment over other investments. And the closer you work on your own deals, the more knowledge you'll accumulate to help you with your future deals.

Having an effective team working together is essential to accomplish your investment goals. Not only can you delegate tasks to people skilled in other areas, but you benefit—and learn—from their base of experience. Experience and updated knowledge are crucial because the only constant in real estate is change. Keeping informed is a lifetime pursuit. With knowledge comes power and self-confidence. The more you know, the more you will grow. And the way to begin growing your wealth is to get started—but that takes money. Chapter 4 details many of the ways—some of them surprising—to put together the investment money you'll need.

4

Getting the Money

When I was growing up, I thought a millionaire was a person who earned $1 million a year. I was in awe of how anyone could possibly make this much money. Many years later, I found out it didn't refer to how much money the person made, but that the person had a net worth of $1 million. In today's world there are a substantial number of people who are millionaires or multimillionaires.

Money seems to be the part of real estate investment that confuses people, and perhaps more than anything else, unnecessarily keeps them from getting on the path to wealth. I've heard people say, "I would like to buy a property, but I only have $60,000 in a certificate of deposit at my bank." They'd be surprised if I were to tell them that they could buy a five-unit apartment building for $300,000—with just $60,000 cash down and get a 10 percent to 20 percent return. And this return is only a small part of the deal. If they resold the building after a year for 10 percent more than they paid, they would make a profit of $30,000. That's equal to a 50 percent return on a $60,000 cash investment. Add to that the 10 percent to 20 percent cash flow return and the total annual return now equals 60 percent to 70 percent. That's called leverage, which you'll read about in Chapter 9. This is evidence of the incredible opportunities available in real estate with only a small amount of cash.

Forget those stories you hear about cousins who buy a property for all cash. First of all, that's not smart investing. And more importantly, it wrongly gives the impression that you need piles of money before you can even consider real estate as an investment.

Real estate investments are not just for the rich. Ride down any street and look at the small store buildings, apartment buildings, and office buildings. Who do you think owns them? Small investors. Some may own several buildings, but they started with one building and then resold it at a profit before buying more buildings to create a multimillion-dollar net worth. You can do the same thing and become wealthy. But you'll need seed money to get started.

You may be surprised at how easy it is to get the cash for your first down payment. Many people are worth much more than they think. Sit down and list your assets. Assets are things of value such as your home, furnishings, art, antiques, stamp collections, and jewelry, as well as the money that you have built up in your IRA, 401K, or other similar accounts. Assets also include money in bank accounts, stocks, bonds, mutual funds, and the cash value of life insurance—in short, anything you own that has a value. When listing your assets, use the current value and not what you paid. Now make note of the money you owe, which are your liabilities. The difference between your assets and liabilities is your net worth.

Let's take a look at the net worth statement of a businessman who wants to invest in a piece of commercial real estate but has only $20,000 in his savings account (see Figure 4.1). Aside from the dearth of cash, he focuses on his debt: mortgages, credit card bills, car payments. And they are not insignificant, totaling $197,000. But when he starts to list his assets, led by the real estate he already owns, he is astonished. The value of his property, cars, life insurance, IRA accounts (which can be invested in real estate), his mutual funds, and his certificates of deposit, in fact, *exceed* $1 million. Even when he subtracts his liabilities, he's still worth more than three-quarters of a million dollars.

His assets—and many of yours—can be used as collateral to borrow money from a bank for a real estate investment. This is the way that wealthy investors operate. As long as you can make more money than the cost of borrowing, it is healthy to borrow, and it makes sense to do so.

Obtaining a Home Equity Loan

In spite of the recent housing downturn across the country, most homeowners have seen unbelievable increases in their property values. In response to those rising property values, banks several years

Net Worth Statement			
ASSETS		LIABILITIES	
Cash in savings account	$20,000	Car loans	$30,000
IRA account	$150,000	Mortgage on residence	$100,000
Mutual funds	$50,000	Mortgage on vacation home	$50,000
Automobiles	$60,000	Credit card balance	$7,000
Certificate of deposit	$50,000	Life insurance loan	$10,000
Residence	$500,000		
Vacation condo	$150,000		
Life insurance cash value	$15,000		
Personal property	$25,000		
TOTAL	$1,020,000	TOTAL	$197,000

ASSETS	$1,020,000
LIABILITIES	$197,000
NET WORTH	$823,000

Figure 4.1   Net Worth Statement

ago came up with an idea that has caught on like wildfire: the home equity loan. A home equity loan is a second mortgage on your home. The second mortgage, when combined with your existing mortgage, can equal as much as 80 percent of the value of your home. Let's assume that your home today is worth $500,000 and the balance of the first mortgage is $100,000. For the second mortgage, the bank calculates that 80 percent of $500,000 is $400,000. Subtract the $100,000 first mortgage from $400,000. The difference is $300,000, which is the amount of your equity loan. You can draw from that loan at any time you wish and at any amount up to $300,000.

You'll pay interest only on the money you draw, and the interest rate is generally the prime rate, the lowest rate that banks charge. When you obtain a home equity loan at the prime rate, you are getting the same low interest rate available to the very wealthy. But that is not the end of it. You generally pay no closing costs, and you have up to 20 years to repay the loan. In many cases, you pay only interest for the first 10 years. After that, you begin to pay principal and interest. You can repay the amounts that you borrow at any time and, as soon as you pay, the interest stops. Then you can tap the same credit line again and again, up to $300,000.

You can't beat this kind of a deal, which gives you a ready source of cash and opens the door for you to start investing in properties. Even if you don't invest it all in property, you know that you have up to $300,000 available at any time you need it. One word of caution: Don't fall behind in your payments, because that will detrimentally affect your credit rating.

According to Lawrence Yun, chief economist and senior vice president of research for the National Association of Realtors, "subprime mortgages account for less than 10 percent of total home ownership" in the country. Those of you in the remaining 90 percent will more than likely qualify for a home equity loan.

IRA Accounts

Individual Retirement Accounts (IRAs) can be invested in real estate. Even some of the smartest people in the country mistakenly believe that IRA monies can be invested only in stocks, bonds, annuities, and the like. But it is perfectly legal to use IRA monies for real estate investments and mortgages. You do not withdraw the money from the IRA to invest personally but, rather, transfer it into a self-directed IRA. The IRA itself can then acquire the investment along the terms allowed by the federal government.

When done correctly, this IRA option is very a powerful one. I've been encouraging my cousin to move her $100,000 IRA account into a real estate investment. The return that she is now getting from her IRA is 3 percent from an annuity with a multibillion-dollar insurance company. Real estate investments could boost those returns to 15 percent to 20 percent—or more.

Cash Value of Life Insurance

There are various types of life insurance. They include term life, universal life, and variable life. The one I am referring to here is whole life insurance. With this type of policy, the insured pays a fixed premium until death, at which time the beneficiary may receive the funds over a lifetime or for a fixed number of years.

Three or four years after this type of policy is purchased, the policy owner begins to build up a cash value. It accumulates each time a premium payment is made. The policyholder can borrow in excess of 90 percent of the policy value, but never 100 percent. (The insurance company holds back enough money to pay the interest charge in the event the policyholder does not pay it.) The loan does not have to be repaid until the death of the insured, at which time it is deducted from the amount of insurance received by the beneficiary.

Many people overlook the fact that the cash value of their insurance policy is an asset that they can borrow on quickly without any red tape or costs. Investing this money in income-producing property can result in a much higher return than the interest being paid to the insurance company for borrowing the money.

Customized Creativity

You don't need to have assets to get money. People with virtually no assets can begin the journey into the world of real estate and become wealthy if they have good incomes, good credit ratings, or even good friends open to a smart investment opportunity.

For example, let's say that you find a bargain consisting of 10 small bay warehouses. You don't have the money to buy it, but you know that your attorney, your accountant, and your appraiser friend want to invest when the right opportunity arises. Your appraiser friend agrees that the property is at least 15 percent under the market value. If renovations are made and the property is more effectively managed, the rents can be increased to a level where the property will be worth much more.

You suggest forming a partnership. You will own 10 percent of the deal for finding such an exceptional property, while your three friends will own the rest. In addition, you will receive a fee for overseeing the improvements and managing the property. Here's a case where you have no money in the deal, yet you have created a partnership that will enjoy great profits in the future.

The Use of Options

An option to purchase is a written agreement between an owner of a property (seller) and a prospective buyer. It gives the buyer the right to acquire a property at some time in the future at a fixed price. The fixed price is arrived at when the option agreement is signed. The optionor is the person extending the option (the seller) and the optionee is the person getting the option (prospective buyer). In exchange for this right to buy, the prospective buyer gives the seller an agreed amount of money, referred to as option money. The option money can vary from a nominal amount to a larger amount depending on the size of the deal. The time frame to exercise an option to purchase can range from a few months to several years.

Depending on the deal, the initial fixed price can increase over a period of time. For example, let's say that you obtain a one-year option to buy a small office building for $700,000 with $10,000 option money. You can renew the option for a second year, with the price increasing to $725,000, by paying an additional $15,000 in option money. In 1.5 years, the property increases in value to $950,000, and you sell it to a third-party purchaser for that price. A simultaneous closing takes place, at which time you close on your purchase for $725,000 by paying the balance of $700,000 ($725,000 less $25,000 option money credited to the purchase price) and the third-party purchaser pays you $950,000. The spread is $225,000 ($950,000 resale price less your purchase price of $725,000 equals $225,000 profit). That reflects a 900 percent return on your cash investment ($225,000 divided by $25,000 equals 900 percent).

Many options, if drafted properly by the optionee, will give the optionee the right to sell the option itself at any price during the option period. Many optionees do this and pick up a quick profit without ever closing the deal. There are different types of options but three are commonly used:

1. An option to purchase property.
2. A lease of a property with an option to purchase.
3. A sales contract subject to certain conditions. For example, it might be a sale that is conditioned on getting a property rezoned from residential use to a retail strip store center. If not rezoned, the deal is off and the deposit will be refunded. Although this is actually a contingent sale it is, in effect, an option.

In an up market, options are difficult to obtain because many owners don't want to sell. They think prices will continue to rise. In a down market, when prices are softening and beginning to come down, sellers will be more receptive to giving options. This is the time for you to step in and make big money with a small amount of cash.

OPM

The use of other peoples' money (OPM) may sound like a slick formula for investing, but it's not if it's done in a professional manner with a clear understanding between the parties. There are wealthy people who will lend money to someone they trust and believe will become successful in the business world. A relationship such as this is not common, but it can be established when both parties respect one another and the lending party feels confident the loan will be repaid. Many years ago when I was young in the business, I formed a holding company, O & R Investments Inc., with an attorney friend of mine, Evan Olster, who had a good head for real estate. The purpose of this company was to buy foreclosures on the courthouse steps. We each scratched up $500 to get the company started, but $1,000 wasn't enough. However, we had no assets or banking connections.

Evan had a rich uncle, Ben Chauncey, who liked the idea of Evan and me buying foreclosures. He also had faith in our integrity and abilities. We initially thought we would offer Ben a one-third interest in the company, then decided it would be simpler to sign a promissory note and pay him 17 percent interest—substantially more than he was receiving from his bank accounts. That way, Evan and I could split the profit 50/50 rather than dividing it three ways. Ben liked the simplicity of this strategy and started us off with $100,000. Over the next 10 years we bought 350 properties auctioned on the courthouse steps, fixed them up, and resold them at good profits. Ben continued to increase the loans, eventually cutting the rate of interest in half. Our company went from a $1,000 investment to a net worth of several million dollars over a decade.

Ask Your Banker

Most people believe you must have collateral to apply for a loan, but that's not always true. Ask the loan officer at your bank about a noncollateralized loan. There is no banking regulation that prohibits this. In fact, wealthy customers of the bank do it all the time, borrowing large sums at prime rate or below just on their signatures. They invest it at a much higher rate of interest without using a penny of their own money.

You can do the same thing on a much smaller scale. Explain that you need money to invest in an income property, then ask for a loan on your signature. If you have been a good customer of the bank and have excellent credit, you're likely to get it. Ask for a loan that is more than you expect to get so that there is room for compromise.

The bank will charge you an interest rate of 1 percent or 2 percent over the prime rate. You pay interest on the money only as you draw it. Usually you get a year to repay the loan with the understanding that the loan will be renewed if you pay it off and don't seek another loan for 30 to 60 days. At that point, not only will you likely be able to renew the loan, but you'll have a good chance of increasing the amount of the loan.

If you haven't resold the property within the year or made enough money to repay the loan, what do you do? You will have to be resourceful. Ask a business colleague or a family member for an interim loan (also known as a bridge loan). After all, you'll need it for only the 30 to 60 days before you can return to the bank for another loan. Bankers have helped me over the years. I started off with a $3,000 signature loan early in my real estate career. Ten years later I was able to borrow in excess of $1 million just on my signature.

Present Sacrifice for Future Benefits

The most conservative—and obvious—way to get a down payment for an investment property is to save for it. The biggest obstacle to saving is our consumerism-obsessed culture. The average American has zero savings. In fact, many people spend even more than they make. We live beyond our means, buying expensive cars, big homes, designer clothes, and country club memberships, while taking expensive vacations. Most of us are in such denial that we don't seem to mind paying 18 percent or 20 percent interest on our credit cards. This is a poverty mentality.

By taking a true assessment of our needs, versus our wants, we could devise a plan to help generate down-payment money. We could replace our gas guzzlers with smaller hybrid cars, sell our big houses with strangling mortgages, and move to more affordable homes. We could prepare gourmet dinners at home rather than eat in expensive restaurants. Those lattes at you-know-where add up, too. Take your lunch to work.

Small sacrifices add up to big savings. Come up with a plan, put it in writing, and live by it. Enroll your partner and your family in the dream of what future benefits will come from present sacrifice. This is a prosperity mentality that puts you in charge of your economic life.

The Moped Story

A colleague of mine, Scott Sime, made his first investment without any cash when he was in college. Today he's a multimillionaire investor as well as the managing director of the Miami office of CB Richard Ellis. Here is Scott's story in his own words.

> The delayed gratification theory is something that I started early in my professional career, and it still encompasses a great part of my character and actions today, 25 years later.
>
> My freshman year at Duke University, I ran an advertisement in the local paper to sell my Japanese automobile for $10,000. This car was a gift from my parents after I received an athletic scholarship. I wanted the money to invest in the stock market or real estate. I had done some intern work with a stock brokerage firm earlier that year, and I was anxious to begin my investment strategy. My plan was to sell the car and buy a moped for transportation around campus.
>
> Chip Chesson, a local real estate developer/broker, answered my advertisement. After several rounds of negotiations, I traded the automobile for the down payment on a duplex Chip had recently developed. The duplex price was $60,000, and my $10,000 auto served as the down payment to close the deal. This investment produced approximately $2,000 per year in pre-tax cash flow from the net rentals. Four years later during my senior year of college, the property sold for $70,000.
>
> The upshot was that I doubled my cash investment while receiving a monthly cash flow. Having completed my first real estate deal, I had $20,000 in my bank account, and I was on my way to bigger and better investments. The moped, meanwhile, cost $300 and served me well for my four years at Duke.

After college, I took my $20,000 from the duplex sale and used it toward a $180,000 home in Miami's Coconut Grove neighborhood. My income from my real estate brokerage business was not enough to cover the mortgage, so I converted the utility room into a loft-style half-bedroom—basically a wooden loft above the washer and dryer. This was a detached structure away from the main house. By doing this I was able to rent the main house and cover the majority of my mortgage payment. At the end of the day, it cost me $350 per month to own this home and live in this utility room. Not glamorous, but I sold the house two years later for $225,000. That was a $45,000 return on a $20,000 investment.

This chapter has focused on helping you realize how relatively easy it is to find investment money—in fact, you may already have it without knowing it—and that many financing options may be readily within your reach. We're now ready to move on to the most important strategy in this book, the Big Six. These are the components of the success-driving formula that will ensure that you buy the right property.

The Bottom Line

Most people want to increase their wealth. Then why do so many stop before they even get started? It's because they think they need a lot of cash. If they were talking about stocks, bonds, or most other investment vehicles, they'd be right. But real estate investment is the exception. This is one business area where, with a bit of resourcefulness, you can acquire investments with very little cash of your own.

Much of this springs from a distinction in real estate financing: It's not how much cash you have, it's what you're worth. And according to a government report, Americans are worth more than ever.

The "Flow of Funds" report issued by the Federal Reserve early in 2007 concluded that Americans were 7.4 percent richer at the end of 2006 than they were a year earlier. The measurement focused on household net worth, or how rich a household is after liabilities, such as credit card debt and mortgages, are subtracted from assets such as houses, cars, and retirement accounts. Although many Americans don't save money, consumers' ratio of net worth-versus-income has been rising steadily since 2002.

For first-time investors, arguably the most eye-opening aspects of real estate investment involve financing flexibility. You can borrow against assets you already own, form partnerships, and implement options to buy property, or you can just play off your good credit standing to persuade your bank to extend you a line of credit. These options are available because real estate investment is not a lone-wolf undertaking. Certainly your goal is to make money for yourself. But along the way, banks, mortgage companies, and others also stand to make money—and that is why they are willing, even anxious, to help you find ways to begin your investment. The range of options for finding financing is so amazing that you can even, under certain circumstances, invest in a real estate deal without using *any* of your own money. New investors frequently overlook valuable resources close at hand.

There was a time when financing vehicles were few and straightforward. In recent years, however, a number of new—often innovative—offerings have become staples among the growing roster of financing options. Lenders are willing to work with you to get the investment money you need, but you must be prepared when you approach them. Knowing the workings of the mortgage loan market and understanding all the options you can tap is imperative. If you're creative, there is even an array of customized alternatives open to you. You just have to identify them.

The United States is no longer a cash economy, and real estate investors—including you—should be prepared to embrace that.

PART
II

THE BIG SIX FORMULA

Everyone wants a magic and immediate path to wealth. The bad news? That path doesn't exist. The good news? Wealth is attainable through more conventional means. If you come to understand the real estate industry, if you apply the knowledge you pick up in this book, and if you deepen your own firsthand experience as you buy and sell investment properties, you'll be on the road to success.

Along that road, there are six core principles that will make or break each real estate deal. They are the most important concepts you will learn. I call them the Big Six. If you master these principles, wealth will be within reach. We'll touch on each of the Big Six in the six chapters that follow, explaining what makes them so important and how you must incorporate them into your real estate investments.

When I organize real estate seminars at universities or for members of Realtor associations, the Big Six are the cornerstones of the class. Thousands of people have taken our seminars, mastered the Big Six, and found their road to riches. You can, too. However, it's not enough to just understand and utilize the Big Six. You must execute them *in order*. That's because each builds on elements of the previous component in the sextet.

The Big Six are

1. Location
2. Building quality and design efficiency
3. Tenant profile
4. Upside
5. Financing
6. Price

The elements of the Big Six are graphically illustrated in Figure 5.1.

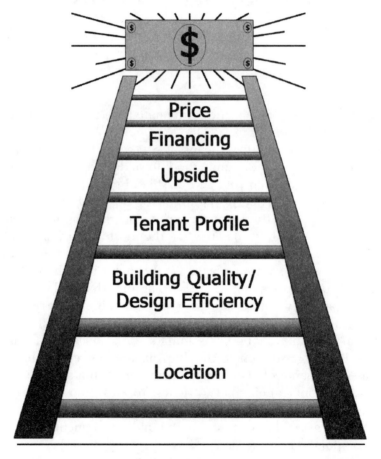

Figure 5.1   The Big Six Ladder to Achieving Real Estate Wealth

I came to identify the six essential components through my own real estate experiences. With each successive deal I negotiated, I grew to recognize the common elements. The Big Six are part of a sequenced step-by-step formula that enables you to identify and purchase the right property at the right price. And your property purchases—more than your property sales—are crucial to attaining your financial goals.

With the Big Six formula, you make your money in buying. That's right. Your "buy"—not the sale of your property later—is by far the key to wealth. Jumping into a deal because you've found a building with dramatic architecture, beautiful landscaping, and in immaculate condition means little if the rents are at the full market rate, leases are long term, and renewal options carry only modest increases. Such a building might impress your friends, but what good is it as an investment if it offers no opportunity to increase your income and, correspondingly, the value of the building?

It doesn't take a rocket scientist to figure out that the value of an income property comes from the income it generates. The best strategy is to buy a building that has rents substantially lower than the market rate and leases expiring in a relatively short period of time with no renewal options. That puts you in a position to raise the rent, increase the income stream from the property, and, as a result, boost the value of the property.

You might be thinking that because I have had more than 30 years of experience investing in real estate, I have an edge over you. That's true, but you eventually can do as well or better than I have done if you start now and you abide by the Big Six. It's really not that difficult.

Remember, none of the Big Six components can stand alone. They fit together snugly to form your customized real estate formula.

CHAPTER 5

Location

PLANTING INVESTMENT ROOTS

As you launch your search for investment properties, one of the big questions you'll have to answer is "where?" Location—the first element in the Big Six formula—is the single most important component of any real estate deal. It is crucial in determining your investment success. Those who buy in well-established locations will be safe and secure with their investment. Rarely will they see their real estate decrease in value. More than likely, they will see it increase at an extraordinary rate over time.

Most successful investors have made their millions by buying in the best locations—although it means that they have to search longer and harder for just the right property. "The money is easy to find. It's finding the deal that is difficult," says Bob Gallaher, a long-time real estate investor in South Florida. That said, the elements that make one location more desirable than another are many. They include the socioeconomic levels of the people who live or work in a particular neighborhood, its proximity to public transportation, crime levels, the nearness of prestigious universities and medical facilities, traffic congestion, zoning restrictions, the quality of schools, fire and police protection, and even the reputation of the local government and its officials.

The type of property you seek—apartment building versus small shopping center or office building versus warehouse—also is important in determining the "where" in your investment strategy.

In addition, you'll need to bear in mind that location is not a fixed characteristic. The appeal of locations can change—good neighborhoods can begin to erode and sketchy neighborhoods can stabilize. Whether a location meets the goals of your investment strategy is not something you'll be able to ascertain without exploring a number of factors.

The appeal of locations has shifted as the country has developed. Before the advent of the automobile, development was focused on cities, because there simply was no easy way for most people to venture into the vast wilderness that surrounded urban centers. Some of the oldest U.S. cities (e.g., Philadelphia and Annapolis, MD) date to the seventeenth century. Like them, urban areas that saw fast growth in the eighteenth century—including Boston, New York, and New Orleans—still have neighborhoods with elegant, well-preserved buildings, many of which are listed on the National Register of Historic Places.

Once automobiles became commonplace, communities began to flourish outside cities. As the U.S. population grew, the country reached a crucial juncture: How would the nation's transportation system be unified? President Dwight D. Eisenhower made it official in the 1950s when he launched a federal highway system. His initiative shaped the way the country grew and changed. Because of the highway system and the automobile culture, suburban areas matured and today are considered prime locations for real estate investors. In some older urban areas, industry and jobs have even shifted out of the inner cities and into the suburbs. In the metropolitan Detroit area, for example, a disproportionate number of commuters drive from suburb-to-suburb for work, rather than from suburb-to-downtown.

These dynamics of population growth have had a direct bearing on the development of commercial properties, including apartment buildings, retail centers, office buildings, and industrial buildings. That is how location has evolved into such an essential factor.

Evaluating Locations

As real estate brokers and investors began to look upon location in terms of its desirability, an informal ranking system emerged. Brokers and investors started to refer to "A" locations, or properties they considered to be situated in excellent areas; "B" locations were good; and "C" locations were fair. These ratings, while not an exact science, combined both objective and subjective considerations. That said, when individuals in the real estate industry refer to a rating, most of their colleagues concur. Think of different areas of your own community and rate them by location. Then ask your friends and neighbors to do the same thing. I think you will find that your conclusions are pretty much the same.

Since there is a subjective aspect to this, not all people will agree all the time on what makes up an "A" location. But it will be rare that you find people putting an "A" location ranking on what most others consider to be a "C" location. Though imperfect, this system is helpful in narrowing down locations that match your investment goals. To better understand how the locations are ranked, let's look at the three categories that investors are likely to consider.

Type "A" Locations

Here we will find prestigious, stable, established communities that have been around for many years. In the downtown areas of "A" locations, it may be that the development of properties took place more than 100 years ago and, within the core of the city, there will be a mix of all types of properties. If there is waterfront, we likely will see high-rise luxury apartments and condominiums leasing at impressive rates and selling at upper-end prices. We will also see skyscraper office buildings rented to high-profile tenants. Any property in such a location will command premium prices because there is little or no land available for new development. In fact, old buildings in disrepair are often torn down to make way for new construction. Be aware, however, that not every area within the downtown section can be considered an "A" location. There may also be "B" and "C" locations surrounding the core.

"A" locations in suburban areas, meanwhile, are usually in close proximity to conveniences and necessary services. Within these non-urban communities, we find neighborhoods with expensive homes and affluent residents. Thus, the tenants renting in "A" location buildings will be pay higher rent than those in other communities.

> **Transportation:** Certainly, transportation options exist everywhere, but in the case of "A" locations—because the homes and commercial properties were developed first—transportation is

generally close by. In many cases, there is no need to travel to a major expressway to get to common destinations. Still, some expressways and major arterial roads will be accessible to the people in the "A" locations. What differentiates an "A" location is the easy ability to get to prestigious office buildings providing professional services or to high-class retail centers in a shorter period of time.

Shopping: The "A" communities are characterized by excellent shopping facilities. Not only will we find major shopping malls with some of the most sophisticated retail stores in the country, but there will be other stores and restaurants catering to just about every need. Retail strip centers within the "A" locations have top-quality tenants and goods in a higher price range than other areas. Also, we will find beautiful professional office buildings. Not only do people who reside in such communities do business there, but residents of less prestigious areas will be drawn to the "A" retail locations.

Medical: As the population ages, affluent people in "A" communities want to travel shorter distances to medical professionals. As a result, the best medical professionals are usually located within these areas. This means medical office buildings here command high rents and usually have close to 100 percent occupancy. The demand for hospitals, of course, exists within all locations. The best hospitals will not always be in "A" locations, but many are.

Cultural and entertainment venues: Another characteristic that marks "A" locations is the presence—within a reasonable distance—of theaters, fine restaurants, cinemas, sports facilities, and cultural venues. The restaurateurs are paying upper-end rents to the owners of the buildings; consequently, their menus feature higher prices than might be found elsewhere. Private clubs, cultural outlets, and performing arts centers carry a particular status or snob appeal.

Schools: "A" location schools, both public and private, usually have reputations for excellence. Many people who can afford to will opt to buy homes in communities where the public schools are top-notch. Universities are often within a reasonable distance (although many of the finest universities in the United States are not in "A" locations).

Houses of worship: Affluent people in top-rate locations want to be within a reasonable distance of prestigious and established churches and synagogues, including those with respected religious schools. Not only do these houses of worship fulfill a spiritual purpose, but they are also used for cultural and social activities.

Supply and demand: The demand for rentals in "A" locations will usually exceed supply. This is across the board and includes rentals of apartment buildings, retail stores, and office buildings. Since the owners of these properties are able to get higher rents, their investments bring increased net incomes. At the same time, the value of properties in "A" locations will normally increase more substantially than properties in other locations. There is also a feeling of security and safety associated with investing in these established and stable communities. Properties in these locations are the hardest to find, but patient and persistent investors will spot opportunities.

Property taxes: Homeowners in these areas generally pay the highest property taxes. Taxes for income property owners in an "A" location will also be higher, simply because the assessed value of the properties is greater. In many cases, the property taxes—and most other expenses—can be passed on to the tenants. For example, the owners of many shopping centers and office buildings have clauses in their leases requiring tenants to pay their pro rata share for increases in property taxes and operating expenses. Thus, as the expenses increase, the landlord does not bear the additional cost alone.

Such clauses are rare in apartment rental leases; since the leases are generally of a short-term nature, building owners can simply increase rents. Owners of real estate in "A" locations pay the highest property taxes for multiple reasons: Schools are generally better run with quality teachers and advanced curriculums; roads are better maintained; police and fire protection is professional with a fast response time; and park landscaping and recreational facilities are usually kept in top condition. So while taxes are high, they are high only relative to properties in less desirable locations. And residents and investors in "A" locations can afford to pay the higher taxes.

Appreciation: Although demand in "A" locations will almost always be greater than the supply, that's not to say there will be no vacancies or turnovers within the buildings. However, when a vacancy occurs, the apartment, store, or office in question is generally rerented quickly. The vacancy factor in an "A" location may be 1 percent to 3 percent annually; it is usually a great deal higher in other locations. Because of the higher occupancy and substantial rent payments, there is security in investing in buildings in an "A" location. Depending on the structure and condition of the leases, the rate of return for investors can be conservative or it can be quite high.

Type "B" Locations

"B" locations have some of the same features as "A" locations, but quality standards are often not as stringent and some characteristics may be missing. The people who reside in a "B" location are generally middle class. Their communities are well kept and their homes, while priced considerably below those in "A" locations, are attractive.

Because "B" locations are not as desirable as "A" locations, there is more land available to build on. That means the supply-and-demand factor is not what it would be in an "A" location. The demand, in some cases, may be greater than the supply, but generally the supply is greater than the demand. One can determine this to a great degree by simply traveling up and down main streets to see how many vacant stores there are within retail strip centers and shopping centers. The presence of numerous empty stores indicates a high vacancy rate in the area. A check of the vacancies in office buildings and apartment buildings can also help determine the location category. It would not be unusual to find a vacancy factor of 5 percent or more within a "B" location.

More homes are likely to be for sale in this location, too. Since commercial properties mirror the residential properties in a location, a higher volume of homes for sale usually means there is a higher vacancy level for apartment buildings, retail stores, and office buildings. There are certainly many exceptions but, as a rule of thumb, the more homes there are and the longer they take to sell, the more vacancies can be found among commercial buildings.

Transportation: People are more likely to use public transportation, including mass transit, if it is available.

Shopping: So-called Big Box discount stores, as well as neighborhood and regional shopping centers—usually with anchor tenants catering to middle-class consumers—are found in this location. Leased strip malls in this area will have convenience stores, small restaurants, shoe repair shops, and the like.

Medical: Doctors, dentists, and other medical professionals in "B" locations may be as qualified as those in "A" locations but, because they treat middle-class patients, they want to lease offices where the rents are more reasonable. Therefore, building design and construction quality are of less importance in "B" locations than in medical offices in "A" locations.

Cultural and entertainment venues: These locations have good theaters, concert halls, and restaurants. However they will not be as glitzy as those in "A" locations, and they will be more reasonably priced. Snob appeal is not a big factor.

Houses of worship: As with "A" locations, people want to be in close proximity to churches, synagogues, and other religious centers. Not only are they used for worship, but they serve as community and cultural gathering places.

Schools: "B" location public schools can be excellent (depending on the quality of the teaching staff and the programs). Magnet schools and charter schools are often found in "B" locations.

Supply and demand: Rents in a "B" location will be significantly lower than those in "A" locations, and commercial property patterns will mirror those of residential properties. Across the board, rents will probably be about 25 percent lower than those in "A" locations, and it will take longer to rent vacant apartments and offices.

Contrary to "A" locations, the supply of properties will outweigh demand. In an "A" location, there is little or no land to build on. In a "B" location, there are many sites available for development. As a result, when new apartments, offices, and retail stores are built, there may be higher vacancy levels in existing buildings and rents could decline.

Where "A" location vacancy rates may be 1 percent to 3 percent, "B" location vacancy rates could be 5 percent or more.

Property taxes: A primary factor in property tax assessments is the net income that buildings generate. Since "B" location buildings normally have lower net incomes, their real estate values—and corresponding taxes—are lower.

Appreciation: Because there is usually greater supply than demand, the vacancy factor in a "B" location could be considerably higher than in "A" locations. An exception is when rents are below market rates. In that case, the buildings will have less turnover, fewer vacancies, and the return on investment may even be greater than otherwise expected. If a building is attractively designed, it may even have an appreciation rate similar to one in an "A" location.

Type "C" Locations

"C" locations are unlike "A" or "B" locations. Homes in this location would be modest, and residents' incomes would be much, much lower than in an "A" location and much lower than in a "B" location. Again, commercial properties would mirror the residential properties, with lower rental rates for both. People would be living in apartments that are somewhat marginal.

Transportation: Although the distance to expressways and major arterial roads might be approximately the same, fewer people in this location will own automobiles. They are more likely to rely on buses, subways, and other public transportation to get to their places of work. As a result, there would be good accessibility to public transportation.

Shopping: Retail offerings in a "C" location will not be as appealing as those in "A" and "B" locations. The shopping facilities will, to a great degree, consist of convenience stores and retail strip centers with retail tenants paying considerably lower rents. Many residents in a "C" location will not shop in their own neighborhoods. Rather, they will travel into a "B" location where there is a wider selection of goods and services.

Medical: Medical services may be dominated by county-owned hospitals reliant on Medicaid or Medicare patients. Some of these hospitals will be first rate and boast exceptional doctors, but this most often occurs when these are teaching hospitals affiliated with a university.

Cultural and entertainment venues: There are fewer cultural venues, although there may be more parks and recreational facilities because of government concerns about providing leisure-time facilities in working-class neighborhoods. Some of the best restaurants, especially those established many years ago, are found in these locations.

Schools: The schools within a "C" location might not match the quality of those in "A" and "B" locations, although there are always exceptions. Young people living in "C" neighborhoods may not necessarily attend nearby schools; they may be enrolled in schools in "A" or "B" locations, especially if their school district offers magnet or charter school options (and corresponding transportation).

Supply and demand: Land and buildings will be in plentiful supply, and property values, as a result, will be considerably lower than in "A" and "B" locations. Apartment buildings, retail stores, and office buildings will have higher vacancy rates, and rental rates will be much lower than in "B" locations. It will not be unusual to find a 10 percent to 20 percent vacancy factor in a "C" location; apartment buildings may have annual turnover rates as high as 40 percent. But vacancy and turnover rates can be kept lower if the stores, office buildings, and apartment complexes are kept in good condition and offer reasonable rents.

Property taxes: Homes will be in the lower price range, and commercial buildings will generally be of poor design and have lower quality construction. These conditions, together with lower rental revenues, will result in lower property taxes.

Appreciation: Property values, in most cases, are not going to increase at a rate comparable with "A" and "B" locations. This is particularly true for buildings with high vacancy rates, whether they are apartments, retail stores, offices, or industrial buildings. The exception could be buildings that are well managed and leased at bargain prices with high occupancy rates. Once sold, these buildings may experience considerable appreciation, because the investors who acquire them can increase the rents to—or close to—market levels. If they do so, the buildings will grow in value.

Industrial Properties

Criteria for ranking a location for warehouses and manufacturing plants differ from those of other investment real estate. What may be an "A" or "B" location for income-producing residential or office properties might not necessarily be considered appropriate for warehouses and manufacturing facilities. Because owners and tenants of these types of buildings cater to a different clientele, they normally look for places where land is inexpensive yet close to transportation conduits. As a result, what would be a "C" location for apartments, retail stores, and offices could well be an "A" location for warehouses.

Properties comprising small bay warehouses, flex space, or public storage facilities might be situated in a separate industrial district within any location (including "A" locations and "B" locations). However, manufacturing plants and complexes for heavy industrial use would not. They are more likely to be situated in "C" locations.

Short-Term Gains and Declines

Even if you find a location that seems right, you still must determine the direction in which it is headed. Some locations are on the upswing, while others are on the way down. If a location has moved up to an "A" from a "B," you need to research whether the rise has been steady. There are many possible reasons for an improvement in the ranking of a location: Higher-end homes (and condos) may have been built in the areas, a prestigious university may have opened a campus nearby, or a public transit link may have been added or improved. On the other hand, if a location has declined from an "A" location to a "B" or even "C" location, that also should be a red flag for an investor. Such a tumble could be sparked by a variety of factors, including haphazard zoning, traffic congestion, increased crime, deteriorating schools, and poor infrastructure.

After looking at a number of properties in different locations and tapping the expertise of the right broker and other professionals, the wise investor can learn a great deal about the dynamics of locations, including where transitions from one category to another are taking place—and whether they are on the rise or on the decline.

Long-Term Gains and Declines

Within any community, large or small, there are established neighborhoods. Some of these locations might have been undesirable at one time but, for a number of reasons, they are sought after today. Take Harlem in New York City. Once viewed as a run-down and dangerous neighborhood with abandoned buildings, the area is undergoing a revival. Former President Bill Clinton has established the William J. Clinton Foundation in a Harlem building with a view of Central Park and midtown high-rises. Harlem townhouses are regularly selling for more than $1 million. And Vornado Realty Trust, which specializes in Manhattan office and commercial space, announced in mid-2007 that it would build the first new office building in Harlem in more than 30 years.

South Beach in the Miami area is another turnaround story. Some 20 years ago, South Beach was a haven for retirees with moderate fixed incomes, including Social Security benefits. The ocean-front area had virtually no attractions, and few young professionals had any desire to go there. In the past 10 to 15 years, the area has gone through a dramatic transformation. Old hotels facing the ocean have been completely renovated or demolished to make way for new construction. Top-rate restaurants and entertainment, trendy nightclubs, and designer shops have joined a renourished sandy beach—now wide and beautiful. Touted around the globe as a hip and happening destination for a vacation or for a second home, the area is now known by the trendy moniker SoBe, short for South Beach.

Concurrently, there are once-attractive locations that have deteriorated in value and attractiveness. A decade ago, the Seattle suburb of Bellevue, Washington, was a community on the upswing. Developers were putting up buildings as fast as they could, bullish about the growing local economy and the nearness of Microsoft's world headquarters, a catalyst for Bellevue's burgeoning tech industry. Then the Internet bubble burst. There are signs that Bellevue is resuscitating, with new construction projects and office building vacancies at 4.5 percent in early 2007. That's a big change from the

28 percent vacancy rate during the bust, a time when the Seattle area lost an estimated 20,000 technology jobs.

And there's Roxbury, a suburb of Boston that was once known as a solid middle-class location. Problems with violent crime have caused housing price declines there. First quarter 2007 figures from the Multiple Listings Service Property Information Network, a real estate database, found that Roxbury condo sales prices were down more than 29 percent. And don't forget Three Mile Island, the nuclear power plant accident that, among other things, ravaged property values in a big swath near and through Middletown, PA.

So locations can—and do—change, both in the short term and for the long term. But there are ways to determine whether an area is on the upswing or, conversely, is showing signs of decline. That said, when you seek an area for your real estate investment, you're not necessarily looking for a location that is being gentrified. Your goal is to find an area that is solid and stable. Money can be made in any location, but the surest way is to invest in "A" locations. My own investment strategy has been to buy good quality buildings in rock-solid "A" locations. What I mean by a "good" building is the subject of our next chapter.

The Bottom Line

One thing that makes property investment so interesting is the dynamism of the real estate landscape. There are myriad factors to look at when it comes to selecting income-producing properties, but one—your ability to choose the right location—will be absolutely paramount to your real-estate success. This is your first and most important step as you begin the journey to create wealth. If you buy a property in the right location, then follow up by adhering to the additional elements of the Big Six, you'll be a winner.

All investors wish to make money and to see their properties generate a substantial cash flow and increase in value over time. There are ways to make money from investments in nearly any location. However, as we create a real estate investment strategy, we want one that not only is successful in the long-term but also safe and solid. That strategy is to buy in "A" locations.

You may be able to modify or redesign a house. You may be able to tear down a building on a property you own and build a new one from scratch. You may even be able to change the use of an investment property. But there is one thing you can never change—the location. For that reason you must be certain you're putting your money in a solid neighborhood.

Drive up and down streets in any community, and you'll be able to spot the areas that are thriving. These will be places where there are few—if any—vacancies, where the buildings are well designed and well maintained, where people of means congregate, and where the community has major cultural and entertainment facilities, top fire and police protection, and quality schools. This is the type of location that you should be looking at to invest your money.

But you also need to remember that neighborhoods can change in a heartbeat, for better or for worse. Or they may slowly evolve into a different location category. Before you invest, it is your job to identify if the location is in the process of shifting—and the direction it is trending. Your judgment in selecting the right location must be exceptional.

Never underestimate the importance of this decision. The foundation for real estate investment is location. Of course, you need to adhere to the other five elements in the Big Six. However, if you don't begin by choosing the right location, the remaining steps become meaningless.

CHAPTER 6

Building Quality and Design Efficiency

ENSURING THE LONG-TERM VIABILITY OF YOUR PORTFOLIO

There are two parts to the second element of the Big Six. The first, building quality, refers to the craftsmanship and construction standards used in a building. The second element is design efficiency—that is, the combination of special features that add to a structure's overall value and attractiveness. Design efficiency interfaces with building quality. When you find an investment property you'd like to buy, you will need to scrutinize both elements.

Some owners or developers instruct their architects to design buildings that can be built at the lowest possible cost. The resulting buildings meet minimum standards at the time of construction, with no regard for features that the market may consider desirable in the years to come. Forward-thinking owners and developers, on the other hand, erect buildings that far exceed minimum construction requirements, and they grace their buildings with useful and innovative design elements. Using imaginative and creative architects and well-established contractors to design and construct their buildings, they embrace the philosophy that building quality and design efficiency not only make their buildings attractive to tenants when they're inaugurated but add value to the buildings in the future.

Design features that stand the test of time include walk-in closets, large kitchens with windows, and his-and-her bathrooms. When it comes to commercial properties, strong design features run the range from higher-than-normal ceilings and wider hallways to overhangs above store entrances. Parking is also an important feature for commercial buildings, particularly stores. Rear parking for employees and plentiful general parking for customers is a value-added feature now and in the years to come. High-ceilinged warehouses configured so they are easily adaptable to office use are another example of buildings with forward-looking characteristics. All these amenities add value to the properties, and they attract top-level tenants. That means the building owners can obtain considerably higher rents than they would in a marginal building.

Do not mistakenly assume that a building must be brand new to meet the highest quality standards of a Class A building. Throughout the country, many people reside in buildings of superb quality that are fifty or a hundred years old—or older. These are buildings that were originally constructed to meet high standards and have been regularly updated to retain their charm, elegance, and character.

To understand the value and importance of quality construction and design efficiency, let's look at an inexpensive building that cost $50 per square foot to build 15 years ago and is now worth $100 per square foot. That's a 100 percent increase, or a little more than 6 percent appreciation per year. But a quality building that cost $90 per square foot to construct 15 years ago would now be worth $270 per square foot. That is equivalent to a 300 percent increase, or a 15 percent appreciation rate per year. It's easy to see which was the better long-term investment.

You should invest in a quality building. It gives a higher rate of return, and it appreciates in value at a faster rate, both goals in our wealth-creation strategy.

But how can you be sure you have a quality building? Not only do construction standards span a broad range, but they change over time. They also change from community to community. For that reason, you'll need time to thoroughly examine the building before you conclude the purchase. When you make an offer, you and the seller will execute a contract with a contingency: You will be given the opportunity to conduct a due diligence that includes physical inspections of the property. Depending on the size of the deal, the time period for this will typically run from 30 to 60 days.

This is the point when you'll tap the expertise of the professional team we discussed in Chapter 3. Working on your behalf, your CPA, attorney, and professionals such as an engineer or a general contractor will review such things as financial data, leases, service contracts, and building-code compliance and violations. The due diligence provisions state that if for *any* reason you determine that the building is unsatisfactory, you can cancel the contract and have your deposit refunded in full.

This chapter will help you understand what factors determine the "class" of a building and why each element is important for the long-term strength of your investment.

Class A Buildings

Less than one minute after seeing the exterior of a building, I already know whether I like it or not; I do not have to deliberate. Years of experience have taught me that it either has the right look or it doesn't; but you won't have to rely on your instincts. Just as real estate industry insiders assign a ranking to locations, they also have a system for rating buildings. They use alphabetical designations— classes A, B, and C—that take into consideration a combination of factors, including construction quality, architectural beauty, physical details, design efficiency, and tenant amenities. The differences among A, B, and C buildings are both objective and subjective. However, like location, most investors and brokers are pretty much in agreement with the criteria that define each classification.

Class A buildings feature the best architecture and construction. They are well designed and use the finest materials, workmanship, and finishes. Investors are attracted to them, and their rental space is scooped up by prestigious tenants. These buildings are excellently maintained and well managed. Attractive and efficient, they command the highest rents.

Class A buildings cater to tenants seeking ultra-luxurious apartment buildings, state-of-the-art office buildings, upscale retail centers for nationally known retailers, or industrial buildings suitable for major local companies. Big banks, large law firms, insurance companies, and other image-conscious firms that want their offices to exude prestige are drawn to Class A structures. These buildings will have large lobbies and common areas, good restaurants, water fountains, sculptures, and other beautiful artwork. If they are office buildings or apartment complexes, they may feature fitness centers and private dining clubs.

Class A buildings are the costliest to build and, because of their prestige and superb locations, they command high rents. But they also are likely to be out of a new investor's price range. They could cost from $25 million to several hundred million dollars. Often they are owned by institutional investors such as large insurance companies, financial institutions, pension funds, or real estate investment trusts (REITs). In the cases of corporate-owned buildings, the corporation may be more concerned with its own business performance and bottom line and less concerned about its real estate investment. Returns on these buildings are modest.

Class B Buildings

Class B buildings are well designed, well maintained, employ good materials, and exhibit fine workmanship. They also share some, although not all, of the features of Class A structures. They span a wide spectrum of prices, from $500,000 and up, and they usually generate a much greater rate of return than Class A buildings. Because of this, Class B buildings are in great demand by investors. The tenants who occupy these buildings don't want or need extreme luxury, glitz, or an abundance of amenities. As a result, they pay substantially less in rent than tenants in an A building. Our focus throughout this book will be on Class B buildings, because they give us the biggest bang for the buck.

Class C Buildings

Class C buildings offer few or no amenities and are usually older than Class B buildings. Their maintenance and management are just average, and their mechanical, electrical, plumbing, and ventilation systems are passable. If apartment buildings, they may have inexpensive materials and finishes. Parking will be minimal and landscaping, if there is any, will be basic. Class C office buildings, retail stores, and warehouses would have been constructed to meet minimal quality requirements and will have no frills.

These buildings generally attract low- to moderate-income tenants seeking affordable space. Initially the rate of return on Class C buildings may be significantly higher than those for Class A or

Class B buildings. However, the risk factor is high—especially in bad times—because this type of property is subject to high vacancy rates, high turnover, and tenants who are not paying rent.

In summary, we might say that A buildings are excellent, B buildings are very good, and C buildings are fair. Since Class B buildings will be our focus, you'll need to understand in detail what differentiates them. Class B apartment buildings will have details that vary from Class B offices, while Class B warehouses will have yet other construction and design features. As we examine some typical characteristics of a range of commercial real estate investments, bear in mind that key design features may not be consistent across all geographic areas of the United States.

Class B Apartment Buildings

Apartment buildings in the B category may consist of five-unit buildings or several hundred units in a single complex. They may be one-story or multilevel structures. However, they have fewer design flourishes than Class A buildings and a shorter list of amenities.

By way of example, let's take a look at Sophie Manor, a two-story, 24-unit, Class B apartment building with rental units. This 13-year-old building is close to a suburban "A" location. The design features that help define it as Class B include the following:

- Good architecture
- Attractive landscaping
- Security cameras at building entrances
- A principal door for each apartment that opens to a foyer instead of directly into a living room
- Windows in kitchens and bathrooms to provide natural light
- Walk-in closets
- Central air-conditioning and heat
- Open balconies (in temperate climates)
- Storage areas
- At least one parking space for each one-bedroom apartment, two spaces for each two-bedroom apartment, and three spaces for each three-bedroom apartment, along with ample visitor parking
- His-and-her bathrooms
- Kitchens with modern appliances

- Separate dining rooms
- A washer and dryer in each unit

Class B apartment buildings should also have a well-conceived and user-friendly floor plan. Many years ago, I bought a 76-unit apartment building, Kendall Manor, for $25,000 per unit, or a total price of $1.9 million. It was a C building in an "A" location. All the apartments were very small two-bedroom, one-bath units with only 575 square feet. I planned to convert the building to condos and sell the units for $49,900. But I changed my mind because there was a major elevated highway under construction that came so close to the building that it would have created an intolerable noise factor. There was also a very serious design flaw: The sole bathroom in each unit was located so that to use the bathroom, you had to walk through someone's bedroom. It was a terrible layout. I kept the building for about three years, increased the income and, because of inflation, was lucky to resell it at a reasonable profit.

Class B Retail Strip Store Centers

When I refer to retail strip centers, I'm talking about everything from clusters of a few stores to small shopping centers where there are lines of stores contiguous to each other under a common roof. Most retail strip centers are found in the suburbs. They generally are open-air complexes facing a main street. Most have one story, but there may be some two-story buildings that contain retail stores on the first floor and a combination of offices and service-related businesses on the second floor. Those second-floor businesses may include private mailing services, print shops, specialty shops, or bookkeeping services. They rent their offices at rates that are considerably less than those on the first floor.

The second-story businesses may see less traffic since some customers don't like walking to a second floor or even using an elevator. As a result, even if there is 100 percent occupancy on the first floor, the second floor might have a considerable number of vacancies. On the other hand, if the property is a larger shopping center of a mixed-use nature, there may be attractive apartments and professional offices on upper floors. (Large regional shopping centers and malls, a different category of real estate, are not the subject of this book.)

Let's look at Julia's Place, a one-story neighborhood strip center. Some of the desirable design features of Julia's Place include

- Stores facing a main street.
- Stores with uniform easy-to-see signage.
- Customer parking in front of the stores and employee parking behind. Julia's Place has a good ratio for customer parking— four spaces for every 1,000 square feet of rentable building area.
- An architecturally pleasing exterior façade with roof over-hangs to protect customers from inclement weather.
- Stores that are about 15 feet wide and 50 feet deep. If they are deeper, you will not get that much additional rent per square foot.
- Separate electric meters for each store.
- Separate water meters for each store.
- Individually controlled central air-conditioning and heat for each store.
- Security cameras at entranceways.

Class B Office Buildings

Class B office buildings come in all shapes and sizes. We'll use Gina's Plaza as an example as we look at the characteristics that distinguish it as Class B. This five-story office building with 30,000 rentable square feet sits close to commuter travel routes in an established and growing "A" location in a suburb. Individual offices within the building range in size from 500 to 2,500 square feet. Attorneys, account-ants, real estate brokers, psychologists, consultants, and insurance agents are among the tenants. For their clients and patients, the building is easy to find.

Gina's Plaza also has plenty of parking. Unlike some Class A buildings with parking structures, visitors don't have to shuttle up and down on elevators after parking in order to access the first-floor entrance. The parking system here is uncomplicated. There is surface parking on the same level as the building, making access convenient and simple. You might call it a user-friendly building.

Gina's Plaza has the following notable features:

- Good architecture.
- Attractive landscaping.

- A dignified backlit sign on the front of the building.
- A good parking ratio—four customer parking spaces for every 1,000 square feet of rentable building space, with more than ample visitor parking.
- Tiled or carpeted corridors.
- Common areas—hallways, bathrooms, lobbies, and storage rooms—equal to approximately 15 percent of the total gross square footage of the building. Space within an office plus the common area percentage equals the rentable square feet (RSF), on which the rental space is based. If the common area exceeds 20 percent, there can be tenant resistance to this.
- Corridors decorated with framed art posters or other wall décor.
- Tasteful and uniformly designed signage at the entrance to each office.
- Uniform signage and graphics in common areas.
- An attractive tenant directory at the entrance to the elevator listing the name and suite number of each office.
- Immaculately maintained restrooms.
- Many exterior windows.
- A security system that includes a card-entry system to unlock exterior doors after hours and on weekends.
- Security cameras at entrances.

Another type of Class B office building is the campus-style complex with several one- or two-story buildings with surface parking, all on a sizeable tract of land. These are often occupied by medical and other professional tenants with clientele that want and need to access the building easily. In many cases, each office has an exterior entrance rather than interior entrances off hallways.

There are also suburban Class B office complexes of mid-rise and low-rise buildings, with either parking garages in the building or connected to the building (or a combination of covered and surface parking). Most of these buildings have a principal entrance and interior corridors that allow access to individual offices.

Like a Class A building, a B office building may have striking architecture, but it lacks the plush lobbies, restaurants, and fitness centers. Still, B buildings must be continuously upgraded.

My own office building, an upper-end B building with excellent architecture, is in an "A" location. It was built in 1972 and I bought it in 1981. Because I have continually upgraded the building, people think it's much newer. During the past few years, I have modernized the elevator, replaced the hallway carpeting with granite tile, installed new lighting in the corridors, re-landscaped the exterior, repainted the exterior, and modernized the signage and graphics. In the final chapter of this book, "One Good Investment Is Worth a Lifetime of Labor," I will share with you why this building has become so successful.

To recap, here are the rules for choosing the most profitable long-term investments:

- Buy a B building in an "A" location.
- Buy a B building in a "B" location that's improving and destined to become an "A" location.
- Buy a C building in an "A" location provided that the building can be renovated and reconfigured at a reasonable cost to become a B building.

Please bear in mind that these rules are not usually applicable to industrial properties, which service a different clientele. The criteria for evaluating industrial locations are different.

Industrial Properties

Among the most attractive investments in the $500,000 and above price range are small bay warehouses. These are similar to strip stores in that they are contiguous to each other and sit in a row. Less parking is required, and the design features can be plainer than those of strip stores.

When it comes to small bay warehouses, smaller is better. Each warehouse should contain from about 600 square feet to about 2,500 square feet. Most bays generally have a small office within it. Tenants attracted to small bay warehouses include auto mechanics; suppliers of home improvement products such as flooring, electrical, or plumbing supplies; construction firms; and other businesses that need space but not a lot of infrastructure or amenities. For the most part, these tenants supply services or products, many to distributors and local residents. Small bay warehouses can be situated in any location. In "A" or "B" locations, they would be confined to areas designated for light industry.

Flex space warehouses are found in the same type of neighborhoods. Flex space warehouses combine warehouse space and office space within a single unit. The office area may be about 25 percent to 35 percent of the total area. These buildings generally have good exposure on well-traveled streets, usually with lots of glass or window detail and attractive landscaping. They are designed to look similar to attractive retail strip centers.

In recent decades, another type of warehouse—the public storage building—has sprung up. These are places where people can store items, usually on a temporary basis. Variations on this are the numerous mini warehouses available for storage of smaller items. Both types of storage facilities can be considered hybrids because they combine a real estate investment with the operation of a business.

Small bay and flex-type warehouses can be real moneymakers. They are excellent investments, even though they don't carry the glamour of other income properties, and they appreciate substantially in value, especially in areas around the country where there is a limited supply of land. Warehouses with high occupancy rates offer a powerful opportunity for investors who can find them. Within this arena, there have been conversions to warehouse-condos, some of which have been quite successful.

Now that you've found a building with the quality and design efficiency factors that meet the grade and in a location that has passed our Big Six requirements, you're ready for the next step in your journey to wealth—the tenant profile, the subject of our next chapter.

The Bottom Line

At some point, you've probably been on a tour of a historic home. The home may be notable because it was the birthplace or creative space for a famous author, inventor, or celebrity. Or, on a rare occasion, the house itself is the draw—a house so magnificent or filled with such outstanding detail or so marvelously designed that people flock to see it. Thomas Jefferson's mountaintop home, Monticello, is a stunning example. The third president's 43-room masterpiece, which was built, rebuilt, and repeatedly modified over four decades, puts construction quality on the stage. Its beautiful masonry work and carpentry show how finely crafted details can set a building apart.

In western Pennsylvania, Frank Lloyd Wright's Fallingwater proves the power of architectural design. Wright was commissioned to use his architectural vision to build a weekend home. Today the refuge-like haven balanced on a rock cropping over a rushing stream is feted as the best all-time work of American architecture.

Of course, you won't be looking for buildings that win awards or draw throngs of tourists long after you're gone. Your goal is investment property that will generate income and increase in value over time. But the examples of Monticello and Fallingwater show just how important the second element of the Big Six can be.

When you invest in a building, you can always make modifications. But to maximize the return on your investment—as well as the cash flow it generates while you own it—you need to begin with a building that is well built, stylish, updated, and maintained with the future in mind. You want features and amenities that will pass the test of time. And that is where the second step in the Big Six comes into play.

Building quality and design efficiency are the benchmarks that help determine whether a particular building will further your wealth-creation strategy. There are a number of details and factors that you, with the help of your professional support team—made up of your lawyer, accountant, contractor, and engineer—can examine to determine the suitability of a building. These factors range from the quality of the construction materials used to the fluidity of the floor plans. Once you begin paying attention to these features, you'll see that even small details—whether there is a security camera at a building entrance or the parking is easy to reach—are important.

You may be surprised to learn that the very best buildings, Class A structures, are not necessarily the very best investments. Rather, buildings that fall into the B classification generally offer greater return on investment and greater appreciation in value. And to a large degree, they are more accessible to individual investors. Institutional investors often own the Class A buildings, which also carry the highest price tags. Class B buildings—or, in some cases, Class C buildings that can easily be upgraded to Class B—are the ones you should seek to acquire.

Remember, you need not be restricted to apartment complexes, small shopping centers, or office buildings. Less glamorous industrial real estate properties—from small bay and flex-type warehouses to storage facilities—often reap outstanding returns. As an investor, your job is to learn to identify the features that will maximize the strength of your investment over time.

CHAPTER 7

Tenant Profile

THE RIGHT FIT

The term "tenant profile" broadly refers to the terms, conditions, and provisions under which a tenant leases space in a building, as well as to the overall makeup of the tenants within a building. When we buy a building as investors, we acquire a preowned property, one that has been operated by others over a period of time. We were not involved in selecting the location of the building, determining the quality of building standards, or selecting the design criteria. Nor did we choose the size of the building, the number of units, the rental rates, or the terms and conditions of the leases. We also did not select the existing tenants. These are factors that we inherit.

How you handle these conditions—the third element of the Big Six—can dramatically affect whether you generate desired cash flow levels. Certain tenant profile characteristics must be in place, or you must be able to put them in place, if you are to achieve the key goal of increasing the value of your investment.

Each of your investments may have a different tenant profile. For some buildings, you may want tenants in the medical or health care sector who may be interested in seeing you convert their offices into condos and then letting them buy the office space. In retail strip malls, you may want an anchor tenant, such as a high-profile national store chain, that not only signs a long-term lease but lures the kind of walk-in traffic that helps attract other retail tenants. You may even decide to transform a building with large spaces and a few tenants into one with small offices and many tenants.

Even though the puzzle pieces are different, the final picture has one feature that is constant: The tenants are the source of your operating cash flow. Your ability to keep that flow smooth, steady, and at market rates is vital. Attracting and keeping the right tenants is essential.

Following the Big Six's step-by-step formula, you will already have found the ideal location and building combination—a Class B building in an "A" location. Now you'll need to analyze the revenue-generating aspects of the building to see which ones could work in your favor, which could be modified for even better performance, and which would be counterproductive. Let's look at some tenant profile factors and what we can do to turn them into assets in our wealth-creation plan.

Factor No. 1: Rental Rate and Terms

When it comes to rental rates and terms, the perfect scenario is to buy a building with tenants who are paying rents that are significantly below the market rate, have short-term leases, and have no options to automatically renew their leases. Under this scenario, you can justifiably raise rents, and because leases are short term, you can usually do it fairly soon after you acquire the building. If there are no renewal options, you are not locked into extending the previous below-market rents to incumbent tenants.

During the past four years, I purchased four buildings that matched these sought-after criteria. Three of the buildings were subsequently resold for several million dollars more than their original cost. (The fourth building, the latest one I acquired with some excellent partners, is discussed in Chapter 8.)

By way of example, let's take a fictitious example of The Shawn, a 20,000-square-foot office building. The tenants are paying $15 per square foot in an area where the market rate is $22 per square foot. All the leases expire in two years without any options to renew. By increasing the rent by $7 per square foot when the leases expire, $140,000 in cash flow will be added to the bottom line. Based upon an 8 percent cash-on-cash return, this increases the value of the building by $1.75 million (i.e. $140,000 divided by .08). Even if the rent were increased by only $5 per square foot, an additional $100,000 in net income would be generated and the value of the building would increase to $1.25 million. Keep in mind that fixed operating expenses basically remain the same whether or not you raise rents.

Of course, if tenants have signed long-term leases at market rates with renewal options at modest increases, then you would have no opportunity to enjoy healthy bottom-line gains.

Factor No. 2: Gross or Net Lease

In apartment buildings, leases are generally structured on a gross basis. This means that the landlord covers all operating expenses, with the tenants paying only for electricity used in their individual units. Since the leases on apartment buildings usually are not for more than one or two years, the landlord is in a position, upon expiration of the leases, to increase the rent. This increase is not only to cover operating expenses and the rate of inflation, but also to generate an increase in cash flow.

Office buildings and retail strip centers can be on either gross leases or net leases. If they are on gross leases, the landlord pays for all operating expenses, but the tenant generally pays its proportionate share of any increases in operating expenses over the base year, which is the first year of the lease. For retail stores on gross leases, tenants may still pay the cost of utilities if there are separate electric and water meters in the complex. Because of uncertainty about operating expenses such as taxes and insurance, there is now a move toward net leases in some parts of the country. As gross leases expire, they are replaced with agreements that require tenants to pay all expenses. This is simpler because it eliminates the need to bill tenants at the end of each year for increases in operating expenses. It is also more economical for the building owner, because it dramatically reduces bookkeeping costs.

Factor No. 3: Size of Units

When it comes to how Class B apartment buildings are configured, a 40–40–20 mix might be considered a good one, depending on the community and the part of the country in which the building is located. That means 40 percent of the units would be one-bedroom apartments, 40 percent would be two-bedroom/two-bathroom apartments, and 20 percent would be three-bedroom/two-bathroom apartments. Because I recommend buying Class B buildings in "A" locations, the size of the one-bedroom units should be approximately

700 to 750 square feet, the two-bedroom units about 900 to 1,100 square feet, and the three bedrooms should have more than 1,100 square feet (with a maximum of about 1,300 to 1,500 square feet).

In a small retail strip center, there is also a wide variance in the sizes of the stores, depending on the geographic location of the complex. In general, stores that are 15 feet wide and 50 feet deep would be adequate for small retail and service companies. Larger operations may need to store equipment and supplies in the rear of the stores; in that case, a small store of 750 square feet will generate more rent per square foot than a large store of 2,500 square feet.

Let's say you are contemplating the purchase of a 20,000-square-foot office building or retail center. One tenant occupies 50 percent of the building, a detail that could be an advantage as easily as it could be a disadvantage. If the tenant is financially strong, has been in the building for a long period of time, and has paid the monthly rent promptly, you should have no great misgivings about this tenant's occupying such a large space. On the other hand, if the tenant's business has been declining and rent payments have become irregular, this could signal a serious problem. If the tenant abandons the lease or declares bankruptcy, you could find yourself with a building that is half vacant.

Sometimes a large space can be divided into smaller retail spaces, but not always. When building configurations make such a modification not feasible, you face the prospect of a large block of space remaining vacant for a considerable length of time. This could result in a substantial negative cash flow. Alternatively, if you have a 20,000-square-foot building rented to a number of tenants occupying offices from 500 to 1,500 square feet, you can accommodate vacancies without a severe economic impact. One or two unoccupied units would result in a nominal vacancy factor. So you must be careful in acquiring buildings in which one tenant occupies a large block of space.

Many years ago I had a tenant, a large insurance company that occupied an 8,700-square-foot floor in my office building. This tenant was already renting for several years before I bought the building. Then suddenly this insurance company filed for bankruptcy and went out of business, leaving the entire floor vacant. I unsuccessfully tried to rent the space for more than one year. I couldn't find a tenant to rent even just half the floor. Desperate to solve this problem, I came up with the idea of altering the floor and reconfiguring the space into small offices ranging from 150 to 300 square feet. I also added a reception desk and secretarial area, as well as a conference room that any tenant could use simply by making an appointment. This configuration of space is commonly referred to as an executive center.

It cost me in excess of $200,000 to build out the space, but I was able to increase my income by doubling the rent and targeting small individual tenants. To this day, this floor is still in operation and is very profitable. Most of the tenants are one-person operations. Virtually all are professionals.

Factor No. 4: Impact of a National Tenant

One might assume that a well-known national tenant, such as a fast-food restaurant or coffeehouse chain, would be a great asset to a retail strip center. The presence of a top national tenant will usually draw more customers to the retail center. That, in turn, increases the building's appeal to other tenants who rely on heavy foot traffic. However, you should not be swayed solely by the fact that you have a national tenant unless the presence of that national tenant has a positive economic impact on your investment. By way of explanation, let's look at two scenarios.

First Scenario

If the lease with the national tenant is set at a low rental rate with multiple options to renew at modest increases, and the other tenants are paying top rents with options to renew at modest increases, this will limit the resale value of the property. An income property's value is based not only on today's income but on the future income it will generate over a period of years. So in this case, even though there may be great pride of ownership, the future value of the property is limited.

Second Scenario

Again, let's assume that the same structure of the lease with the same national tenant exists. Let's further assume that virtually all of the other tenants moved into the center years before the national tenant did. Their leases are far under the market rate and will expire in a relatively short period of time with no options to renew. This places you in a strong position. You can substantially increase the rents to the market rate, generate significantly more income, and almost certainly ensure an immediate gain in the value of the property.

Factor No. 5: Right of First Refusal

A few years back, I came across a two-story retail strip center. It was a Class B building in an "A" location. There was no land left on which to build in this area, and the location was central, near a major highway, and only 15 minutes from downtown. I liked this particular building and had driven by it many times. Because the area was beginning to flourish, I thought it would be a good investment if the price and terms were right. The owner said he would consider selling it. After I looked at the rent roll, I entered into a $900,000 deal to acquire the building. The 30-day due diligence period revealed something that really surprised me: One of the tenants, a laundromat, had the right of first refusal to buy the building.

I have always disliked this type of clause, but this was only the second time I'd been involved in a deal with such a restriction. (The first time was many years ago, and the deal eventually fell apart.) The right of first refusal is a disadvantage for investors. Basically, it means that when you enter a contract to buy a property, the seller is obliged to reveal the price and terms of your proposal to a third party—in this case, the tenant who owned the laundromat. For an investor, it is a bad position: Your contract is shown to a tenant who can then snap up the deal and leave you out in the cold.

To make matters worse, this building also had another tenant, a locksmith, paying a rental rate that was about 40 percent below the market level. Furthermore, the lease agreement gave the locksmith the option to renew—with no increases—for 10 years. The building owner had drafted all these leases and agreements on his own, with no professionals involved. It is unwise for building owners, with the exception of real estate professionals, to draw up their own leases. Ill-conceived and onerous clauses in lease agreements can drastically reduce the value of a building.

Needless to say, I canceled the deal during my due diligence period. If the leases had been structured properly, it would have been an excellent investment. To this day, the building has not been sold.

Factor No. 6: Potential Condo Buyers

For about 10 years, beginning in the early 1970s until the early 1980s, I specialized in converting rental apartments to condominiums. At the time, such conversions were relatively new. I was one of the first real estate investors to get involved in them, and my philosophy was to sell as many condo units as possible to the existing tenants. In the span of a decade, with the legal expertise of my attorney, Joe Reisman, I converted 1,700 rental units in 22 buildings into condos. The percentage of tenants that bought their units ranged from 30 percent to 70 percent, with an average of about 50 percent.

In more recent years, apartment conversions have swept the country, sometimes at a near-frenzied pace. Converters bought up mega-complexes; in many cases, the tenants were scared off and the converters catered to outside buyers.

When it comes to large apartment complexes, the condo craze ended in late 2006. But small apartment buildings of 8 to 24 units, with the right tenant profile, lend themselves to conversions. A huge amount of money can be made if you can identify the type of buildings to buy for conversions. I will give you the know-how for this in Chapter 13.

Factor No. 7: Parking Considerations

I purchased my own office building in 1981. The previous owners had assigned parking spaces for each tenant in the leases. As it turned out, those clauses were impossible to change: The tenants insisted on retaining their assigned spaces. The building today still has assigned parking spaces.

For most of the other office buildings and apartment buildings that I have been involved in, there were no assigned parking spots. The tenants, under the terms of the lease, had the right to park a certain number of cars (depending on the square footage of the office they were leasing or the size of their apartment unit). Tenants simply parked where they found open spaces, and there were no problems with this arrangement.

When I walk through my building's garage and upper deck, it is not unusual to find numerous assigned parking spaces that are not in use. A conservative estimate would be that 30 percent of the spaces are vacant at any given time. Experts have told me that you can accommodate, as a practical matter, 20 percent more parking in a building with unassigned parking. In many cases there is a charge for tenant parking, so unassigned parking spaces can result in higher parking revenue.

That is not to say that you should steer clear of a building with assigned parking. Everything else being equal, it is not a huge disadvantage. But you will be better off with unassigned parking. At this point, we are talking about office buildings and apartment buildings; assigned parking is not applicable to retail centers or industrial warehouses, because the bulk of the spaces are for customers doing business at the centers.

Factor No. 8: Undesirable Mix of Tenants

There are pockets within "A" locations that may be designated for light industrial use, including warehouses, flex space, and a structure that is a combination of retail stores and offices. These sites usually cater to the industrial market as well as to people in the communications, computer, and high-tech sectors. Within some of the retail strip stores in areas like this there might be tenants such as gun shops, pawn shops, X-rated video stores, and the like. Usually you will not find these stores side by side at one strip center but spread out within a building. If it is a two-story building, there could be a massage parlor upstairs. The tenant profile of a building like this could be problematic.

A few years ago, an old-time investor offered to sell me his office building. It was a five-story Class B building in a "B" location, but the area was improving and headed toward becoming an "A" location. The building was beautifully designed, and it was situated on a large parcel of land with a big parking area. I immediately liked the look of it from the exterior and thought it would be a good investment.

But when I entered the lobby, I saw a guard and numerous people entering and exiting. I was curious about the reason for this busy flow of people. I discovered that within this building, consisting virtually of all professional offices, one tenant occupying a large amount of space was a county agency dealing with drug addicts and former convicts on parole. There had been several serious skirmishes and assaults on the premises, thus the need for a guard. Once I understood this—and found out that the county agency was on a long-term lease and the cost of rotating the guards from early morning to late in the evening was very high—I decided that this building did not match my investment goals. The building stayed on the market for at least two years before someone bought it. This is an example of a good building in a good location but with a diminished value because one tenant was not compatible with the remainder of the tenants.

If you can combine Class B buildings in "A" locations with a desirable tenant profile, you're ready for next element in the Big Six—upside.

The Bottom Line

In a good real estate deal, everyone comes out a winner. The sale of a prime piece of New York City real estate not only serves as an example of how this can happen, but it underscores the crucial importance of the tenant profile, the third element in the Big Six formula for building wealth.

This 42-story office building drew prestigious tenants and had a coveted address on Avenue of the Americas with a direct underground connection to Rockefeller Center. Its vacancy rate was very low, and several important leases for large rental spaces within the building were about to come up for renewal, giving any new owner the opportunity to renegotiate leases at a significantly higher rate.

It was a perfect investment scenario. The current investors were ready to reap the rewards of their years of ownership, and a new investor recognized that the property would immediately see its cash flow—and value—jump significantly. The critical force at play in this was the tenant profile.

The Big Six strategy is designed to increase the value of a building in a short period of time, usually one to three years. Tenants can represent either an asset or a liability in an investment. When you invest, your mission is to make sure your tenant profile is the former and not the latter. In the case of the New York building, the combination of high-profile renters, leases on the verge of expiration, and skyrocketing market rental rates resulted in a textbook-perfect tenant profile.

Different investors will analyze tenant profiles in different ways, but always with an eye on making their income property work for them as they have envisioned. What we are focusing on in this book is finding an income property that offers the opportunity to increase rental income and, by doing so, multiply the value of the building so that you can resell it at a substantial profit. Just as you want a well-constructed and well-designed building, you'll want stable tenants who are a good match for your building and have appropriate lease agreements.

Layers of factors go into a tenant profile. Analyze the lease agreements held by the current tenants. Find out how much rent is generated and whether it is at market rate or under market. Examine the configuration of the building, and study whether the biggest tenants are the right tenants and whether there is a complementary mix of tenants in the building. As you do this, keep in mind that there are two aspects to the tenant profile. One is what the profile looks like when you buy the building. The other is the ease with which you can take advantage of or modify the profile to maximize your revenue stream.

8

Upside

MAXIMIZING THE RETURN ON YOUR HOLDINGS

As one of my college professors used to say, "a building can be architecturally perfect with sound engineering, but if it doesn't make money, nothing else really counts." Real estate appraisers will tell you that the most important factor in determining the value of an investment property is the income it will generate. A building may cost $800,000 to construct, but if it brings in only the income of a $600,000 property, then it is worth only $600,000. That's how real estate works.

Upside, the fourth element in the Big Six, refers to the cash flow growth possibilities offered by a particular property along with the likelihood that the property will increase in value. This chapter is designed to help you determine whether a property has upside— and how to maximize it. As we've said before, the best way to make big money is to buy a property where rents are below the market rate and tenants have short-term leases with no options to renew.

Why would any building owner charge rents that are less than the market rate? It happens frequently, especially when an owner has held on to a building for a long time. Generally, there are two reasons. The first is that owners get to know the tenants personally over a period of time and are hesitant to raise rents. They have had virtually 100 percent occupancy for many years with long-term tenants and don't like the idea of vacancies. The second reason is that these owners base their targeted rate of return on their original investment, not on today's market value.

Let's look at the example of Egmont Gardens, a Class B apartment building in an "A" location. The owner of Egmont Gardens bought the property 15 years ago for $300,000. Today it is worth $1.1 million. You make an offer of $1 million, which the owner accepts. You determine that the Egmont's rents are 30 percent under the market rate. You also see that the leases expire within the next year, and the tenants have no options to renew.

The current annual gross income for Egmont Gardens is $140,000. The operating expenses are $49,000. That leaves a net operating income (NOI), of $91,000. You put down $200,000 in cash and obtain an $800,000 mortgage at 7.5 percent interest, payable $71,000 annually including principal and interest. Since your NOI is $91,000, that leaves a cash flow of $20,000.

Now let's look at the value a year later after you have raised the rent by 20 percent. The operating expenses remain basically the same, because increasing rents does not generally increase expenses to any great degree. Although you have raised rents by 20 percent, your rents are still 10 percent under the market rate, so the rent increase should result in little or no turnover of tenants. As a general practice, it is not wise to suddenly hike rents up to the full market rate because that can shock tenants and precipitate a rash of vacancies. A better approach is to wait until vacancies arise and then bring the rents up to the market rate. (There may be some cosmetic improvements needed in the apartments for new tenants, but those costs will be more than offset by the rent increases.)

The value of a property is based on the rate of return a buyer would expect in a given marketplace at a given time. Let's assume that a buyer would expect an 8.5 percent return if the property were purchased for all cash with no financing. To determine the value of a property, you divide the net operating income by the expected rate of return, or capitalization rate, which I discuss more fully in Chapter 10.

What is the value of Egmont Gardens a year later? After you raise the rents by 20 percent, the resulting NOI increases to $119,000 from $91,000. That puts the value of Egmont Gardens at $1.4 million. That's $119,000 divided by 8.5 percent. But is the rate of return 8.5 percent? The answer is no. Most investors leverage their investments with mortgage financing rather than paying all cash. A leveraged deal will generally increase the rate of return by a significant amount because it is based in this case on cash flow, not on the net operating income. After Egmont Gardens' income is increased by 20 percent, its cash-on-cash return is 24 percent (see Figure 8.1).

Based on a value of $1.4 million at the end of one year, and assuming that Egmont Gardens will appreciate in value by 5 percent each year thereafter, your equity in the property will grow by leaps and bounds (see Figure 8.2). At some time in the future, if you should choose to increase your mortgage, you could easily recoup your original $200,000 cash investment, wind up with no money in the deal, and enjoy what is known as an infinity return. (Infinity returns are discussed in Chapter 9.)

Tenants Can Set the Price of a Building

Recently, I looked at a campus-style medical office complex with 56,000 rentable square feet (RSF) situated on five acres. The complex consists of five one-story buildings with attractive and functional interiors, all beautifully designed by a well-known architect. There is ample parking, with six spaces per 1,000 square feet of building area. This is a high-end, Class B property in an "A" location. Virtually all the tenants are paying rents that are 25 to 35 percent under the market rate. But the tenants have options to renew their leases for long periods of time at modest increases. The sale price desired by the owner would have been in line if the tenants had been paying market-rate rents. But because the tenants were not and their leases provided them with long-term options to renew with only modest rent increases, the return on that building would have been minuscule. It was a real estate investment that would have had no upside.

Remember what my college professor said: "A building can be architecturally perfect with sound engineering, but if it doesn't make money, nothing else really counts." "The *price* of an income property is the amount the seller is asking. The *value* is based on the income stream it generates," says Tom Dixon, a prominent Realtor, consultant, and educator. When unsophisticated property owners draft their own (usually long-term) leases without the input of their expert team of consultants, they create a situation in which—by default—tenants actually set the price of a property. That is what had happened with this medical complex. To acquire it as an investment property would make no sense.

Egmont Gardens **Class B Apartment Building in an "A" Location**

Economic Impact of Increasing Rents by 20% at the End of the First Year

Assumptions: Purchase Price $1,000,000. Down Payment $200,000.
Mortgage $800,000 at 7.5 percent fixed rate 10-year Term plus 25-year Amortization
($71,000 Annual Debt Service).
Value of building predicated on an 8.5 capitalization rate.

	Existing Rents		**Raising Rents 20 Percent**	
Income	$140,000		$168,000	
Operating Expenses	$49,000		$49,000	
Net Operating Income	$91,000		$119,000	
Debt Service	$71,000		$71,000	
Cash Flow	$20,000		$48,000	
Cash-on-Cash Return	$20,000 $200,000	= 10.0 percent	$48,000 $200,000	= 24.0 percent
Value of the Building	$91,000 NOI 8.5% cap rate	= $1,070,588	$119,000 NOI 8.5% cap rate	= $1,400,000

Equity Buildup over a 10-Year Period

Assumptions: Property value is $1,400,000 at the end of the first year.
At the end of the second year, the property appreciates by 5 percent each year thereafter.

End of Year	**Value**	**Mortgage**	**Equity**
0	$1,000,000	$800,000	$200,000 Cash Investment
1	$1,400,000	$788,673	$611,327
2	$1,470,000	$776,466	$693,534
3	$1,543,500	$763,312	$780,188
4	$1,620,675	$749,136	$871,539
5	$1,701,709	$733,860	$967,848
6	$1,786,794	$717,398	$1,069,396
7	$1,876,134	$699,659	$1,176,475
8	$1,969,941	$680,542	$1,289,399
9	$2,068,438	$659,940	$1,408,497
10	$2,171,860	$637,740	$1,534,120

REMEMBER YOU MAKE YOUR MONEY IN BUYING!

Figure 8.1   Egmont Gardens

Upside Strategies

There are numerous ways that the income of a building can be increased and increased substantially. The logic is simple. The more income, the bigger the bottom line. And the bigger the bottom line,

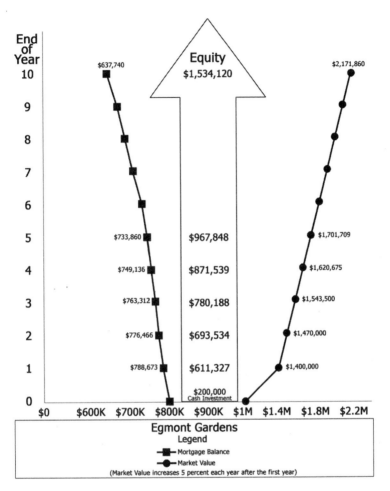

Figure 8.2   Egmont Gardens: Equity Buildup

the bigger the resale value. As you think about upside you should remember: You make your money in buying! Now we'll explore some of the upside strategies.

Converting Buildings from One Use to Another

Converting buildings to different uses can be a good way to increase the upside of a building. Do not confuse this with condominium conversions. In a condo conversion, we are not altering the use. A rental apartment that becomes a condo is still a residence. The only difference is the legal form of ownership. The conversions we are now discussing would entirely change the property from one use to another use.

Many times these conversions focus on schools, hospitals, government buildings, warehouses, and other structures that have become outmoded and nonfunctional. Sometimes a school building can be purchased and reconfigured into rental apartments or condominiums—or even into a hospital.

A vacant hospital, by contrast, can be converted to offices, apartments, or hotel rooms. And an abandoned industrial warehouse can have a range of uses: art museum, flea market, or even a vocational school. The owners of these buildings are motivated to sell them because the properties are no longer suitable for their original use. For this reason, a buyer can often pick them up at bargain prices. Of course, a detailed analysis has to be made of the costs of the conversion, as well as the rental income that would be generated, to see whether the deal makes sense.

Creative Thinking

Sometimes unusual—and unexpected—circumstances affect the value of a building. That's what happened in California, where a woman owned a 20-unit apartment building—appraised at $1 million—about a mile from existing railroad tracks. The state decided to extend the rail line, and the new tracks ended up right in front of her building. The noise became so unbearable that all the tenants moved out.

The noise had such a negative impact on the property that its value dropped dramatically. It was on the market at $650,000 for a year with no buyers. Eventually, an astute investor entered into an option-to-buy for $400,000. He then offered the property to a school that needed a residential facility and classrooms for deaf students. The school, which had found no existing buildings adaptable for its use and was planning to construct a $3 million complex, was very interested in the deal. The investor assigned his option to them for $150,000 profit.

That meant the school paid $550,000 to acquire the building. The projected cost of converting it into classrooms and dormitories was about half the price of a new building. Furthermore, the complex could be up and running in 6 to 12 months, rather than the two years or more it would have taken to build a new school.

Expansion Potential

You may be able to buy a property with a building that has rents at market rates but where there is still room to construct additional units. By adding more units, without paying for more land, you can generate greater net income. When the additional income is added to the net income from the existing building, the result is an increase in the total cash flow. That, in turn, increases the value of the overall property.

Mismanaged Buildings

There are opportunities to pick up buildings that have been poorly managed. Sometimes it's because the heirs of an estate are fighting among themselves, out-of-town or out-of-country owners are employing unskilled managers, or local owners are putting the job in the hands of a low-paid manager whose performance they don't monitor.

You can spot these buildings quickly. This mismanagement is characterized by unkempt grounds and rundown buildings—both exteriors and interiors; lots of deferred maintenance; tenants for whom there have never been background or credit checks; tenants who pay their rent late; poorly drafted leases; and frequent evictions.

If you can find buildings like this (and there are more of them than you might think) that are structurally sound in top locations, you can make some big bucks. "While location is the No. 1 criteria in evaluating real property, one of the secrets of finding undervalued properties is to look for mismanaged buildings," says Jorge Cantero, a nationally known broker and management expert. "The property management function should preserve the asset. But it can either enhance or erode its value."

Executive Centers

We live in a high-tech world and, increasingly, we have become a "virtual" society. That includes workers. In greater numbers than ever, they are working remotely from home offices or in small offices within executive centers. Working away from corporate headquarters eases rush-hour congestion and eliminates long commutes in some urban areas. It gives flexibility to families, especially those with small children or those facing medical challenges, and—in these days of rising gasoline prices—it can help cut workers' expenses while giving a boost to air quality. Furthermore, by letting employees work from home or satellite offices, companies can keep their headquarters smaller and more efficient.

For the real estate industry, corporate downsizing has fueled a market for executive centers, which I referred to earlier. These are collections of small offices. Some are set up with shared secretarial services, phone lines, and conference rooms. Typically, air-conditioning and heat, reception areas, nightly janitorial service, and parking are folded into the rental deal.

Many of these executive centers are carved out of large blocks of space in existing office buildings and industrial buildings. These full-amenity spaces are reconfigured and divided into small offices that can be rented at approximately double to triple the rental rate of conventional large offices. The appeal? Even with the higher relative rents, tenants still pay much less than they would if they had to rent a larger office. This is a win-win situation for both the landlord and the tenant.

Turnaround Buildings

Four years ago, I was the highest bidder at a sealed auction for a 52,000-square-foot office building that included a two-level underground parking garage on a tree-lined boulevard. It was a Class B building in an "A" location in one of Miami's historic and prestigious neighborhoods, an area known as The Roads. The U.S. government had seized the building from offshore investors who had been found guilty of illegal acts. The all-glass building on a corner lot was eight stories high and had 31,000 RSF and spectacular views of the city. It had magnificent architecture, and its interior was beautifully designed.

I bid $3.6 million, which equated to $116 per RSF, and my offer was accepted. Other buildings in the area were selling for more than $200 per RSF.

I brought in a partner, Jim Pollack, a successful attorney-investor who had been in other deals with me. We each took 40 percent of the deal. Sandra Goldstein, one of the outstanding Realtors in town, and two dentists took the balance. This sounds like a dream deal—but there were a number of negatives to overcome. First, the building was only 25 percent occupied. It had also been badly neglected. During the 30 days we had to check out the building, we found that saltwater intrusion into the garage had caused the walls to deteriorate; in addition, there was an underground environmental contamination problem and the building needed a new roof. Remedying those problems, which involved renovating the common areas in the interior of the structure, replacing a generator, installing new signage, improving the landscaping, and generally putting the building in first-class condition, was going to cost an additional $1 million.

Sandra agreed to supervise all the work, which took more than a year to complete. She also agreed to relocate her real estate office in the building and be an on-site leasing agent and property manager. During the year of construction, rehabilitation, and renovations, the disruptions were so great that we could not rent any of the vacant space. In fact, we were lucky to keep the few tenants that we inherited with the building. I think the main reason for this was the strong rapport that Sandra developed with the tenants and her ability to convince them that the improvements would benefit their businesses.

Once the building was transformed, we changed its name to The Roads Professional Center (see Figure 8.3). The small spaces, ranging from 300 to 1,500 RSF, were easy to rent. The vacant sixth and seventh floors, each with 4,000 RSF, were also very desirable. They were just underneath the penthouse floor but above the tree line. Both those floors had glass exteriors on all sides; the views were magnificent. We offered to rent the floors to law firms, insurance agencies, real estate firms, stock brokerages, and other companies. We had some hot prospects, but nothing materialized.

So, after six months, we decided that our best bet was to divide these two floors into small offices. We weren't exactly sure what size spaces the market really wanted, so when people came to the building to rent space, we showed them the two vacant floors and signed them up for leases based on the amount of space they needed. Most of them wanted between 500 and 1,500 square feet, so we began to redraw and build out the space with the understanding that the tenants would move in upon completion of each office. Other offices in the building ranged in size from 500 to 2,500 RSF.

Within a year, we filled the building at the prevailing rental rate of $23 per square foot. We felt that we could get even higher rent rates within the next year or two, so we did not enter into any long-term leases, nor did we give options to renew. As time went on, we

Figure 8.3   The Roads Professional Center

increased the rent between $25 and $27 RSF and were fully rented with a waiting list.

We were able to increase the existing mortgage with the bank by approximately $1 million to cover the costs of all the improvements and alterations, with the understanding that once the building was 95 percent rented, the bank would increase the loan to $4.1 million. Based on our purchase price of $3.6 million plus the $1 million that we spent on improvements, that loan increase meant we only had $500,000 of our own cash in the deal.

We recently sold the property to a South American investor in an all-cash deal worth $7.3 million. We walked away with a $2.7 million profit.

Let The Building Talk to You

In mid-2007, Tony DeRosa, Steve Bernstein, and David Rosen, all successful investors in their own right, joined me in the purchase of 3901 Doral, a two-story Class B office building comprising 25,632 useable square feet (USF). There is no common area in this building so USF is the same as RSF in this case. We paid the owner $4.75 million, or the equivalent of $185 per USF. We invested $1 million cash and financed the balance with a local bank. The building is situated on a 1.42-acre corner lot in an "A" location in the city of Doral, a suburb of Miami and a very active area. The building is close to two major expressways and the Miami International Airport and is adjacent to a Marriott Courtyard Inn (see Figure 8.4).

When we first saw 3901 Doral, it was run-down and barely visible from the street. A tall, broken-down fence with unkempt vines

Figure 8.4   Location of 3901 Doral

blocked the view, and only the tenants knew of the building's existence. The building was structurally sound, but it needed upgrading and improvements on the exterior façade and the grounds.

We repainted with a striking color combination, did extensive landscaping (including the planting of 25 royal palm trees), resealed the parking lot, tiled the walkways, and installed professionally designed signage and graphics. These improvements cost us $200,000, but they transformed a drab, tired, and seedy building into a good-looking office complex (see Figure 8.5).

I always recall something one of my real estate colleagues, Leonard Kaplan, said many years ago. He told me that when you buy a building and are not sure what you want to do with it, you should "let the building talk to you." In effect, he meant let the market tell you what it wants.

The offices in the Doral building range in size from 541 to 2,162 USF. The tenants pay for electricity and their own janitorial services. This results in operating expenses about 40 percent lower than

Figure 8.5   3901 Doral

the standard. The market gave us multiple options for handling the building, each of which would provide for substantial upside.

- The rental rates are 30 percent under the market rate and most of the tenants have short-term leases and no options to renew. This gives us the opportunity to raise rents, thereby increasing both the income from the property and the value of the property.
- The building is well suited to a condo conversion. Each office has a separate outside entrance. Each also has a separate bathroom within its offices. There is a shortage of physicians in the area so small condo units would be especially appealing to medical professionals, although the building should attract a variety of other professionals and businesses, too.
- The property recently was rezoned for 23 commercial uses, including a multistory hotel and office building. We knew this was a strong possibility before we entered into a contract to buy the building. There are 72,000 cars that pass this property on a daily basis. Several firms have expressed interest in demolishing the existing office building and redeveloping the site. In fact, the land alone is now worth substantially more than what we paid for the entire property.

This building is continually talking to us. The conversations are becoming more serious. Who knows what tomorrow will bring.

If you cannot spot the upside in a potential real estate investment, then it is not the investment for you. The upside of a property can already exist—or you can create it—but a property *must* have upside. If it meets all the other requirements of the Big Six but there is no upside, you'll never meet your goal of creating personal wealth that will enable you to live the life of your dreams. But if you met the first three requirements of the Big Six and then found a property with strong upside, you're ready for the fifth element of the success formula: Financing. We'll explore it in depth in Chapter 9.

The Bottom Line

Real estate does not exist in a vacuum. When manufacturing jobs leave an area, the demand for manufacturing facilities and support properties will likely move as well. When a small city lures medical companies or technology-service firms, then those companies will need office space—but maybe not the traditional kind. Developments in the overall economy, even the global economy, have a spillover effect on real estate. And that, in turn, adds dynamism to commercial real estate investment.

Whether you can make money during these trends and changes all depends on upside—and your ability to identify and magnify the income growth potential of a property.

Sometimes the upside is easy to spot. You may find a building with large offices that could generate far more revenue if they were modified into smaller office spaces catering to small businesses. Or you may learn that a medical office complex is up for sale and, because you've followed developments in that industry, you know the building would be perfect for a conversion into office-condos. Other times, your creativity and vision will be the key to the upside. In this era of global trade, for example, there is a growing demand for distribution warehouses near key U.S. airports, seaports, and trucking centers. At the same time, the need for manufacturing facilities has declined in some parts of the country. Goods are being produced outside the country and then shipped in. Increased interest in global warming and environmental issues has sparked demand for "green buildings"—those that already have or easily can incorporate solar energy and other eco-friendly details and features.

Seeing a property that fits a trend is not enough, however. Always remember there is great flexibility in terms of the ideas that you can come up with to make a property more valuable. The key to increasing value lies in buying a Class B building in an "A" location where the rents are under the market, the leases are short term, and there are no options to renew the leases. This will give you the income stream necessary to realize your goal of becoming financially independent.

CHAPTER

Financing

CHOOSING THE FISCAL FORMULA
THAT MATCHES YOUR GOALS

The economic activity of our country is based on borrowing and lending money. Virtually everyone is borrowing for one reason or another, and money is continually being recycled, which is important to a free market economy. Without that free flow of money, our society, as we know it, would cease to function.

The dynamics of borrowing and lending money are multilayered, and the key players include banks, financial institutions, mortgage companies, corporations, the federal government, and private investors. Banks borrow from their depositors and then loan those borrowed funds to customers. The government, meanwhile, borrows money—which it uses to operate the country—by selling bonds, Treasury bills, notes, bonds, and other securities. Developers borrow money to construct buildings and create communities; consumers borrow money to buy products. In addressing the fifth component of the Big Six, this book will help you understand your role in this chain—specifically, how you can obtain the best financing possible.

Before You Begin: Your Credit Report

Before you get started, you'll need to get a number of finance-related items in order. Most important among them is your credit score. The first thing you should do before applying for a mortgage loan is to review your credit reports and your credit scores.

Basically, a credit report is a detailed document that traces your credit history using information from banks, retail outlets, credit card companies, car dealerships, and other businesses. It takes into account your employment history and tracks everywhere you have lived. It also may include tax liens, bankruptcies, or other public record information that could affect your ability to pay loans. The purpose of the report is to establish your creditworthiness, in part by examining your reliability when it comes to repaying past loans and obligations.

Credit-reporting bureaus use complex algorithms to evaluate all the aspects of your credit history and come up with a credit score. There are several systems in place, but generally a credit score can range from about 300 to 850. Nearly one-third of the score is usually linked to how much debt you have, while another 30 percent or so is related to whether you've paid past bills and loans on time. The remainder of the score is affected by how long you've had credit and by how many credit report inquiries have been made. If you've been applying for a lot of credit cards or loans, your credit score could be affected. Few people ever achieve a perfect score of 850.

Credit reports used to be kept secret from consumers and were available only to lenders and businesses. But the laws have changed, and now consumers can get copies of their scores. You should obtain your credit information at least 45 days before you intend to apply for a mortgage. This allows time to correct mistakes or misinformation. If you know in advance that you have problems with your credit rating, you should resolve them as soon as possible so that the credit bureaus can report a new score before your lender sees the reports.

Credit reports can suffer from two types of problems: incorrect information and missing information. According to the one-time, groundbreaking report "Millions of Americans Jeopardized by Inaccurate Credit Scores," prepared by the nonprofit Consumer Federation of America (Dec. 17, 2002), about one-third of consumer credit reports contain inaccurate information, which results in lower credit scores. At the same time, 78 percent of reports omit positive information; those omissions can also result in lower scores. The research found that one-third of the reports overlook a mortgage account that has never been paid late, and more than three-quarters of the reports omit a revolving credit account in good standing. Several years ago, I ordered my credit report and was astonished to see the items that turned up on it. They included a mortgage in excess of $1 million that I had paid off many, many years ago. I had to search through my files for documents that showed the loan had been repaid and send the evidence to the reporting bureaus, at which time they removed the item. There were other inaccurate items, and it took me several weeks to get the reports of all three credit bureaus cleaned up. Since that time, all my reports have been correct.

The web site of the Consumer Federation of America (www. consumerfed.org) does annual research involving credit reporting and consumers' understanding of it. The federation's reports explain factors that affect credit and how credit ratings can be improved. These reports, as well as brochures and other information about credit bureaus and credit ratings, are available online and can be useful tools when you are learning about credit scores and the steps to take to ensure that your score is as high as it should be.

The easiest way to check your credit rating (and find out your score) is on the Internet at www.annualcreditreport.com. You can use this web site to order a credit report from each of the credit bureaus: Equifax, Experian, and TransUnion. You can also reach the credit bureaus by phone at 877-322-8228. Once every 12 months you are permitted under the Fair Credit Reporting Act to order one free credit report from these credit bureaus. Although the annual credit report is free, you will have to pay a small fee for the credit scores. If you have already used up your free credit report entitlement for this year, you can still order additional paid reports from the web sites of the three bureaus: www.equifax.com, www.experian. com, and www.transunion.com.

One of the criticisms of credit scores is that they frequently span a wide range, differing as much as 50 points depending on which bureau is doing the calculations. In evaluating your application for a loan, lenders will use the middle of the three scores from the credit bureaus. Your goal should be to achieve at least a 730 credit score, which is excellent. A score above 680, which is considered good, is the minimum that you should have if you want to obtain a loan with a competitive interest rate.

Financing Components and Dynamics

Without mortgage financing, the real estate business would cease to exist. That said, in order to succeed in the financing of properties, it is essential that we as investors know and understand the ins and outs of the financing process. A mortgage is a loan secured by real estate. The mortgagor is the party that pledges the property to the lender as security for the loan. The mortgagee (lender) is the party that accepts the property as security for the loan. People often confuse these terms.

The term institutional lenders refers to banks, insurance companies, mortgage companies, real estate investment trusts (REITs), credit unions, corporations, pension funds, conduit lenders, and various other institutions. That term is used to distinguish these lenders from private parties that lend money. Our focus will be on dealing with banking institutions.

As you begin your journey through the financing components of the Big Six, you need to understand the role interest rates play in your loan, the loan-to-value (LTV) ratio, what the debt service coverage (DSC) ratio is, how a balloon mortgage—the most common bank mortgage available to you—works, what bankers mean by "points," how prepayment penalties can affect your investment, and what's involved in assuming an existing mortgage.

Interest Rates

More than 50 years ago, savings and loan (S&L) institutions were the most common mortgage lenders for real estate. At that time, the interest rate had held stable for several decades at about 6 percent. During the real estate shakeout in the late 1980s and early 1990s, most of the S&Ls, as well as some other lenders, went out of business after making too many bad loans, mostly on marginal commercial properties. Numerous properties were foreclosed and taken over by lenders who, in turn, conveyed many of them to a governmental subsidiary known as the Resolution Trust Corporation (RTC). The RTC subsequently sold the properties on the open market at deep discounts.

In the early 1980s, the prime rate of interest was 20.5 percent, and the fixed rate for mortgage loans was about 16 percent but gradually decreased over a period of time by a significant amount. Since 1995, the rates have dropped dramatically. The present sub-prime crisis has not only caused the economy to take a deep dive, but it has also resulted in a record number of foreclosures nationwide. This time, the bad loans were made on homes.

The demand for Class B buildings in "A" locations today is as strong as it ever has been. Few choice properties are actively on the market. Paradoxically, the sub-prime situation has caused a major reduction in interest rates, but bankers are being careful about loaning money to buyers of residential properties. At the same time, there is an ample supply of low-interest bank funds for high quality commercial properties. In some cases, the rates are as low as 5.25 percent. But it would be fantasy to think that these rates will last into the future.

Loan-to-Value (LTV) Ratio

Normally a bank will loan up to 80 percent of the purchase price of the property. The bank will require a qualified appraiser to confirm that the purchase price is the market value of the property. Let's take a case where the purchase price is $1 million and the appraisal amount is equal to or greater than $1 million. The bank typically will loan 80 percent of this amount, or $800,000.

In some instances, the bank will agree to a loan up to 90 percent of the purchase price based on an amortization period of up to 30 years. But a loan of this kind would be made only to a good customer of the bank, someone with a good net worth and an excellent credit rating. If the bank were unwilling to accept a 90 percent LTV ratio, an investor may be able to obtain a second mortgage from a private party for five years for 10 percent of the purchase price. While a second mortgage would bear interest at a higher rate than the first mortgage, it would be well worth it to the investor who can come up with only $100,000 cash to structure the deal on this basis. Bear in mind, however, that most banks will have to consent to an investor placing a second mortgage on the property, particularly if they feel the income from the property may be insufficient to cover the payments on both mortgages.

Assuming that the bank consents, and assuming that the $1 million property appreciates in value by approximately 5 percent annually, the value in five years would be $1.276 million. At such time, the investor should be able to revisit the bank and request that the bank increase the loan of $800,000 to about 80 percent of $1.276 million, or about $1 million at the prevailing rate of interest. Now the investor is in a position to pay off the second mortgage of $100,000 with $100,000 to spare in that investor's pocket.

In such an instance, the bank should charge only closing costs on the increased amount of the loan. Let's say those closing costs are $5,000. That means the investor would still have $95,000 left over. Structuring a deal such as this would allow an investor with a limited amount of cash to acquire a $1 million building using just $100,000 in cash, rather than $200,000 in cash. (For simplicity, this example ignores amortization on the $800,000 mortgage.)

Debt Service Coverage (DSC) Ratio

Institutional lenders have divergent policies regarding the DSC ratio. This ratio reflects the relationship between net operating income (NOI) and the annual debt service. As explained in previous chapters, NOI is the income from a rental property after operating expenses have been deducted. Debt service consists of the mortgage payments on the property. Simply put, the ratio gives an indication of whether the deal will generate enough NOI to pay the debt.

Usually a bank will require a DSC ratio of about 1.20. This means that the bank wishes NOI to be 20 percent greater than the debt service. For example, if debt service is $80,000, the NOI should be $96,000, or 1.20 × $80,000. The bank wants the 20 percent cushion to provide a margin of safety against factors that can adversely affect the property's cash flow, such as a decrease in occupancy or an increase in expenses.

But what happens in a situation where today's NOI only equals the debt service but, a year from today, because of substantial upside, the NOI will be considerably greater? Is the ratio based on today's NOI or the NOI a year from today? If you are able to use reasonably hard data to convince the bank that one year from now the ratio will be 1.20, if not more, you may be able to wrap up the deal based on a 1.00 DSC ratio. Documentation that might persuade a bank includes evidence that your lease rates will adjust upward as leases are renewed during that year. That way, the bank could underwrite the loan on a pro forma basis.

Astute bankers understand that when you bring them a Big Six property to finance, they have to be realistic and flexible if they want to make the loan.

Most investors want to obtain the highest possible loan amount for the longest period of time, thus affording them maximum leverage. But there are investors who may want to pay off the mortgage more quickly and own the property free and clear sooner. They may wish to obtain a loan for an LTV ratio of only 50 percent or 60 percent payable over a shorter term of time. Because lower LTV-ratio loans afford the lender more security than the norm, you can usually negotiate a lower interest rate and, possibly, reduce the number of points.

Life insurance companies and some other financial institutions loan money at a fixed rate of interest for up to 30 years on income properties. Such loans are virtually nonexistent in bank financing. A typical bank loan in today's world would be 80 percent of the appraised value of the property based on a 25-year amortization period with a balloon payment (one lump sum) at the end of 10 years. The interest rate for the first five years is usually set at a fixed rate; for the second five years, it is generally based on an index-rate formula tied to a percentage over the prime rate—the Treasury rate, or another agreed-on index. You may be able to negotiate a cap or ceiling, which is a limit on the maximum interest rate that the bank can charge. But in such an instance, the bank will also want to negotiate a higher minimum interest rate, commonly known as a floor rate.

Balloon Mortgage

Because balloon mortgages are the type you'll encounter most often in bank financing, it is critical that you understand how they work. Although the amortization period for a bank loan is generally predicated on a 25-year stretch of time, the banks usually require that the loan be paid off in one lump sum at the end of ten years. In the real estate and banking industry, this arrangement is also often referred to as a 10/25 mortgage, as compared with a mortgage that would be equally amortized over a period of 25 years. Don't be afraid of a balloon mortgage on a Big Six property. You will usually be able to pay the loan off in a much shorter period than 10 years if you refinance the property prior to the end of 10 years.

Let's take the case of Jason's Place, a professional office building that an investor buys for $1.5 million with $300,000 cash and a mortgage of $1.2 million. It is a 10/25 mortgage with an interest rate of 7.5 percent for the first five years and an interest rate of 8.5 percent for the second five years. The balloon balance at the end of 10 years amounts to $970,096. Assuming that the property appreciates at the rate of 3 percent or 5 percent annually, the existing mortgage could easily be paid well before the end of 10 years by either increasing the loan with the existing bank or refinancing with another bank. The investors who have made fortunes will generally increase or refinance the loan for a maximum LTV of 80 percent, recoup their entire purchase price, and still have tax-free money to put in their pockets. Based on scenarios A and B in Table 9.1, you will be able to see how this is done.

Loan Points

Just about every bank charges points to obtain a loan. Points are nothing but additional interest that the bank charges. One point is equal to one percent interest. The points can range from less than one point to two points or more, depending on the bank, the type of property, and your creditworthiness. You can negotiate the points, as well as all other terms of the mortgage, including the amount of the loan, the interest rate, whether there is a prepayment penalty, the assumption clause, and the like.

Prepayment Penalties

These penalties may be based upon some type of index, or they can be set at a specific rate that diminishes as the period of time for the mortgage lessens. For example, a prepayment penalty might be 5 percent of the principal balance of the mortgage if prepaid in the first year, with the prepayment penalty rate declining by one percent each year until the end of the five-year period, at which time the prepayment penalty would be zero.

Investors generally dislike loans with prepayment penalties, and some banks attract customers by agreeing to waive prepayment penalties. Still, prepayment penalties do exist, and, if you get the right mortgage with the right terms, there are circumstances when it might be better to have a loan with a prepayment penalty than one with other less appealing terms. Of course, if the loan terms are basically the same at two different banks, then you would want to do business with the bank that does not impose a prepayment penalty.

Assumption

Most banks will not generally permit a new buyer to assume an existing mortgage. However, there are certain situations in which

Table 9.1   Jason's Place: A Professional Office Building

Assumptions:

Price: $1,500,000; Cash down: $300,000.

Mortgage loan: $1,200,000, based on 25-Year Amortization Period; 10-year balloon.

Interest for first five years is 7.5 percent and 8.5 percent for the second five years.

Scenario A: Assume an Annual Appreciation Rate of 3 percent

End of Year	Value of Building	Principal Paid	Balance of Loan	New Loan at 80 percent LTV*
0	$1,500,000	$0	$1,200,000	$0
1	$1,545,000	$16,991	$1,183,009	$1,236,000
2	$1,591,350	$18,310	$1,164,699	$1,273,080
3	$1,639,091	$19,731	$1,144,968	$1,311,272
4	$1,688,263	$21,263	$1,123,705	$1,350,611
5	$1,738,911	$22,914	$1,100,791	$1,391,129
6	$1,791,078	$21,908	$1,078,883	$1,432,863
7	$1,844,811	$23,845	$1,055,038	$1,475,849
8	$1,900,155	$25,952	$1,029,085	$1,520,124
9	$1,957,160	$28,246	$1,000,839	$1,565,728
10	$2,015,875	$30,743	$ 970,096	$1,612,700

Scenario B: Assume an Annual Appreciation Rate of 5 percent

End of Year	Value of Building	Principal Paid	Balance of Loan	New Loan at 80 percent LTV*
0	$1,500,000	$0	$1,200,000	$0
1	$1,575,000	$16,991	$1,183,009	$1,260,000
2	$1,653,750	$18,310	$1,164,699	$1,323,000
3	$1,736,438	$19,731	$1,144,968	$1,389,150
4	$1,823,259	$21,263	$1,123,705	$1,458,608
5	$1,914,422	$22,914	$1,100,791	$1,531,538
6	$2,010,143	$21,908	$1,078,883	$1,608,115
7	$2,110,651	$23,845	$1,055,038	$1,688,521
8	$2,216,183	$25,952	$1,029,085	$1,772,947
9	$2,326,992	$28,246	$1,000,839	$1,861,594
10	$2,443,342	$30,743	$ 970,096	$1,954,674

*By increasing the loan with the same bank or refinancing with another bank, the balance of the loan can easily be paid off well before the end of 10 years.

experienced investors who do a lot of business with various banks can negotiate a loan that is assumable. This arrangement usually carries the condition that the bank approves any buyer who assumes the loan and that the buyer pays necessary fees and closing costs. An assumable mortgage loan is beneficial to both the seller and the buyer when the interest rate on such a loan is less than the prevailing rate with other lenders—thus representing a substantial cost savings over a period of time. And the assumption of a loan reduces the closing costs by a significant amount. Because of these benefits, a property that has an assumable loan may bring the seller a higher sales price.

Appraisal

After a bank receives an application for a mortgage loan, it will require an appraisal, usually by a Member of the Appraisal Institute (MAI). MAIs are viewed as appraisers at the top level of their profession, and the banks feel comfortable using these professionals. The buyer pays the appraisal fee, which will be quoted beforehand, and the appraisal will be made on the bank's behalf and issued to it. Often the appraisers will contact the owner of the property or the buyer of the property to request information to help in the appraisal. This information can include such things as a copy of a sales contract, income tax returns, and rent rolls.

The Advantages of Dealing with Local Banks

As we've said, mortgage money can come from a variety of sources. But a strong relationship exists between the banking industry and the real estate industry, and banks are one of the principal places to obtain financing. Where else in the world can an investor obtain a long-term mortgage at a competitive interest rate for 80 percent of the value of a property? Lenders know that virtually all prime commercial real estate will increase in value over time. And while the LTV ratio at the beginning may be 80 percent, that ratio becomes less and less with amortization and appreciation.

In late 2007 and 2008, few lenders were enthusiastic about loaning money on residential properties because of the subprime mortgage crisis. "Most lenders will not make a residential loan today unless the home is in a top-notch location and the buyer has excellent credit and is making a down payment of at least 20 percent," says Jose Gaviria, president of Worldwide Lending Corp. Residential mortgage brokers with whom I have spoken say their business is off up to 80 percent. On the other side of the coin, there is still an excellent supply of mortgage money available to creditworthy borrowers on Class B income properties in "A" locations. Although there are many places you can go for mortgage money on income properties, this book primarily deals with local banks. That's because there are a number of advantages in working with local financial institutions. They include

Simplicity: It is easier to talk with bankers within your local community because, simply put, they are accessible. Rather than deal with a home office that is out of state, you'll negotiate with bankers you may know as members of clubs, social organizations, professional associations, religious institutions, and community activities.

Market knowledge: Local bankers know the real estate market inside out, including which locations are prime, which locations are on the rise, and which are on the decline. They are also familiar with proposed changes in planning and zoning as well as governmental ordinances that affect the value of real estate. As a result, they'll recognize when a smart investor comes to them with a deal. A distant bank approached with the same deal might not appreciate the profit potential.

Quick results: The time period to obtain a mortgage commitment will usually be quicker. A loan from an out-of-state lender may require 90 to 120 days for approval, but it can usually be done in 30 to 60 days with a local bank.

Rapport: In dealing with a senior loan officer at a local bank, you can develop a relationship of trust and confidence. The loan officer's job is to generate business for the bank. Once your loan request is approved, the loan officer will look to solicit more business from you. I frequently run into a senior vice president of a bank at the gym. I do considerable business with him. Just about every time he sees me, he wants to know when I will bring him my next deal.

Renegotiating: Local banks don't usually sell their commercial mortgage loans on the secondary market. Rather, they retain these as portfolio loans. That means that you are usually negotiating with the same bank where you originally secured your financing.

In 1998, I placed a mortgage for $3.75 million with a local bank on an office building that I owned. The interest rate was 8 percent, which was the prevailing rate in the marketplace. A few years later, interest rates started to drop, and I was able to go back to the bank and get it to reduce the rate to 7.25 percent. Then, a year later, when the rates continued to drop, I got the bank to cut the rate to 6.75 percent. This reduced my mortgage payments by $47,000 per year. Based on an annual 8.5 percent rate of return (the norm at the time), the $47,000 in additional cash flow increased the value of my building by $550,000. I logically expected reductions of this kind to come with sizeable fees and geared myself up for that eventuality. The amazing thing is that it cost me only $5,000 each time, or a total of $10,000, to lower the interest rate. I was able to recoup the $10,000 in less than three months.

With an out-of-town lender, a renegotiated deal like the one described would be virtually impossible, because it would result in a substantial monetary loss in interest income for the financial institution. The out-of-town bank would have no motivation to do it. But because I was a good customer of the local bank and had done considerable business with it, its officers agreed to an exceptional deal. The spread between their cost of funds and what they were charging me still gave them a nice profit.

Other renegotiating possibilities that you could more easily take advantage of with a local bank include increasing the amount of the loan based on increasing income, lengthening the remaining term of the loan, and reducing the amount of the prepayment penalty. Renegotiations like this would be rare with out-of-town lenders. Once they make a loan, they don't normally change the terms.

Ideal Financing

Like other kinds of real estate transactions, your loan request will be marked by back-and-forth negotiations with your bank. You should start by asking for what ideally suits your needs, knowing in the back of your mind that you probably won't get all the terms you request. Here is a template for what you should seek:

- **Amount of loan:** Eighty percent of the purchase price.
- **Terms:** Thirty-year amortization with a 15-year balloon.
- **Interest rate:** The rate of interest for the first 10 years should be a fixed rate. The rate for the last five years should be based on a specified type of index, whereby the rate is based on an agree percentage above the prime rate, Treasury rate, or any other index mutually satisfactory to you and the bank.
- **Prepayment penalty:** None.
- **Assumption clause:** Permissible to future buyers at a 1 percent transfer fee.
- **Points:** One-half point.
- **Future advance clause:** Such a clause in the mortgage permits you to increase the loan in the future without having to renegotiate a new loan. This is beneficial to you because you will pay only modest closing costs on the new funds generated. (The bank has already charged you points and closing costs on the existing loan.) If you refinance with another bank, however, you will have to pay points and closing costs on the entire new loan obtained.
- **Secondary financing:** To be permissible. This simply means that you can place a second mortgage on the property.
- **Banks attorney's fee and appraiser's fee:** Mutually agreed beforehand; it normally is your responsibility to pay these fees.

In addition to submitting your loan request to one bank, it makes good sense to submit it simultaneously to a second bank. Let each bank know that you are submitting your request elsewhere. That knowledge may increase each bank's motivation to make a deal and shut out the competitor. Remember, you are in a strong negotiating position because bankers want to make loans on properties that meet the criteria of the Big Six. Don't settle for anything less than a loan that meets your specific needs. "A good deal can turn bad with the wrong financing," says Joe Martinez, president of Vesta Commercial Mortgage, Inc., a successful South Florida mortgage brokerage firm.

Getting Your Loan Approved

It isn't enough to simply call your loan officer and give him or her some brief information on the property. Although you make take this step simply as an introduction to your investment plans, you need to follow it up immediately with a detailed package of information that includes

- Address and legal description of the property
- Size of the building and the land area
- Date the building was constructed
- Copy of the sales contract
- Condition of the building and proposed improvements, if any, as well as estimated costs of the improvements
- Narrative of the location
- Narrative regarding the quality of the building and its design
- Narrative of the tenant profile
- Narrative of the upside potential
- Occupancy rate for the last five years
- Current rent roll
- Copy of an appraisal (if one exists)
- A demographic report
- Owner's statement of income and expenses for the property for the past three years
- Your income tax returns for the past three years
- Your personal financial statement
- Photographs of the property
- Aerial photograph of the property and the surrounding area

Private Lenders

Some investors may choose not to seek a mortgage from a bank. They would rather deal with private lenders for various reasons. Perhaps the investor is reluctant to reveal a lot of personal financial information, or he or she is interested in a bargain property but needs the money more quickly than a bank can manage. There are also investors who need only a short-term mortgage—for three to five years, for example. This would be a property that has substantial upside but requires two years or more for making improvements, increasing rents, and implementing more effective management. A bank is unlikely to give investors the terms they'd like. But by going to a private lender and taking steps to substantially increase the value of the property, these investors can later negotiate bank loans for larger amounts and better terms than if the investor had initially dealt with a bank. Other instances where a private loan may be easier to obtain could include the construction of additional units on a property.

A loan from a private party will carry a substantially higher interest rate than a bank loan, but the savings in points and other bank closing costs will, to some degree, offset the higher interest rate paid. Many private lenders will require the borrower to pay at least one year's interest if the loan is paid off during the first year. After that, the loan can in many cases be prepaid without penalty. In the following chapter, seller financing and its unique advantages are discussed. Getting the seller to hold a mortgage is an excellent way of financing a property.

The Romance of Leverage

Leverage is the heartthrob of real estate investment, a magnificent tool for achieving great wealth. Most investors buy with leverage. They want to put up the least amount of cash and obtain the biggest mortgage possible, for the longest period of time and at the lowest interest rate. Even if an investor is a billionaire, the law of leverage is too good to pass up. The rate of return for an investor with leverage will, in the majority of cases, be significantly higher than for one who uses his or her own funds and pays all cash for a property (see Table 9.2).

Leverage also affords you the opportunity to buy several properties with the same amount of cash that you would be expending if you bought only one property. We'll look at it using two scenarios. Under the first scenario, Buyer A pays a price of $500,000 all cash to buy a small income property. The net income is $50,000, so Buyer A would be receiving a 10 percent return ($50,000 ÷ $500,000 = 10 percent). At the end of one year, Buyer A sells the property for 10 percent more than the purchase price—or $550,000, which represents a $50,000 profit. The profit of $50,000 plus the

Table 9.2   The Romance of Leverage

Assumptions:

Buyer A pays $1 million for an apartment building (all cash).

Buyer B pays $1 million for an apartment building ($200,000 cash).

Mortgage Loan for Buyer B is $800,000 based on 25-Year Amortization Period; 10-Year Balloon. Interest for first five years is 7.5 percent and 8.5 percent for the second five years.

Property sold at the end of one year for 10% more than the original purchase price.

		Buyer A	Buyer B
1	Purchase price	$1,000,000	$1,000,000
2	Cash	$1,000,000	$200,000
3	Rental income	$150,000	$150,000
4	Operating expenses	$50,000	$50,000
5	Net operating income (NOI)	$100,000	$100,000
6	Mortgage amount	$0	$800,000
7	Mortgage payments (debt service)	$0	$70,944
8	Cash flow (Line 5 minus Line 7)	$100,000	$29,056
9	Cash-on-cash return (Line 8 divided by Line 2)	10 percent	15 percent
10	Resale price at end of one year	$1,100,000	$1,100,000
11	Profit (Line 10 minus Line 1)	$100,000	$100,000
12	Return on initial cash investment (Line 11 divided by Line 2)	10 percent	50 percent
13	Overall return (Line 8 plus Line 11) divided by Line 2	20 percent	65 percent

net income of $50,000 equals $100,000. That $100,000 divided by $500,000 equals an overall 20 percent return.

Under the second scenario, instead of buying one income property for $500,000 cash, Buyer B takes the same $500,000 cash to buy five income properties for a total of $2.5 million (obtaining a mortgage loan for the $2 million balance). After operating expenses and mortgage payments, Buyer B's cash flow is $50,000 from all the properties combined. That represents a 10 percent return.

At the end of one year, Buyer B sells the five properties for 10 percent more than the purchase price, or a total of $2.75 million, which represents a $250,000 profit. The new buyer assumes the mortgage of $2 million and pays the differential of $750,000 in cash. The profit of $250,000 plus the cash flow of $50,000 equals

$300,000. Based on a $500,000 cash investment, this represents a 60 percent cash-on-cash return to Buyer B. Many investors in this second scenario would hold their properties for more than one year, arranging to sell them at different times depending on their needs as well as on market conditions. This affords a great deal of flexibility and potential for greater profits. When we leverage a property, we are able to deduct the interest paid on the mortgage as an expense. And each time a mortgage payment is paid, the amount applied to principal is building equity in the property.

Please keep in mind that when we compare the rate of return on a stock market investment, it is usually based on buying for cash and selling for cash, just like the situation described in our first scenario. It doesn't take into account the law of leverage and, as we already know, leverage generates a greater rate of return than a deal based on all cash. There are two reasons that investing wisely in commercial real estate is so much better than investing in stocks: the law of leverage and the control of your own money. These characteristics are nonexistent in an investment in stocks.

Infinity Return

The ultimate dynamic in investing in income properties is the attainment of an infinity return. An infinity return is a rate of return that is boundless and immeasurable. In essence, it refers to a situation when there is no cash invested in a property but the owner still receives a return. Leverage and an infinity return work in concert with one another. They are like a peanut butter and jelly sandwich. There is no greater return in the world. And because you have bought a Big Six property, an infinity return is achievable. Not only can you fully recoup your initial cash investment but, in many cases, you can put additional cash in your pocket.

Let's say that you buy a small retail strip center for $1 million, using $200,000 cash and an $800,000 bank mortgage. Your initial cash flow is $30,000, or a cash-on-cash return of 15 percent ($30,000 divided by $200,000 equals 15 percent). Because of excellent upside, you are able within four years to increase the cash flow from $30,000 to $60,000. And let's assume that the property has increased in value at this point, to $1.4 million from $1 million.

You visit your banker and he or she agrees to increase the $800,000 loan to 80 percent of $1.4 million, or $1.12 million, subject to an updated appraisal to confirm the value of the property.

Here is the new position you're in:

Increased loan	$1,120,000
Old loan	$ 800,000
Proceeds before costs	$ 320,000
Bank costs	$ 10,000
Net cash proceeds	$ 310,000
Recoup of initial cash investment	$ 200,000
Additional cash in pocket	$ 110,000

By increasing your mortgage from $800,000 to $1.12 million, your mortgage payments are higher. As a result, the cash flow is reduced to $40,000 from $60,000. That $40,000 divided by zero cash investment equals an infinity return.

You have gotten back your initial cash investment of $200,000 plus $110,000 additional cash, or a total of $310,000. Additionally, you still have a $40,000 per-year cash flow, which should continue to increase each year. All the money you have received is tax free because no sale has taken place. You are now ready to make your next investment, while still owning the retail strip center.

By repeating this process, you can wind up with millions of dollars in equity and a cash flow well into six or seven figures. By implementing this strategy, you'll continue to have infinity returns, even if you opt to sell some of the properties along the way.

In Chapter 11, you'll see how one investor obtains an infinity return by partnering up on a $4.25 million deal using only $200,000 cash. But one word of caution: Don't expect an infinity return overnight. It usually takes four to five years provided you have invested in a Big Six property.

All-Cash Buyers

Some investors prefer owning properties free and clear, and they are in a position to do that if they have substantial amounts of money in bank accounts, stocks, and bonds they wish to liquidate, or other sources of income. Leverage is absent from their investment formula. There is nothing wrong with this philosophy. I know some all-cash investors who have done well. It is a much more conservative way of investing, but it works for people who don't like the idea of debt.

That said, there are many investors with a lot of cash who still want to leverage their deals. This gives them an edge especially in a down market where "cash talks" and they are able to pick up buildings at prices substantially under the market.

Burn the Mortgage Quickly

In between highly leveraged investors and the few investors who pay all cash are investors who put down as much cash as they can and then pay off the mortgage with the cash flow from the property as quickly as possible. The fact that they get a shorter amortization period (15 years rather than 25 years, for example) means that their monthly mortgage payments will be greater but the loan will be paid off sooner. They believe, and rightfully, that as soon as they burn the mortgage there should be enough income to live the life of their dreams without having to work for a living anymore. This, too, is a perfectly sound way of thinking. We must remember that we have different objectives and perspectives. What works for one may not work for another.

In getting a shorter-term mortgage with higher payments, you can usually bargain for an interest rate and closing costs that are lower. The reason for this is that the lender knows your equity is building much faster than it would with a loan that had a long payout.

Mortgage Brokers

A good mortgage broker can perform a great service. In general, a mortgage broker has contacts that you don't have and access to numerous institutional lenders that will make loans on the type of property you are buying or refinancing as an owner. It is well worth it to pay a mortgage broker's fee because brokers are in a good position to get you the financing you need. The fee, depending on the size of the deal, can range from about one-half of one percent to one percent of the mortgage. If you are just getting your feet wet in investing, it might be a good idea to employ a successful mortgage broker. Not only will you likely obtain better financing, but you can learn a lot about the ins and outs of the financial world.

Healthy versus Unhealthy Debt

It would be virtually impossible for us to achieve great wealth in real estate without incurring debt. But what kind of debt? Mortgage financing on a Big Six property is healthy debt. The reason, of course, is that the tenants, in effect, are making our mortgage payments and, after operating expenses, we are receiving a cash flow return on our investment. However, if a second or third mortgage is placed on the property it could result in a negative cash flow. And it doesn't usually make sense to take money out of our pocket each month to carry the debt. Such a situation could result in a loss of the property by foreclosure—and this wouldn't look good on a credit report.

The Bottom Line

In the musical *Cabaret*, there is a song with the lyrics "Money makes the world go around." It could just as easily be used to describe real estate's role in the economic landscape. The free flow of money and access to credit is what adds vibrancy to property investment. Money can be made, but how and how much money you, as an investor, realize depends greatly on the financing you arrange for your investments.

Real estate investment is flexible enough that it can accommodate a number of philosophies: investors who want to use as much of the bank's money as possible to create their portfolio and eventually achieve an infinity return; investors who want to pay cash because they dislike debt; and those who put down a large amount of cash and pay off a mortgage as soon as possible. If you fully understand the financing component of the Big Six, you may find yourself suspending some of your notions about debt. Debt can be healthy if it also generates income.

But money is where real estate can be intimidating for new investors. The way to overcome that fear is proper preparation. Learn the terms, understand the components of a mortgage and how they interact, and be open to the full range of financing options available.

Along with that preparation comes the confidence to bargain. Banks and other financial institutions make money from mortgages. They *want* your business. That means they're willing to negotiate. Be creative—you may be surprised at the terms you're able to obtain from a bank or private lender.

A wealth of financing options are at your door. Big Six deals are hard to find. But we have given you the tools to know where to look for a Big Six property and to recognize one when you see it.

CHAPTER 10

Price

LOOKING BEYOND THE PRICE TAG
TO SEE THE BIG PICTURE

When consumers turn on the television, they are bombarded with pitchmen selling get-rich-quick seminars on buying and selling houses, along with testimonials from people claiming they have made piles of money from the knowledge they gained in these courses.

Newspaper articles and other news reports focusing on housing investments complement these paid "infomercials." What the media fail to present are the success stories of small investors who have done well with income properties. I don't believe the media are doing this on purpose. Like too many laypeople, reporters, radio personalities, and television anchors erroneously think that real estate means houses while investment means stocks. Rarely will you see an investment story that pertains to income properties, and certainly not one directed toward small investors who otherwise would buy only stocks.

As a result, although many people can toss around opinions on buying houses, most of them have little knowledge of commercial property investment. And misconceptions abound. For starters, the majority of people think these properties are beyond their reach as investors. But commercial portfolios are not the monopoly of moguls. Around the country, millions of small investors own small-income properties. These are the little apartment buildings, small office buildings, neighborhood shopping centers, and clusters of warehouse buildings you pass—probably without noticing—when you drive down streets across the country.

Many of these small investors started with one building. Today they may own several buildings—enough to make them financially independent. In fact, most people are not aware of the fortune they can make by investing in income properties. These are investments that can be grabbed for as little as $500,000 with only $50,000 to $100,000 in starting cash.

The Price-Is-Too-High Syndrome

Throughout my career, I've heard the same statement over and over: The price is too high. But that begs the question, "Too high compared to what?"

When people talk to me about good deals they passed up, I frequently ask them why they didn't jump on the purchase at the time. Inevitably, they say the price on the property was too high. Then I follow up with the question, "Have you ever bought any investment real estate?" In most cases, except for their own home, the answer is "no." These are the coulda', shoulda', woulda', people. My advice is to avoid them. They are negative thinkers, and for the rest of their lives most of them will sit on the sidelines while others make the fortunes. The investors you should associate with are the people who bought properties, managed them, took care of them, and increased the income of their properties. Eventually these properties became very valuable.

These people were successful because they took action when they found the right deal. You want to emulate them, and the way to start is to understand that the right time is now. People of action are the success stories not only in the real estate investment field but in life.

The Louisiana Purchase

Arguably one of the greatest real estate deals in the history of the United States was the agreement brokered by Thomas Jefferson and Napoleon Bonaparte in 1803. At that time, France owned most of what is now the United States of America. Because France was in dire need of money to wage war against the British, Napoleon considered a proposal to sell to the 13 American colonies some 530 million acres to which France laid claim. Negotiations between Jefferson and Napoleon went on for almost a year. Napoleon was holding out for a price of $21 million, or about four cents per acre, while Congress had authorized Jefferson to negotiate the deal at $11 million, or about two cents per acre.

Jefferson, representing the United States, and Napoleon, representing France, agreed on a price of $15 million but Congress balked—although later it approved the deal at $15 million, or the equivalent of three cents per acre. and the size of the country more than doubled. The transaction also marked the beginning of widespread land acquisition by everyone from farmers to businessmen. With so much land now available in the country, people began homesteading 640-acre tracts for which they paid next to nothing. The American notion of owning property became an institution.

You Got Here Too Late Young Man

When I moved to Miami many years ago, local people told me that all the good deals had already been made. I heard stories about parcels of land that had sold for $1,500 and were now going for $15,000. All the good property had already been gobbled up, they said. I arrived at the wrong time, they concluded. Twenty years later, people were saying I was successful because I arrived in Miami at just the right time.

They were wrong, of course. I was successful because a salesman taught me an important lesson—a lesson fundamental to making money in real estate during both up times and down times.

Many years ago, this salesman, Benn Zack, came to work for me. He had grown up in the real estate business in Detroit and had worked for his father, who was a multimillionaire real estate investor. Benn had a talent for finding good properties, some of which he sold to me, and others that we bought together. In fact, he sold me the first building I ever converted, an 18-unit complex that we named Plaza Maria, located a few blocks from my office at the time.

Benn had an instinct for fine real estate deals, but whenever he submitted one to me, I would say, "It's way overpriced. I could have bought that property for half that price a couple of years ago." Benn would then show me comparable properties that recently sold for more money than the deal he was offering me. This went on for many months. He would bring properties to me, and I would tell him how much the property had sold for years ago. Finally, Benn persuaded me to buy a few of these properties he'd found.

Those investments proved very profitable and they broke me of my defeatist attitude. Benn and I went on to make lots of money together over a period of a few years. He helped me kick a bad habit and changed my future in real estate.

It's all about price amnesia. One of the reasons that out-of-town and foreign investors make such vast fortunes in real estate is that they neither know nor care what properties sold for in the past. All that interests them are the present and the future.

In buying a property, don't let what others paid for it previously affect the price you pay. It doesn't matter if their rich aunt willed it to them, or if they won it in a craps game. The only question you should ask yourself is, "What is this property worth on today's market, and what will it be worth in the future?"

Things to Know

Once you've nailed down what you think is a fair price, you can begin your negotiations with the seller. At this point, it is important to be prepared. Information is the tool that will give you a better handle on dealing effectively with the seller. The details you need to determine are discussed in the following subsections.

Length of Ownership

The first thing to find out is how long the seller has owned the property. Although you may not think it, this can be a crucial factor in your negotiations. If the seller has owned the property for 20 years or more, the seller is usually willing to sell for a lower price than if he or she has owned the property for a just a few years.

Over the past few years, income properties have increased in value at a substantial rate, as much as 20 to 30 percent per year in certain areas of the country. Let's look at Seller A, who bought an office building 20 years ago for $1 million. Today Seller A's building is worth $3 million, free and clear of any mortgage. Owners like Seller A, who have owned a property as long as this, are often renting the offices in their buildings below the market rate. As I earlier discussed in this book, there are many owners who get attached to their tenants and like to keep their buildings 100 percent occupied. They can charge much lower rent because their income—although below market—represents an inordinately good return on their original investment.

In this case, I would try to buy this office building for less than the $3 million. If that weren't possible, however, I would probably agree to the $3 million, provided that I could foresee sufficient upside.

Another reason for dealing with a seller like this? He or she may wish to finance the deal by holding a first mortgage in order to spread most of the capital gains tax on the sale over the term of the mortgage. This is beneficial to me as the buyer because it means I won't have to pay points and closing costs to a bank, thus saving myself a substantial sum of money.

Now let's look at Seller B, who bought an almost identical office building just three years ago for $2.5 million. The property carries a $1.9 million mortgage. The properties of both Sellers A and B are in good condition, and both buildings are in the same location. But the tenants in Seller B's building are paying rent at the market rate. That means there would virtually be no upside to the deal—and no incentive for me to buy.

It is my experience that people who sell a property they have owned for five years or less will want a price that many buyers don't wish to pay. Of course, there are exceptions. If a seller bought a property during the past few years at a bargain price, he or she could sell it at a price that would still give a buyer room for a good profit. I had such an experience recently. The two-year owner of an office complex was willing to sell it for a price well under market value because it needed major improvements and upgrading. When he didn't get the offer he wanted, he made the improvements and—because of the excellent original deal he made—he still was able to sell the property under the market value.

So, there is no hard and fast rule that, because a seller purchased a property in the past few years, the price is always going to be too high. But I generally prefer dealing with a seller who has owned the property for many years because many times I can negotiate a deal at a lower price.

Motivation

It is helpful for us to know the motivation behind an owner's decision to sell. In other words, you should try to find out why a property is on the market. There may be numerous reasons: a relocation out of town, a shortage of money, a big life change like a wedding or a divorce, the desire to buy another property, partnership disputes, ill health, old age, retirement, or the settlement of an estate. Some sellers will not to want to disclose why they are selling. However, if you can find out the motivation for the sale, it may give you insight that will help you more effectively negotiate a deal. Still, regardless of the motivation, it all comes down to buying the property using the Big Six formula.

Decision-Maker

Before you begin to negotiate, make certain you know who will make the final decision for the seller—in other words, who will be signing the contract. You may expend a lot of time negotiating with a person you think owns the property only to discover that he or she owns the property with partners and is not authorized to sell the property alone. Alternatively, if a property is owned by a husband and wife and you are negotiating with only the husband, you may spend days, weeks, or even months in discussions before you find out that the wife is not willing to sell the property. If you had known this from the start, or even better, had met with both the husband and wife, you could have saved yourself a lot of time.

In cases where corporations own property, you may be dealing with a mid-management person or even someone slightly higher in the corporate hierarchy. But the chairman of the board or the executive committee will make the final decision. In these situations, simply ask, "Who is the decision-maker on this deal?" If the transaction has to be approved by a board of directors, then there is no other alternative but to wait until the board has made the decision. But if the deal does not require board approval, then you should identify the decision-maker for the company and deal directly with that person.

In other situations you may want to buy a property owned by an estate. Again, you should try to identify the decision-maker. Is there an executor of the estate who has the authority to make the deal subject to court approval? Or does the executor need the consent of all of the heirs? How many heirs are there? Your best bet is to consult with the attorney representing the estate and get all the facts beforehand. It would be a good idea to read the documents recorded at the courthouse to see the provisions in the last will and testament of the deceased. Many deals have been lost, after lengthy negotiations, simply because the investor did not correctly identify the decision-maker.

Seller Financing

The notion of *seller financing*, frequently referred to as holding paper, comes as a surprise to many investors. That's because they are under the impression that it is virtually impossible to get the seller to hold a mortgage on a property that is for sale. While it is true that the vast majority of sales are made by a buyer paying cash thanks to financing from a bank, there are certain circumstances when it is beneficial for a seller to hold paper.

Not all sellers may be cognizant of the advantages of holding paper but, once they understand it is to their benefit, you may find that they are disposed to doing it. Many sellers who have owned properties for a long period of time may prefer to hold paper rather than pay a big capital gains tax all at once, especially after their well-informed CPA has pointed out the benefits for them to do so. And there are times when a seller may hold a second mortgage, usually for a short period of time, in order to clinch a deal. So don't think that seller financing is out of the question.

Let's take the case of the Smiths, a husband and wife who bought an apartment building, Sarah Ruby's Cove, for $500,000 about 25 years ago. Today the property is valued at $3 million and they wish to sell it. Because of the depreciation of $2.9 million taken over the period that they owned the apartment building, the cost basis for the property is $100,000. After paying capital gains tax on this sale of, let's say, $435,000, they would net $2.465 million.

But the Smiths are in their late 60s and want to retire. They do not want to make any further investments and, therefore, have no need for such a large lump sum of cash. What they really want is a substantial and steady income so they can travel and spend more time with their children and grandchildren. They also prefer to pay their capital gains taxes over time, rather than all at once. Because they know Sarah Ruby's Cove is a solid Class B building in an "A" location, they are willing to hold a first mortgage.

A buyer comes along and is willing to pay their price of $3 million, net to them, provided he can make a deal with $600,000 cash down. The Smiths would hold a first mortgage for $2.4 million at 8 percent interest based on an amortization period of 25 years with the balance due in full at the end of 10 years, (In other words, a balloon mortgage). The monthly principal and interest payments owed the Smith would be $18,524. This investment represents a much greater return than they could obtain on a safe investment such as government securities.

The Smiths enter into the sale contract. The mortgage stipulates that there is no prepayment penalty for the first five years. The prepayment penalty for years 6 and 7 is 2 percent, for years 8 and 9 it is 1 percent and for the tenth year there is no penalty. The buyer agrees to the prepayment provision because he expects to keep the property as a long-term investment. The mortgage also provides for no assumability except with the Smiths' consent. Not only is the buyer getting excellent terms, he is eliminating the red tape of a bank mortgage and saving about $50,000 in closing costs. Everyone walks away a winner.

In some cases where there is seller financing, you may be wise to pay a higher price than you would for bank financing. For example, if you were able to structure a seller-held mortgage for a long term at a very low rate of interest, payable interest-only and providing for an assumption clause, you might get a higher rate of return, despite the fact that you paid more for the property. I will never forget the wise words of Bill Strickfaden, who taught investment real estate courses: "You can pay any price for a property as long as you can dictate the terms."

Quick All-Cash Deal

By all cash, we are not referring to a deal where the investor obtains a first mortgage from a bank and, together with a cash down payment, gives the seller all cash. We are referring to a situation where the investor has funds in the bank or in stocks or other securities that could be liquidated quickly into cash. Often there are sellers who want to make quick deals for all cash rather than sell to an investor who ties up the property by making the deal contingent on obtaining financing.

In effect, a contingency to obtain financing kills a deal if the necessary financing is not obtained. The time period to obtain financing is usually 60 to 90 days. But there are sellers who simply can't wait that long to find out whether or not they have a deal. In these circumstances, an investor with cash funds can sometimes, with an offer that carries no contingency for financing, get a property at a lower price than another buyer who might take several months to close the deal.

It is important to know how fast the seller wishes to close the transaction. Some sellers might want to close within 15 to 30 days after you have obtained a firm mortgage commitment. For tax purposes, if negotiations begin in the latter part of a year, some sellers may prefer to close in early January or February of the following year. This way the profit on the sale would not have to be declared until the year after the closing. That would, in effect, give the seller use of the tax money for an additional one-year period. There may be other tax reasons or personal reasons why a longer closing would make sense to the seller. Sometimes buyers prefer a long closing if they think, because they obtained the property under market value, they can assign their contract to another buyer before closing and pick up a good profit.

Capitalization Rates

In the real estate industry, we often hear about capitalization rates—"cap rates" for short. In effect, this is a calculation linked to the estimated rate of return. It sets a standard of measurement that evaluates the property on the basis of a buyer's paying all cash for a property. If we were only to look at the cash flow of deals and arrive at a value, we could easily end up with three different values on three similar buildings with three different forms of financing. The most valid way of arriving at the value of a property is to use a common denominator, NOI.

As we know, NOI is the difference between the gross income and the operating expenses. Thus the formula will be the same for each property: the NOI divided by the cap rate to determine the value of the property *before* financing. A good cap rate many years ago was 10 percent. Virtually everyone back then was looking to make investments in income properties on the basis of a 10 percent cap rate. That means that if the NOI was $100,000, an investor seeking a 10 percent return was willing to pay $1 million for a property.

Over the past 10 years, poor returns and substantial losses in non-real estate investments prompted investors to pour billions into real estate. Large insurance companies, pension funds, corporate entities, foreign companies, and the general public began to buy income properties. Because of the tremendous demand, the cap rates started to drop significantly and that, in turn, caused the price of income properties to increase substantially. Figures from Real Capital Analytics from mid-2007 showed cap rates ranging from 5 percent to 7.8 percent depending on the areas of the country where these properties were located (see Table 10.1).

Average cap rates can be deceiving. A $50 million Class A highrise office building in an "A" location might be sold to an

Table 10.1 Nationwide Capitalization Rates

Property Type	Region	Average Cap Rate (%)	Average Price ($)
Multifamily	Mid-Atlantic	6.1	107,800/Unit
	Midwest	7.1	70,400/Unit
	Northeast	5.5	216,100/Unit
	Southeast	6.6	80,800/Unit
	Southwest	6.5	74,100/Unit
	West	5.5	145,500/Unit
Office	Mid-Atlantic	6.8	281/SF
	Midwest	7.5	171/SF
	Northeast	6.3	438/SF
	Southeast	7.2	164/SF
	Southwest	7.2	158/SF
	West	6.6	305/SF
Retail	Mid-Atlantic	6.8	155/SF
	Midwest	7.6	148/SF
	Northeast	6.6	238/SF
	Southeast	7.1	144/SF
	Southwest	6.9	139/SF
	West	6.4	214/SF
Industrial	Mid-Atlantic	7.4	62/SF
	Midwest	7.8	49/SF
	Northeast	7.1	75/SF
	Southeast	7.3	53/SF
	Southwest	7.3	69/SF
	West	6.7	104/SF

(Source: Real Capital Analytics, May 2007)

institutional investor such as an insurance company or bank that would be content to buy based on a 5 percent cap rate. The prestige of owning the building can help elevate the company's profile and generate bigger profits. On the other hand, an investor who buys a marginal C property in a "C" location might expect to purchase it based on a 20 percent cap rate.

The lower the cap rate, the higher the price. And the higher the cap rate, the lower the price. The buyer of a boutique retail center in an "A" location, with an NOI of $500,000, would be satisfied paying a price based on an 8.5 percent cap rate—or $5.882 million. But a buyer picking up a C retail enter in a "C" location generating the same NOI of $500,000 might want a price based on a 20 percent cap rate, or $2.5 million. Thus, when we talk about cap rates, we have to compare similar properties in similar locations in the same areas of the country.

When I buy a B property in an "A" location, which is the type of property I focus on in this book, I don't rely on cap rates. I often will buy a property based on a cap rate of less than 4 percent, predicated on the *existing income*. But the property must have exceptional upside, with tenants paying rents that are substantially under the market rate with short-term leases with no options to renew. There must also be an opportunity to improve management, reduce expenses, and make improvements that will enhance the value of the building. I will buy such a property at a low cap rate because I know I can eventually increase the value of the property to an extraordinary level and obtain an infinity return. This is how you make your money in buying.

Knowing the Numbers

If you have reached this point, you will already have successfully executed five steps of the Big Six. This puts you at the crucial point where you want to buy a property at a price that will afford you the opportunity to increase income and, accordingly, increase the property value. A successful real estate investment is based on the income it will generate as well as what it will be worth in the future. You should review the following documents and details to calculate whether the math works for you:

- A statement from the seller noting the property's income and expenses for the past two years

- The seller's income tax return relating to the property for the past two years
- A current rent roll with the name of each tenant, the unit occupied, the date each original lease was signed, the current rent, the expiration date of the lease, the security deposit, and the terms of any option to renew the lease

Often sellers furnish statements of income and expenses that are unrealistic. I have seen statements from the sellers that show no management fee or a nominal management fee. The best way for you to project the income and expenses is with your broker and CPA. More than likely, because the sales price exceeds what the seller paid, the real estate taxes are going to increase. In addition, your insurance premium will be greater because you will have to carry a larger amount of insurance. These factors must be taken into account when projecting the operating expenses for the property. An income tax return that the seller has provided will not reflect the increased taxes and insurance premium for a new owner.

You have come this far because you have climbed the first five steps of the Big Six ladder. You have found the right property. You have worked long and hard for six months, searching, analyzing, and expending an enormous amount of time and energy. It hasn't been easy to find a property because few of them are on the market. Now you are negotiating the sixth step of your strategic formula, which is buying the property at a price that you feel affords you a secure and wise investment.

In the next chapter, "Anatomy of a Big Six Deal," you will vividly see how the first five criteria of the Big Six set the foundation for arriving at the right price and terms. And you may be surprised at the rate of return that can be achieved. After you read the next chapter you will understand better why *you make your money in buying.*

The Bottom Line

Knowledge—not hard cold cash—is the currency of Big Six real estate investment. For that reason, the successful evaluation of a property's price has more to do with how much information you can gather about a seller and the property than it does about the price tag on the real estate deal.

To understand this, you must look at the value of the property, which is not the same thing as its price. Too many would-be investors back away from an excellent deal because they think the price is too high. The crucial concern is not just how much the property costs, but what kind of income it can generate for you. A property that sounds like a bargain is useless if it doesn't have the upside you need.

As you negotiate a price, a multitude of factors come into play. Generally speaking, a property that has been in the same owner's hands for a long period of time is likely to have potential for a bigger upside.

You'll also have to be proactive and make your own assessments about the data you receive. A seller's documentation of income and expenses is only a beginning point—and often not an accurate one. You must calculate your own projected income and expenses to determine the real value of the property.

And the price you settle on can also vary depending on the type of financing you have available to you. Seller financing, for example, holds great advantages for a buyer. It also has advantages for a seller and can be a win-win bargaining chip.

To put in place the final element of the Big Six, you'll be doing plenty of number crunching, but strategy and forward-looking calculations will be more important than simply the seller's asking price. It's not about what the property costs you; it's about what it generates for you.

CHAPTER 11

Anatomy of a Big Six Deal

You can talk about how the Big Six formula works, but it's another thing to watch it in action. A case study is a perfect way to see—and understand—how each of the Big Six elements meshes with the others. Contrary to what you have assumed as a result of infomercials or hyped-up pitches about making fast money from real estate, Big Six deals are thoughtful and carefully executed. A Big Six case study also makes more vivid the reasons you need all six components of our formula. Four or five just won't cut it. Sure, you may make money from a deal that doesn't have all the elements, but you won't create the revenue that moves you forward on your wealth-producing strategy. And that means you won't open your life to the new possibilities you dreamed about.

To get an in-depth understanding of how a Big Six deal works, with all elements in place, we'll look at the fictional case of the sale of Adam's Manor.

Adam's Manor

The Adam's Manor apartment complex was developed in 1985 by a firm known for its quality construction and excellent craftsmanship. The property sits in the Southeast section of the country in a well-established suburban area. Spread over four acres of land, Adam's Manor consists of 4 two-story brick buildings, each containing 10 apartment units. There are 105 parking spaces, of which 80 are allocated to the tenants and 25 are earmarked for visitors. There is sufficient land to construct an additional 10 apartment units.

The 40 units in the complex represent a range of sizes and layouts. Sixteen are one-bedroom, one-and-a-half bath apartments, each 800 square feet in size. Another sixteen are two-bedroom, two-bath apartments, each comprising 1,100 square feet. The remaining eight are three-bedroom, two-bath units, each with 1,300 square feet.

The rents are substantially under the market rate. The one-bedroom, one-and-half bath apartments are rented for $655 per month, the two-bedroom, two-bath go for $880 per month, and the three-bedroom, two-bath rent for $1,100 per month. Those rent levels bring in annual income of $400,320, which we'll round to $400,000. The annual rent increase is linked to the CPI, which makes it roughly 3 percent or, approximately, $12,000 each year. The operating expenses, meanwhile, are 25 percent of the total income.

The property owners have, within the past three years, re-roofed the entire complex, painted the buildings' exteriors, and replaced old appliances with new appliances in each apartment.

In its entirety, the complex has 45,000 square feet of space, including the common areas. Most of the current tenants have lived in the complex for more than 10 years, and the majority are middle aged. The tenants are on year-to-year leases with no options to automatically renew, but the owners have always renewed the leases as a standard procedure of their operation.

The Sellers

The sellers, John and Jane Johnson, are in their mid 60s. Both were born and raised in the area. They bought the complex in 1985 from the original developer for $800,000 with $400,000 cash and a $400,000 bank mortgage that was paid off in 1999. John Johnson works as a mechanical engineer for a large company, and Jane Johnson is the chief accountant for an insurance company. They named the building for their grandson, Adam Jared Johnson, who is now a senior at the state university, majoring in real estate and finance. The motivation for selling the complex? The Johnsons wish to retire.

They have self-managed the property. John has done most of the maintenance and upkeep, and Jane has handled the books and financial matters. They have taken only short vacations during the past 23 years because they didn't feel comfortable leaving the property in someone else's hands while they were away. After they sell the property, they have a number of plans: They intend to buy a home in the area, they wish to take a cruise around the world, and they hope to spend more time with their children and grandchildren. Jane has a real estate license and plans to work part time for a local firm. John will keep busy as a part-time consultant for engineering firms in the area.

Listing the Property

The Johnsons have given an exclusive right of sale to Roland Richards, a well-known and successful broker. They have listed the property for $4.4 million. The terms call for 25 percent cash down; for the balance of the purchase price, the Johnsons will hold a 75 percent first mortgage at 7 percent interest, payable interest-only on a monthly basis, with the principal balance due in full at the end of five years. In other words, this will be a balloon mortgage. The mortgage will be prepayable without penalty at the end of the third year. The agreed-on brokerage commission is 5 percent of the purchase price, with the understanding that 50 percent will be paid to Roland and 50 percent to the buyer's broker.

The Johnsons have a compelling reason for wanting to hold the mortgage. The large gain on the sale of the property will result in a hefty capital gains tax, somewhere in the range of $500,000 to $600,000. If the property were sold on an all-cash basis, the entire tax would be payable all at one time. But since the Johnsons are getting 25 percent cash and the balance in the form of a mortgage, they can defer most of the capital gains tax until such time as the mortgage is paid off. In the interim, they can put the amount of the tax obligation (what they would have had to pay if the property was sold for all cash) into an interest-bearing account.

The Johnsons have instructed Roland that they don't want the property listed on the Multiple Listing Service. In fact, they do not wish for it to be advertised in any way. Roland is permitted to offer the property only on a confidential basis to prospective buyers and to work with other brokers who may have clients interested in this type of property. Roland is enthusiastic about getting the listing of this property and feels confident that he can find a buyer in a relatively short period of time. He considers the listing to be the equivalent of MIB, or "money in the bank," an expression I used many years ago when I was brokering deals and had several sales agents working for me. Whenever we obtained an exclusive right of sale on a property that had all the attributes to make it saleable, we called it an "MIB property." I never realized those attributes would become the keystone of the Big Six, the bible for my investment career in real estate.

Adam's Manor is a textbook example of a Big Six property for the following reasons:

- **Location:** Adams Manor's location is a solid "A." The building sits in a prestigious, well-established area with virtually no land left for development. There are only a few apartment complexes in the area, so demand is far in excess of supply. This is a neighborhood where middle- to upper-middle-class residents live in elegant homes, close to transportation, good schools, and high-end retail centers. The area has a number of good restaurants and cultural venues.
- **Building quality/design efficiency:** The complex was built by a top developer known for quality construction and excellent craftsmanship. Both the developer and the architect working on Adam's Manor were savvy professionals who recognized that the trend was toward larger apartments with his-and-her bathrooms, entry foyers, washing machines and dryers located within the apartments, and kitchens and bathrooms with windows that allow light in.
- **Tenant profile:** The residents are an excellent mix of middle-aged and slightly older tenants. For the most part, their children are grown. These tenants enjoy living in the complex and form a harmonious group. There has not been an eviction of a tenant in 23 years. This type of profile is ideal for a condominium conversion sometime in the future. (Condo conversions of small apartment buildings are discussed in Chapter 13.)
- **Upside:** There is room on the site to construct an additional 10 units, which would generate more income. There is also the potential for a future condo conversion. During their ownership of the property, the Johnsons have become friendly with virtually all the tenants in the complex and have socialized with several of them. Since the time that they bought the building, the only increases in rent have been based on the annual CPI. The leases are on an annual basis with no options to renew. The rents are substantially under

the market rate. Although the Johnsons knew that they could have increased the rents, they just didn't feel right about doing so because of their affinity towards the tenants. The rate of return they had been receiving over the years was more than they ever dreamed of getting.

- **Financing:** The financing on this deal reflects the best of both worlds. The Johnsons are willing to take back a first mortgage at an interest rate of 7 percent per year, with interest-only monthly payments and the principal balance due at the end of five years. This mortgage would be assumable provided the Johnsons approved the buyers. In addition, after the third year, the mortgage would be prepayable at any time without penalty. This type of seller financing offers substantial savings to the buyer because, unlike a bank loan, there would be no points or closing costs. At some time before the end of the five years, a new mortgage would have to be obtained from a bank in order to pay off the Johnsons' mortgage. However, since banks always have a strong interest in financing Big Six properties, a buyer should be in a position to negotiate excellent financing.

- **Price:** Adam Manor's listed price of $4.4 million appears to be a realistic price. Prices in the Southeast area of the country where Adam's Manor is located average $80,800 per unit. But Adam's Manor is far above the average. Based on 40 apartments, the listed price for Adam's Manor is $110,000 per unit. Of course, potential buyers must analyze the income and expenses to determine the real value of the property, but it is likely that at this price, together with the advantage of seller financing, this property is certain to be gobbled up by any astute investor. In fact, even if Adam's Manor were listed for all cash, most investors would buy it because banks would be pleased to provide financing for such a property like this. There are few investment properties in that market that measure up to the Big Six criteria as consistently as this one, and Adam's Manor is in excellent shape and has been well managed.

The Buyer

Forty-five-year-old Mark Miller founded a computer company and has been in business for 10 years. He is married with two children.

He owns a six-unit apartment building that he bought five years ago. His brother-in-law looks after the property and collects the rents. The building has doubled in value since Mark bought it. He plans to keep the building for about two more years then sell it.

Mark has $200,000 cash he wants to invest and has been actively searching for the past six months for another apartment building to buy. He envisions a complex of about 20 units. His broker, Sarah Silver, has shown him several properties but none have appealed to him. Then Sarah learns that Roland Richards, a broker with whom she has made many deals, has the Adam's Manor listing.

Adam's Manor is a property that almost every broker in town has dreamed of listing, but the Johnsons never wanted to sell. Roland hasn't even begun to contact brokers when he thinks of Sarah, knowing she has a buyer interested in an apartment building. He gives her a call, assuming that it could start the groundwork for a quick deal.

Sarah in turn contacts Mark and enthusiastically tells him about Adam's Manor. They meet, and she furnishes him with all the information about the property. After looking over the material, Mark is flabbergasted, "A deal for $4.4 million is way too big for me. How do you expect me to handle something like this with only $200,000 cash?" he asks Sarah. "You know it's way beyond my means. I don't think I should even look at the property."

But Sarah, who recognizes that this could be an outstanding opportunity for Mark, explains that there may be a way to put together a deal. "My CPA wants to go into a good real estate deal, and maybe he will partner up with you," she says. "Let's look at the building and allow things to take their course. What do we have to lose?"

Sarah sets up an appointment with Roland, the listing broker, to show the property to Mark the following morning. Mark is enamored with it and tells Sarah, "If you can show me a way to get into this deal with $200,000 cash, I'll buy it in a minute." Sarah calls her CPA, Ben Burke, and makes an appointment for Mark and Ben to see the property together.

Setting the Stage

Sarah, Mark, and Ben meet at Adam's Manor the next morning, and Ben, too, falls in love with complex. Sarah explains that Mark doesn't have enough cash to buy the complex on his own, and she suggests that Ben and Mark become partners. She adds that if it weren't for Mark's tenacity in searching for a good investment, they wouldn't even be looking at Adam's Manor.

Sarah points out that the deal requires about $1 million cash, so each man would have to come up with about $500,000 to be 50/50 partners. "Mark is on his way to becoming a successful real estate investor and will make an excellent partner. But he only has $200,000 cash," she tells Ben. "Would you consider loaning him $300,000 based on his pledging his 50 percent partnership interest as collateral for the loan?"

Ben agrees to entertain the possibility, but says he wants to see Mark's net worth statement and his credit history before he makes any final decision. Mark responds, "I think it's only fair that Ben furnishes me with the same information." The next day, the two men exchange financial data, and both are satisfied with what they see.

Ben agrees to make the loan to Mark at 6 percent interest, to be accrued and payable together with the $300,000 loan at the end of five years. He and Mark have already established a good rapport, and he feels that they will form a great partnership. Mark and Ben then meet to orchestrate the process for acquiring Adam's Manor.

The Buyers' Strategy

Mark and Ben are convinced that Adam's Manor easily meets the criteria for the first five elements of the Big Six. They also know that if they take too long to come in with a signed offer, another buyer may snap up the property.

The Johnsons have listed the property at $4.4 million. Roland has furnished both men with a statement of income and expenses for the past year. Based on the Johnsons' figures and a capitalization rate of 7.25 percent, which is the acceptable standard in the area for Big Six properties such as Adam's Manor, the property has a value of $4,262,069 (see Table 11.1).

Because the rents are substantially under the market, Mark and Ben project that, in addition to the annual CPI rent increase, which they expect to run about 3 percent, they will be able to increase the rental income by another 10 percent each year for the first five years they own Adam's Manor.

The Johnsons' financial statements for the property indicate that the operating expenses are 25 percent of the rental income.

Table 11.1 Valuation Based on the Johnsons' Income and Expenses

Income/Expense	Value
Rental income	$400,000
CPI increase (3 percent)	$12,000
Adjusted rental income	$412,000
Operating expenses (25 percent)	$103,000
Net operating income	$309,000
Value based on 7.25 percent cap rate	**$4,262,069**

Mark and Ben know that these expenses will increase given that the real estate taxes and insurance will go up as a result of the sale. The Johnsons have been self-managing the property at no fee; Mark and Ben estimate that they will incur a management fee equal to 3 percent of the rental income. Because of this, they estimate the operating expenses for Adam's Manor under their ownership will be 35 percent of the rental income. With these calculations, they determine that the property has a value of $4,052,414 (see Table 11.2).

Table 11.2 Valuation Based on Mark and Ben's Projected Income and Expenses (First Year)

Income/Expense	Value
Rental income	$400,000
CPI increase (3 percent)	$12,000
Increase in rents (10 percent)	$40,000
Adjusted rental income	$452,000
Operating expenses (35 percent)	$158,200
Net operating income	$293,800
Value based on 7.25 percent cap rate	**$4,052,414**

After some discussion, the two partners agree that a reasonable offer for the property should be $4 million. But, before making any offer, they wish to calculate the figures on the income, operating expenses, and mortgage payments so they know what the projected cash flow will be for the first five-year period (see Table 11.3).

Table 11.3   Mark and Ben's Projected Five-Year Cash Flow (Offering Price $4,000,000)

Assumptions

Offering price: $4,000,000

Terms: 25 percent cash, 75 percent mortgage at 7 percent interest; payable interest-only over a five-year period

Entire mortgage due in full at the end of five years

Previous year's rent: $400,000

Annual rent increases: CPI increase of 3 percent and rent increase of 10 percent each year for the first five years

Operating expenses: 35 percent of adjusted rental income for the first year and increasing 3 percent each year thereafter

	Year 1	Year 2	Year 3	Year 4	Year 5
Rental income	$400,000	$452,000	$510,760	$577,159	$652,189
CPI increase(3 percent)	$12,000	$13,560	$15,323	$17,315	$19,566
Rent increase (10 percent)	$40,000	$45,200	$51,076	$57,716	$65,219
Adjusted rental income	$452,000	$510,760	$577,159	$652,189	$736,974
Operating expenses	$158,200	$162,946	$167,834	$172,869	$178,055
Net operating income	$293,800	$347,814	$409,324	$479,320	$558,919
Debt service	$210,000	$210,000	$210,000	$210,000	$210,000
Cash flow	$83,800	$137,814	$199,324	$269,320	$348,919
Cash investment	$1,000,000	$1,000,000	$1,000,000	$1,000,000	$1,000,000
Cash-on-cash return	8.38 percent	13.78 percent	19.93 percent	26.93 percent	34.89 percent

After reviewing these figures, Mark and Ben decide to move forward with their offer of $4 million. They project the value of the property at the end of the five years will be $6,575,513, based on an 8.5 percent cap rate (see Table 11.4).

Table 11.4   Value at the End of Year Five

Projected Value	Year Five
Net operating income	$558,919
Valuation cased on cap rate of 8.5 percent	$6,575,513

Note: No one can predict what the cap rate will be at the end of Year Five. Thus we have used 8.5 percent as the projected rate.

The mortgage with the Johnsons will come due at the end of five years, but Mark and Ben expect to obtain a bank loan six months prior to that deadline. They expect the bank mortgage will be for 80 percent of the then value of the property, or a loan of $5,260,410 ($6,575,513 × 80 percent = $5,260,410). They project the new mortgage will be based on a 25-year amortization, with an interest rate of 8 percent for the first five years and 9 percent for the second five years. They estimate the cost will be one point plus bank closing costs and their own attorney's fees—an amount they approximate to be $125,000. They plan to negotiate a loan with no prepayment penalty and a provision for the bank to release individual units, as they are sold, if at some time in the future the complex is converted to condos.

With the $5,260,410 bank loan, Mark and Ben will be able to pay off the Johnsons' mortgage and still wind up with cash in their pocket.

Sealing the Deal

Mark and Ben have now decided, based on their projected cash flow from Adam's Manor, that they should make a purchase offer of $4 million, with 25 percent cash. The offer is based on the Johnsons' holding a 75 percent mortgage at 7 percent interest, payable interest-only monthly, with the entire principal balance of the mortgage, together with accrued interest, due at the end of five years; the mortgage would be prepayable without penalty after the third year. The men realize that their $4 million offer is $400,000 less than the listed price of $4.4 million. However, based on their calculations for projected income and expenses, they feel that it is a reasonable offer.

As experienced investors, Mark and Ben know there are few sellers who get the price that they are asking and few buyers who get the property with their first offer. In the back of a seller's mind, there is a minimum price that he or she will accept for the property. In the back of the buyer's mind, there is a maximum price that he or she will pay for the property. Somewhere in between is what most likely will end up being the price of the property. I have rarely seen deals where there is no wiggle room in the price.

It is common to see offers and counteroffers in any deal. Even though the seller and buyer both have their final figures in mind, in order to seal the deal they will, in many cases, still go beyond what they set as their limit. Throughout my career, in virtually all cases, I have had to pay more for a property than the maximum price I had in mind. This dynamic exists because there are so few Big Six properties available to buy. If I didn't stretch to make a deal, another buyer would come in and snap up the property.

In the case of Adam's Manor, Mark and Ben decide on their offer and then contact Sarah to advise her, as well as to let her know that they plan to have their attorney, Stephen Samson, draft the contract. Stephen drafts a purchase and sale contract with the terms that follow.

Purchase price: $4 million.

Terms: Twenty-five percent cash down, of which all deposits shall be a part. The balance of 75 percent is to be payable at the end of five years. Interest shall be at the rate of 7 percent payable interest-only monthly. The mortgage is prepayable after three years without penalty.

Deposit: Five percent deposit of $200,000 upon signing a contract; an additional deposit of 5 percent of $200,000 to be made within three days from the end of the due diligence period.

Escrow agent: Stephen Samson, P.A.

Interest bearing: Deposits to be held in an interest-bearing account with all interest credited to Mark and Ben at time of closing.

Due diligence/contingency: Mark and Ben shall have 30 days from the date the contract is accepted by the seller to review all data in connection with the property as well as to make a physical inspection of the different components of the building, including an environmental report. If Mark and Ben, for any reason during the period of the due diligence, find the property to be unsatisfactory, in their sole judgment, they shall notify the Johnsons in writing, at which time the contract will be canceled and all deposit monies refunded. Otherwise, the contract shall be in full force and effect and closed in accordance with the terms and conditions provided in the contract.

Brokers: The brokers in the transaction are Roland Richards and Sarah Silver, who will be paid a total brokerage commission of 5 percent of the purchase price to be divided equally between them.

Closing date: The closing shall take place within 60 days after the end of the due diligence period.

Assignability of contract: The contract will provide for Mark and Ben to have the right to assign the contract to a limited liability corporation (LLC), which they will form.

An LLC shields the partners in the LLC from personal liability but allows the partners to pass through all income and expenses to their personal income tax returns. Since LLC legislation was enacted, I have taken title to all the properties that I have purchased in the name of an LLC. I form a different LLC each time I close on a property.

Brokers Meet the Sellers

In negotiations between the seller and buyer, it is paramount for the brokers to be sincere, honest, and forthright. They should also use the utmost courtesy. The right rapport is essential. In no way should any broker ever badger or talk down to a principal. Sarah and Roland arrange a meeting with the Johnsons; they present the offer, and they attach a copy of the check in the amount $200,000, representing the deposit on the property. (As an investor, your best bet in getting the attention of the sellers is to attach a healthy check to the contract. Some buyers put up a small deposit, which can be counterproductive to making the deal.) If the Adam's Manor deal doesn't go through, Mark and Ben's $200,000 will be refunded anyway, so there is no risk in putting up a substantial deposit.

The Johnsons react negatively to the offer. "This offer is $400,000 less than what we want! These guys are wasting their time," they tell the brokers. "They must not realize that we have a fantastic property here and there's no other property in town like it." Roland agrees with the Johnsons. "Because of the excellent way you have operated the building over the last 20 years, this is a special property, no question about it," the broker says.

Establishing greater rapport with the sellers and demonstrating his sincerity, Roland adds, "I am representing you as your broker, and I appreciate the fact that you had the confidence in me to give me the exclusive right of sale on this fine property. Please realize that as a broker, the license law requires that I must submit any offer made by a buyer to the seller. I have already told Sarah that this offer is much lower than it should be, and I didn't think it stood a chance of being accepted."

But Sarah steps up to defend the buyers. "With all due respect, Mr. and Mrs. Johnson, Mark and Ben really like this property and want to be as reasonable as possible with you and consummate a deal," she says. Sarah tells the Johnsons that Mark and Ben have made an offer considerably lower than the listed price because:

- Real estate taxes on Adam's Manor will increase from the present assessment to an amount based on a property valuation close to Mark and Ben's proposed purchase price for the property.
- The cost of property insurance will also increase to reflect the increased valuation of the property. Mark and Ben will have to carry sufficient insurance just to cover the amount of the mortgage, not only to protect the Johnsons as the mortgage holders but also because the insurable value of the property is greater.
- Unlike the Johnsons, who managed Adam's Manor on their own without collecting a management fee, Mark and Ben will have to hire a professional management company to run the property. The men estimate that the fee for this will be a minimum of 3 percent of the total rental income.

Sarah also explains that Mark and Ben's operating costs for running the building will be 35 percent of the total income, rather than 25 percent of the total income, which is the amount the Johnsons recorded in their statement.

Despite Sarah's explanation, the Johnsons turn down the offer. Roland urges them to consider making a counteroffer "especially in light of the fact that the property will cost more to operate than it did under your ownership."

The Johnsons ask Roland what he has in mind.

Roland turns to Sarah, "These buyers are your clients. Give me an idea of how high you think they will go," he says. Sarah replies, "I really don't know, but if the Johnsons make a specific counteroffer now, sign the contract, and initial the change in price, I'll do everything I can to get Mark and Ben to increase the offer."

Roland tells Sarah that he and the Johnsons need to excuse themselves to discuss the matter privately. Once in the Johnson's study, Roland suggests a counteroffer strategy.

"I have met these buyers and I know that they are ready, willing, and able to act—and to act quickly," Roland tells the sellers. "I have also seen their financial statements and both of them have substantial net worth, as well as excellent credit histories. So you should have no concern about their ability to make the payments on your mortgage and run your property in a first-class manner." He recommends that the Johnsons sign the contract, change the price to $4.2 million, and give Mark and Ben until 5 PM the following day to agree.

"When you listed this property, we asked you your opinion as to its value," the Johnsons respond. "It was you, Roland, who suggested the price of $4.4 million and, even though we thought it was on the low side, we went along with it." The Johnsons then excuse themselves to discuss the matter. When they return, they advise Roland that they will not agree to $4 million. The least they will accept is $4,250,000. They sign the contract, then change and initial a price of $4,250,000 with the stipulation that Mark and Ben accept this counteroffer by 5 PM the following day.

It is my experience that, when sellers say that they will not take "a penny less," most of the time they will take many pennies less. In addition, when buyers declare that they will not pay a penny more, they usually will pay many pennies more. In this particular case, however, the Johnsons may very well be unwilling to take anything less. If the buyers try to continue the negotiations by coming back with another counteroffer, they may agitate the Johnsons and find themselves left out in the cold.

Roland and Sarah race back to meet with Mark and Ben and present the Johnsons' contract reflecting the sellers' counteroffer. "You know Mark, for six months we have been looking at deal after deal, and nothing made any sense," Sarah says. "We've now found a Big Six property—a real gem—and I think that both of you should consider making this deal and initialing the increase in the price. The differential is not that great, and you are buying a superb property." Mark and Ben, realizing that another counteroffer might prove unproductive, tell Sarah that they would like to run some numbers based upon the $4,250,000 price before they agree. Sarah reminds them that they'll have to act quickly because there is a 5 PM deadline the next day, "and we don't want to wait until the last minute."

Mark and Ben go back to Ben's office, run the numbers again, and project a cash flow for the first five years. They calculate that at the end of the first year, they will have a cash flow of $70,675, and by the end of the fifth year, their cash flow will be $335,794. That reflects a cash-on-cash return in Year Five of 31.6 percent (see Table 11.5). Furthermore, based on a net operating income of $558,919 at the end of five years, and a cap rate of 8.5 percent, they estimate the value of the building will be $6,575,513. Based on this, they project that they will be able to obtain an 80 percent loan from a bank amounting to $5,260,410.

From the proceeds of the loan, they will pay the closing costs of $125,000 and the Johnsons' mortgage of $3,187,500, recoup their initial cash investment of $1,062,500, and still have $885,410 in tax-free money left over (see Table 11.6).

After seeing these numbers, Mark and Ben are convinced that they should proceed with the deal at $4,250,000. "I think we can do some stretching and not let this deal blow because of $250,000. It's virtually impossible these days to find a property with all the features this building has," Ben says. Then he adds: "But, why don't we try to make one change—and get the mortgage at 6 percent interest for the first two years then 7 percent interest for the last three years?"

As Mark thinks about this, he reminds Ben that in addition to raising the rental income, there is also the opportunity to build an

Table 11.5   Mark and Ben's Projected Five-Year Cash Flow (Offering Price $4,250,000)

Assumptions

Offering price: $4,250,000

Terms: 25 percent cash, 75 percent mortgage to be held by the Johnsons at 7 percent interest; payable interest-only over a five-year period

Entire mortgage due in full at the end of five years

Previous year's rent: $400,000

Annual rent increases: CPI increase of 3 percent and rent increase of 10 percent each year for the first five years

Operating expenses: 35 percent of rental income for the first year and increasing 3 percent each year thereafter

	Year 1	Year 2	Year 3	Year 4	Year 5
Rental income	$400,000	$452,000	$510,760	$577,159	$652,189
CPI increase (3 percent)	$12,000	$13,560	$15,323	$17,315	$19,566
Rent increase (10 percent)	$40,000	$45,200	$51,076	$57,716	$65,219
Adjusted rental income	$452,000	$510,760	$577,159	$652,189	$736,974
Operating expenses	$158,200	$162,946	$167,834	$172,869	$178,055
Net operating income	$293,800	$347,814	$409,324	$479,320	$558,919
Debt service	$223,125	$223,125	$223,125	$223,125	$223,125
Cash flow	$70,675	$124,689	$186,199	$256,195	$335,794
Cash investment	$1,062,500	$1,062,500	$1,062,500	$1,062,500	$1,062,500
Cash-on-cash return	6.65%	11.74%	17.52%	24.11%	31.60%

additional 10 units on the property. "That is an important facet of this deal," Mark says. "This is a very good deal. I've been looking around for six months and Adam's Manor is way, way, way better than anything I've seen. Let's not push the envelope and quibble about the interest rate. We may upset the Johnsons so much that they call off the deal."

Table 11.6   Mark and Ben's Total Projected Cash Proceeds after Refinancing at the End of Five Years

	Year 5
Valuation based on cap rate of 8.5 percent	$6,575,513
Bank loan 80 percent	$5,260,410
Closing costs	$125,000
Balance of Johnson mortgage	$3,187,500
Net proceeds of loan	$1,947,910
Return of initial cash investment	$1,062,500
Total Cash Proceeds	**$885,410**

Ben agrees and the next morning Mark calls Sarah to tell her that they want to proceed with the deal at $4,250,000. The two buyers meet at Sarah's office and initial the $4,250,000 million price in the revised contract. Sarah then calls Roland with the good news. She delivers to Roland the executed contract and Roland, in turn, takes it to the Johnsons.

"We were able to convince the buyers to accept your counteroffer," Roland announces to the Johnsons. "We've got a deal, and you can start thinking about that around-the-world vacation!" Although the Johnsons had thought they might get more money for the property, they are happy with the deal.

The due diligence begins the next day. Over the next 30 days, Mark and Ben learn that Adam's Manor is in impeccable condition and all the financial data are in order. They put up the remainder of the deposit monies, and the deal closes 60 days later. Ben and Mark take title in the LLC that they have formed. They see this as a long-term investment—a hard-to-find gem that will ensure their future wealth just as it did the Johnsons'.

Five Years Later

Mark and Ben, in the name of their LLC, refinance the property with the bank for $5,260,410, pay the closing costs of $125,000, and pay off the Johnson mortgage in the amount of $3,187,500. Mark and Ben have $1,947,910 remaining. That is not only sufficient to recoup their cash investment of $1,062,500, but it leaves $885,410 in their pockets—and that money is tax-free because they still own the property and no resale has occurred.

For his part, Mark Miller, at the end of five years, has greatly improved his position. As we saw in Table 11.6, after paying the closing costs and the Johnsons' mortgage, the LLC is left with $1,947,910 to be split evenly, with Mark and Ben each receiving $973,955. However, Mark and Ben didn't invest the same amount. Mark owes Ben $331,250 (increased from $300,000 due to the adjustment of the final sales price) plus interest accrued at 6 percent, or $443,288. After Mark pays that back, he is left with $530,667 net cash proceeds (including his $200,000 initial cash investment), plus five years of rental cash flow from the property of $486,776.

Mark has received more than $1 million—or $1,017,443 to be exact—in total cash. The property's market value of $6,575,513 minus the mortgage of $5,260,410 equals total equity of $1,315,103. Mark's 50 percent share is $657,551. Therefore, Mark's total cash received plus his equity equals $1,674,994 (see Tables 11.7 and 11.8).

The most amazing thing? Mark now has zero cash of his own invested in Adam's Manor. He's abiding by the Big Six credo that you make your money in buying!

Table 11.7   Mark Miller's Cash Flow and Cash-on-Cash Return for the First Five Years

Assumptions

Initial cash investment: $200,000

Loan from Ben: $331,250 at 6 percent interest, accrued, payable at the end of five years

	Year 1	Year 2	Year 3	Year 4	Year 5
Mark's 50 percent Split of cash flow	$35,338	$62,345	$93,100	$128,098	$167,897
Initial cash investment	$200,000	$200,000	$200,000	$200,000	$200,000
Cash-on-cash return	17.67%	31.17%	46.55%	64.05%	83.95%

Table 11.8   Mark Miller's Position after Refinancing

	Year 5
Bank loan	$5,260,410
Closing costs	$125,000
Balance of Johnson mortgage	$3,187,500
Cash proceeds to LLC	$1,947,910
50/50 split between Mark and Ben	$973,955
Repayment by Mark of Ben's loan plus accrued 6 percent interest	$443,288
Mark's net cash proceeds (includes $200,000 initial cash investment)	$530,667
Mark's total five-year rental cash flow	$486,776
Mark's total cash received	$1,017,443
Mark's 50 percent equity in Adam's Manor	$657,551
Mark's total cash received plus his equity	$1,647,994
Mark's cash invested in Adam's Manor	**$0**

Now What?

Mark has come a long way. He started with a $200,000 cash investment and now has $1,017,443 cash available to do whatever he wants, as well as 50 percent equity of $657,551 in a Big Six property. But it doesn't stop there. We have followed Mark only through the first five years of this investment.

Over the next five years (Years 6 through 10), Mark and Ben estimate that the rent increases will slow down to 5 percent per year. They also project that the operating expenses will increase by 5 percent, and the cash flow will significantly increase year by year. Unlike the previous interest-only loan the men held with the Johnsons, the current bank mortgage includes principal and interest. That means the mortgage balance is decreasing every month and the equity is increasing—important details that are not reflected in the projection.

With rents steadily going up, the operating expenses are under control, and that gives the building a healthy NOI. Since this NOI is growing and is greater than the debt service, the cash flow is also increasing nicely.

Remember, in order to obtain a cash-on-cash return, you divide the cash flow by the cash investment. However, since Mark and

Table 11.9   Mark and Ben's Projected Five-Year Cash Flow (Years 6–10)

Assumptions

Mark and Ben obtain a mortgage at the end of Year Five for 80 percent of the value of Adam's Manor, or $5,260,401

Terms: 25-year amortization period; 8 percent interest

Annual rent increases: 5 percent in Years 6 through 10

Operating expenses increase by 5 percent per year

	Year 6	Year 7	Year 8	Year 9	Year 10
Rental income	$736,974	$773,823	$812,514	$853,140	$895,797
Annual rent increase (5 percent annually)	$36,849	$38,691	$40,626	$42,657	$44,790
Adjusted rental income	$773,823	$812,514	$853,140	$895,797	$940,586
Operating expenses	$186,958	$196,306	$206,121	$216,428	$227,249
Net operating income	$586,865	$616,208	$647,018	$679,369	$713,337
Debt service	$487,208	$487,208	$487,208	$487,208	$487,208
Cash flow	$99,657	$129,000	$159,810	$192,161	$226,129
Cash Investment	**$0**	**$0**	**$0**	**$0**	**$0**
Cash-on-Cash return	**Infinity**	**Infinity**	**Infinity**	**Infinity**	**Infinity**

Note: The above cash flows are split 50/50. For simplicity, I have not included a vacancy factor in any of my computations. A factor of 3 to 5 percent would be realistic.

Ben's cash investment is $0, the cash return for them is immeasurable and amounts to an infinity return (see Table 11.9). There is no return in the world that can beat this!

The Bottom Line

When legendary Vince Lombardi became head coach of the Green Bay Packers, he told the team, "Winning isn't everything, it's the only thing." This may be true in sports where there is a winner and a loser, but it is not true for a real estate investment. In a Big Six real estate deal, everyone should—and can—come out a winner. Both seller and buyer should walk away from the table feeling well satisfied that a fair deal was made for both of them. And the brokers and other professionals who worked with them should also feel that they played a significant role in making it all happen.

Before they get to that point, however, both the buyer and the seller have plenty of work to do. Each must obtain and carefully analyze critical information including, in the case of the seller, the smartest way to deal with any tax obligations that arise from the sale of the property. Then, well prepared, the courtship begins, with both sides presenting their positions while each side waits for the other to accept.

A Big Six real estate investment is not about one-upping the other side or outsmarting the person on the other side of the table. It is about identifying the Big Six elements in a deal and evaluating whether the property in question will take you closer to your goal of personal wealth. A Big Six deal is a well-handled deal where everyone stands to gain, and the negotiations can and should be civilized, respectful, and productive.

In a Big Six deal that is properly executed, there are no losers.

PART

III

MOVING FORWARD

Like anything you want to see flourish, you'll need to give your real estate investment sufficient care and attention.

Finding and acquiring a Big Six property is essential to the goal of building wealth for the future, but keeping your investment viable, agile, and constantly growing in value is also important. The way you'll do this is to manage it well, to understand when you need to modify or enhance your holdings, and, finally, to take action when it's time to divest properties that no longer match your goals—because you have shifted your strategy or because market forces and other factors have changed the profile of the property.

The third—and final—section of this book focuses on how you can maximize the value of your property and the revenue you receive from it. It's all about controlling and nurturing your Big Six investment.

This section of our book starts with Chapter 12, where we look at what constitutes good management and appropriate leasing of the property. We explore this through interviews with experienced managers who share their stories. Real estate has potential for a long economic life, but market conditions and other factors are not carved in stone. That means you need to be prepared for circumstances in which markets change. The market is softening; do you hold onto your investment? Under what circumstances do you think about selling? What about making changes to the property to help it hold—or even increase—its value?

There were hundreds of thousands of rental apartments, mostly large complexes, converted to condos in the period from 2000 to 2007, at which time the conversions came to a halt. In spite of that, you will read in Chapter 13 that there is still money to be made in converting small apartment buildings to condos. I will tell you how to find the ideal buildings to buy as well as how to sell out the units quickly and make a whopping profit.

In real estate, as in all industries, there are ups and downs. But in buying Class B buildings in "A" locations, you will be able to weather the storms because these types of properties are virtually recession proof. You will always want to look for the ways to *add* value to your property. By constantly improving your property, you're pushing up the level of rent you can charge and, as a result, increasing the value of your property. Not only that, but if you can nudge up your revenue while holding down your operating expenses, you're improving the rate of return on your commercial property. And that is the key to fulfilling your goal of wealth.

In the final chapter, "One Good Investment Is Worth a Lifetime of Labor," you'll meet real-life investors. Each started with very little money yet achieved financial independence from one single investment. You'll learn that with the right information, an understanding of the Big Six formula, motivation, dedication—and a little patience—wealth is easily attainable. Once you have it, you can begin living the life of your dreams.

12

Management and Leasing to Enhance Your Investment

Once you acquire a property such as Adam's Manor, you must be judicious about the next step—its management. A Big Six building, effectively managed, will be a successful profit center for you. You have several options when it comes to management. You can hire a management firm that will oversee your property's operations from a central office, you can hire a firm that will install an on-site manager, you can hire your own manager, or you can manage the property yourself.

In the case of a building such as Adam's Manor, the best strategy is to hire a professional management firm not only to run the building but to handle the leasing of any vacancies that arise. Such a decision takes the management responsibility from the investor and puts it in the hands of an entity with deep expertise in this arena, because it does nothing but manage buildings. There are few investors with the time and know-how of a professional management firm.

The use of a professional management firm can be invaluable for owners: It relieves them of the responsibility of running the building and frees them to pursue other investment deals, to be more active in community affairs, or to spend more time with family and friends. From an economic standpoint, a good property management firm can save you a lot of money, because the firm has access to vendors at better rates than you would be able to arrange on your own. At the same time, because the firm's only business is management, the company is up to date on competition, rental rates, and market conditions. Look for a company with experience in maintenance, leasing, collections, marketing, and budgets—and one with knowledge about local laws affecting real estate.

Property managers can handle the operations of all types of properties, including apartments, offices, industrial properties, mobile home parks, and warehouses. Because they know the real estate market well, they can help minimize vacancies, screen potential tenants, and set rental rates appropriately. They also can keep your property in good condition. Property managers negotiate contracts for janitorial, security, grounds keeping, trash removal, and other services. They monitor the performance of contractors and resolve complaints from tenants when services are not properly provided. Managers also purchase supplies and equipment for the property and arrange for repairs that cannot be handled by regular property maintenance staff.

At the same time, the managers can handle the financial operations of your property. There are a number of property management software programs and professional property managers use them—or their own proprietary software—to efficiently watch income and expenses, track tenant deposits and rent payments, comply with federal and local laws, and even to keep a database of tenant requests.

A good management firm may very well be able to increase the property's income, reduce expenses, and establish such a good relationship with tenants that vacancies are held to a minimum. That means you will be putting more money in your pocket after paying the management fees than if you were running the building yourself. In the case of Adam's Manor, a deal could probably be negotiated with a management firm at 3 percent of the gross income because it would be an easy building to run. As rents are increased at this property and some vacancies occur, the management firm should be entitled to a leasing commission.

If an office building has approximately 50,000 rentable square feet (RSF), there are good boutique management firms that will provide an on-site manager to operate the building. On-site managers take care of the day-to-day operations of a property. They routinely inspect the grounds, facilities, and equipment to see whether repairs or maintenance are needed. They meet with current residents to handle requests for repairs or to resolve complaints, and they show prospective tenants vacant apartments or office space.

On-site managers also enforce the terms of rental or lease agreements, such as rent collection, parking and pet restrictions, and termination-of-lease procedures. Other important duties of on-site managers include keeping accurate, up-to-date records of income and expenditures.

Property managers who are not on site will market rental space to tenants by using a leasing agent, by advertising, or by other means. They align rents to market rates, screen tenants, collect rent, arrange for maintenance and repairs, and ensure that the building and grounds are maintained. All property managers should provide you with monthly statements of income and expenses, as well as an annual report on the condition of the property, inside and out.

A management company is not the only option, of course. There are some investors who can successfully manage their own buildings. They may enjoy doing it themselves or they may employ a family member or close friend to run the operation while they keep a close watch over the process. Under certain circumstances, this can be just as effective as hiring an outside management firm. It will depend to a great extent on the personality of the investor and whether or not he or she enjoys the day-to-day duties of operating a building. Key to this is whether the owner has sufficient time available to properly handle the property's management. Remember, you have invested a lot to acquire the building. Its management is no place to cut corners if you want to generate the income you dream of for the future. You may find an investor who owns a number of properties and employs a full-time staff manager to operate all his or her properties. But until you have acquired a portfolio of investment properties—and maybe not even then—this is usually not the best solution.

Properties that are the most likely candidates for self-management include small apartment buildings, in which case you may consider hiring one of the tenants as an on-site manager. Because this is usually an informal relationship, no written agreement is necessary. If the resident manager is simply handling tenant concerns, looking after the cleanliness and general upkeep of the property, handling the leasing of vacant units, and doing some simple bookkeeping, a reasonable compensation would be a credit of 50 percent of the rent the resident manager is paying and, perhaps, the payment of his or her utilities and telephone. If the resident manager or the manager's spouse can handle minor repairs, painting, and cleaning after an apartment is vacated, then a reasonable compensation would be free rent plus the utility and phone perks.

In my own experience as an investor, I have found that the easiest properties to manage are small retail shopping centers and small bay warehouses. In many instances, I have managed these types of properties out of my own realty office by assigning one person to handle them. For example, many years ago I delegated to my officer manager, Alicia Baro, the responsibility of looking after a small retail center with 12 stores. She was able to keep it virtually 100 percent rented for 10 years and rarely had to visit the property to check on it. We had a person in the neighborhood who, on a daily basis, made sure the grounds were kept clean and did the landscaping maintenance. Alicia's job was to deal with the tenants, mostly over the telephone, and they all fell in love with her. In addition, Alicia deposited all rent checks, paid the operating expenses and mortgage payments, and took care of the simple bookkeeping that was required.

When I sold the building, Alicia told me that she was sad I'd made that decision. She enjoyed operating it and described it as a "wonderful experience." She did a terrific job and, over the years, I paid her a percentage of the gross income. Your goal should be to nurture your investment by giving it the best management possible.

"My accountant once said something I shall never forget: 'If you look after the property, it will look after you.' From that philosophy, I learned that if you don't take care of the property in a responsible manner that works for your tenants and yourself, you will simply not succeed," says Philip Leitman, a partner at Suchman Retail Group, which owns and manages retail centers in South Florida. "We look at a property as a long-term asset and not as a disposable asset. We want to maximize our revenues and control our expenses, but the landlord-tenant relationship is paramount."

For this chapter, I interviewed Leitman and the principals of three other successful property management firms. Their insider experiences and advice help shed light on the ins and outs of managing apartment buildings, small retail shopping centers, small bay industrial warehouses, and office buildings.

Managing Apartment Buildings

Large apartment complexes (about 100 units and up) need a full-time manager located in an office or small apartment used as an office on the premises. There should also be an assistant manager who can handle minor repairs as well the bookkeeping for the operation. There could be a full-time maintenance person or, in lieu of this, an outside maintenance company contracted on a job-to-job basis.

The manager should also handle leasing. Leases in apartment buildings are generally for one year with no options to renew—allowing a landlord to easily increase rents. Although apartment buildings are more intensive to manage, especially the large complexes, their rates of return can be greater than other income properties. Generally, Class B buildings in "A" locations, properly managed, will have a strong occupancy.

Robert L. Valledor, owner and president of the Valledor Company, is a veteran at managing apartment buildings. His South Florida boutique firm specializing in property management was founded more than 50 years ago by his father, Enrique. Valledor is active in community affairs, was president of the Realtor Association of Greater Miami and the Beaches from 1984 to 1985, and holds the prestigious designation of Certified Property Manager from the Institute of Real Estate Management. He spoke with me about the ins and outs of property management.

Rosen: What makes a good property manager?
Valledor: A person who is adaptable, empathetic, and doesn't mind working at night or helping the maintenance man; someone who does what's necessary to get the job done professionally, correctly, and within budget.
Rosen: What is the minimum size building that would warrant a resident manager?
Valledor: I would say 18 to 20 units. However, it really depends on the property and the tenants.
Rosen: Do you encourage owners to have resident managers?
Valledor: It depends on the size of the property. For smaller properties, a resident manager is not necessary. However, for larger properties, yes, we encourage owners to have a resident manager.
Rosen: How long is your typical management agreement?
Valledor: Usually one year.
Rosen: Is the agreement cancelable during this time?
Valledor: Yes. Either our client or we may cancel the agreement upon 60 days written notice.
Rosen: How do you handle accounting?

Valledor: We have our own proprietary accounting software. But you can use a number of other programs, such as Quicken or QuickBooks for apartment bookkeeping. I suggest QuickBooks because it already has a property management template. What is important is being able to understand the information the program provides.

Rosen: How do you handle maintenance? Do you put a regular maintenance person on your staff or do you use an independent contractor?

Valledor: We do it through independent contractors or a licensed company, depending on the maintenance issue and the particulars of the specific property.

Rosen: Are your leases based on a one-year term?

Valledor: Yes.

Rosen: Do your leases provide options to renew?

Valledor: No. But in virtually all cases we will renew the leases for an additional year.

Rosen: Upon renewal, do you increase the rent?

Valledor: Yes, we generally do.

Rosen: By how much?

Valledor: The increase is generally based on the Consumer Price Index. It may be more than the CPI or less than the CPI, depending on the particular circumstances.

Rosen: What is the average turnover for apartment buildings that you manage?

Valledor: Approximately 5 percent to 8 percent.

Rosen: So in a 50-unit building you would have four tenants move out each year, based upon an 8 percent turnover rate?

Valledor: Correct. Maybe more, maybe less.

Rosen: What do you do to those apartments when people move out?

Valledor: We will clean, paint, check the appliances and fixtures, and make the necessary repairs. We also change the flapper in the toilet because it saves on the water bill.

Rosen: Do you ever change any of the locks when a new tenant comes in to prevent the former tenant or anyone with a key from getting in that unit?

Valledor: Always. While our leases provide that the outgoing tenant has to return the keys to us, we make sure all the locks are changed.

Rosen: What is the operating expense ratio on a building?

Valledor: On the larger properties [of 40 to 50 units] it will run 28 percent to 35 percent. On smaller properties [of 10 to 12 units] it can run 38 percent to 42 percent.

Rosen: Do you issue monthly reports to your clients?

Valledor: Yes. We mail them and we post the reports online. We have a secure page on our company's web site that the owners can access using two different user IDs and passwords to log in. Once there, they can read or download reports from the past three months.

Rosen: If you are contacted after hours with an emergency, how do you handle it?

Valledor: I either contact the maintenance person, the proper authorities, or go out there myself to try and resolve the situation. It depends on the emergency.

Rosen: What is the key to keeping a building fully rented?

Valledor: I have found that setting rental rates about 5 percent to 8 percent less than the market rate helps keep the tenants from moving. Trying to squeeze out the last dime in rent is usually counterproductive. If a tenant moves out, the cost of repainting, recarpeting, and other repairs is going to be much greater than the few dollars more that you'll get from large rent increases. Also, you could lose one month's rent or more if a tenant moves out.

Rosen: When you're preparing a budget, what percentage do you allow for vacancies?

Valledor: About seven percent. And that's real conservative. So I'm overestimating what I think it will be the vacancies in the building.

Rosen: What do you think makes you a good manager?

Valledor: I'm available and accessible 24/7. I do what it takes to get the job done. I try to be responsive not only to my clients but to the tenants.

Rosen: How do you find a tenant to lease a vacant apartment?

Valledor: Depending on the market, there would be advertisements in the paper, for rent or vacancy signs on the property, and brochures with the picture of the building, the rental information and a floor plan showing the layout of the apartment. We may have a visual tour of the apartment on our Web site so prospective tenants can see what the apartment looks like and the amenities in the building.

Rosen: What is your fee to manage an apartment building with, let's say, about 40 units?

Valledor: About 4 percent to 5 percent of the gross rents collected.

Rosen: Do you charge a leasing fee in addition to that?

Valledor: Not if we have a resident manager. Otherwise we charge a fee of 6 percent of the contracted rent.

Rosen: Do you bond your resident managers?

Valledor: No, because we do not permit tenants to pay their rent with cash to the resident manager. The rent must be paid either by check or money order. If the tenant prefers to pay with cash, they can pay at our office. So there's no necessity to bond our resident managers.

Rosen: Do you usually select the resident manager from one of the tenants in the building?

Valledor: Sometimes. On some occasions we interview candidates and place them on the property. It depends on the property, and it depends on the available candidates.

Rosen: How much do you pay your resident managers?

Valledor: For a small building we pay about $125 per month. In a larger property we would provide a free apartment plus compensation.

Rosen: How much compensation?

Valledor: About $150 to $200 per month.

Rosen: Are you able to increase the bottom line for your clients over and above the fee they pay you?

Valledor: That is our goal. And in most cases, we accomplish that.

Rosen: How?

Valledor: A good manager will keep the building in good repair with an attractive appearance, which reduces turnover. Good managers make sure that expenses, wherever possible, are reduced. And, most importantly, we are responsive and respectful to the tenants, which also helps reduce vacancies.

Rosen: What percentage of your clients finds you through the Internet?

Valledor: Our Internet inquiries are coming in about 40 percent to 45 percent from people searching for a good property manager in South Florida.

Rosen: How many of those deals do you actually close?

Valledor: We are contracting with about 80 percent of the Internet inquiries.

Rosen: For someone who has bought a building and is looking for a good manager, is the Internet a good place to start?

Valledor: Yes, everybody is on the Internet now. In addition to the Internet, I would also talk to the manager of the nice-looking apartment building in the area about managing my property.

Managing Small Retail Centers

Because a small retail center will be occupied by business people who are generally on longer leases than those in apartment complexes, the management is simpler. Also, the tenants pay common area maintenance (CAM) and increases in the general operating expenses of the building. The supervision of this type of building is not as involved as that of apartment complexes, and often there is no need for an on-site manager. Still, there are many occasions when use of a management firm would be the right choice. Philip Leitman, a partner at Suchman Retail Group, and Ana Vega-Garcia, director of leasing and senior property manager at the company, talked with me about the ways professional management can benefit a small retail center. Suchman Retail Group is a 40-year-old company with retail centers in the Greater Miami area.

Rosen: What size retail centers do you manage?

Leitman: Our centers range from 17,000 square feet to big box centers of about 80,000 square feet.

Rosen: What do you look at to get an overview of the components of your centers?

Leitman: The best way is to prepare a rent roll and keep it current. It gives the owner a quick summary of the terms of each lease, and it is an invaluable tool. It should include the name of the tenant, the store address, the size of the store, the rental rate, the security deposit, the inception date of the lease, the expiration date of the lease, any options for renewal along with the terms of the options, and CPI increases.

Rosen: How do you structure your leases?

Leitman: Usually we require a five-year minimum. The tenant will be entitled to a five-year option just as long as the tenant is in good standing, but the options should not exceed the initial term.

Rosen: What do you consider to be the best mix of tenants?

Leitman: We feel that the best mix is to have both local tenants and national tenants because we feel that it will give us the best return for every dollar invested.

Rosen: What is your average vacancy factor?

Garcia: We budget for a 5 percent vacancy factor overall. But because we are in very strong markets with more demand than supply, our vacancies are actually about 2 percent to 3 percent.

Rosen: Who pays for the CAM, which includes taking care of the parking lot, sidewalks, landscaped areas, irrigation, gutters, roof drains, pump systems, and so forth?

Garcia: The tenants. The amount each tenant pays is predicated on the size of his or her store in relationship to the total size of the entire center. For example, if a center has 20,000 square feet and a tenant occupies a store of 1,000 square feet, then that tenant would pay 5 percent of the CAM.

Rosen: Who pays the operating expenses on the building, such as taxes, insurance, trash pickup, management fees, and the like?

Garcia: Each tenant reimburses us for their proportionate share according to their lease terms. If a tenant maintains their own trash, we deduct that from the charges.

Rosen: Is there a base year for each tenant so that they pay the increase in the operating expenses based on the time that they signed their original lease?

Leitman: No. It's done year to year, predicated on any increases in operating expenses over the previous year. Each tenant pays their proportionate share of any increase just like they do for CAM.

Rosen: How do you budget your income and expenses, and at what point in the year do you do it for the following year?

Leitman: We do it in the fourth quarter, either in November or December. It's really not very hard once you have done it for a while. We look at our expenses line by line. We produce a full financial statement on every property—a profit and loss statement, a cash flow and balance sheet every month. We look at it and do a variance analysis from what we projected. The big things, of course, are going to be taxes and insurance. And then we separate operating expenses from capital items.

Rosen: How about the roof? Who is responsible if the roof starts to leak?

Leitman: Typically the landlord is responsible for the leak unless the tenant physically made a penetration or caused some sort of physical damage.

Rosen: But there is no CAM involved, right? The roof is not part of CAM?

Leitman: Regular maintenance of the roof oftentimes is part of CAM. It depends on how the lease is written. Obviously, replacing a section of the roof or anything that is capital in nature is not a part of CAM.

Rosen: In effect, your leases are triple net.

Leitman: Yes, and that also means tenants are responsible for their store interiors.

Rosen: When do you collect your projected increases for CAM and operating expenses?

Leitman: We collect it each month in advance so that the tenant won't be billed a lump sum amount at the end of the year.

Rosen: Do you have a full-time maintenance person for all your centers?

Leitman: No. Our maintenance is handled on a contract basis with an outside firm. Fortunately, we have enough properties so that we are important to our vendors and we have established good relationships by treating them with respect. We also issue a work order every time we send a vendor out. It's easy in a small business to just call them up and send them out, but we don't do it like that.

Rosen: How do you handle the insurance with a tenant that, because of the nature of their business, may cause environmental pollution?

Leitman: We would require them to carry an environmental pollution insurance policy. Many times a lender will require us to furnish them with a policy from this particular type of tenant.

Rosen: Is there anything in the operation of your centers, whatever it might be, that gives you an edge and helps you?

Leitman: We have a staff person who is responsive to the tenants, whether it is to provide a new lease when someone is interested or respond if a tenant has a problem. We try to have someone available who can take a call. Even if we can't solve a problem immediately, the tenant has to know that we are aware of it and care. We visit properties and tenants regularly.

Rosen: What is your policy with regard to rents that are not paid on time?

Garcia: If the rent is not paid by the seventh of the month we send out a late notice. It includes a late fee or penalty as outlined in the lease.

Rosen: When you have a vacancy in a store, do you put a sign on the window?

Garcia: Immediately.

Rosen: Do you do any advertising in the paper or do you just rely on the signs?

Garcia: We have not used the newspaper in years. We send e-mails to an extensive list of brokers. It is our philosophy that we will pay them a commission. Carrying vacant space is more costly than paying a commission. We are happy to work with other brokers.

Rosen: Other tenants in the center will obviously know when there is a vacant store. Do you send them a letter or e-mail indicating that the store is available and the terms and conditions of the lease?

Leitman: Yes, I would contact the adjacent tenants first.

Rosen: Before you even put up signs?

Garcia: No, at the same time. When a tenant is interested in expanding and they see our sign, they know we are advertising it to the public. If they want to expand, they are going to deal with you because they know you are marketing it to other people. If they think that you are dealing only with them, you are at a disadvantage in your negotiations.

Rosen: What kind of marketing do you do?

Garcia: We e-mail a professional brochure of the center with a photograph of the building indicating the lease price and terms. The brochure also contains a location diagram of the property.

Rosen: Do you provide for an annual CPI increase in your leases?

Leitman: Yes, but we will usually set a minimum rate of increase in the rent.

Rosen: Is the option to renew a lease based on the same terms and conditions that existed on the previous lease?

Leitman: That is negotiable. It could be a continuation of the same rate or, if it's far enough out, we may provide an option to renew at market.

Managing Small Bay Warehouses

There are similarities between managing small bay warehouses and managing small retail centers. However, while the leases for small bay warehouses are usually for one year without options to renew, landlords continue to renew the vast majority of leases for tenants in good standing. It is not unusual to find tenants who have been in buildings for 10 to 20 years. Once these tenants are established, they don't generally want to pick up and move. Like small bay retail centers, the provision for the payment of CAM and increases in operating expenses are generally based on the same formula.

Martin Waas owns Waas Realty, a firm that controls 700,000 square feet of industrial warehouses in the city of Doral, west of the Miami International Airport. His company, founded 36 years ago by Waas's father and mother, manages all of its own warehouses from a central office. When I spoke with him, he detailed the considerations that go into the management of warehouses.

Rosen: Let's say an investor bought his or her first property, a 20,000-square-foot building with a small bay tenant. Who should manage the property?

Waas: If they are operating another business and don't have the time or inclination, they would be better off letting a professional manager handle it. We manage a lot of properties for people in that situation, and they pay us a fee for management. We earn that fee and make more money for them. Generally, somebody that has one building doesn't know what's going on in the marketplace. They don't know they can get another dollar per square foot in rent. Any professional management company would know what is going on in the market, what is happening in the community, and whether something is going to take place that will make the property more valuable. By having a property management company take care of the property, an investor will generally make more money over and above the cost of paying a management fee and leasing commissions.

Rosen: As a professional property manager and also as an investor, what would you say are the most important factors in efficiently managing small bay warehouses?

Waas: Knowing your market, keeping current on the prevailing market rates, being aware of anything that will have a positive or negative impact on the property value, and controlling your expenses.

Rosen: What size are small bay warehouses?

Waas: I consider small bay units to be 1,000 to 2,000 square feet. Once in a while you will see a unit that is less than 1,000 square feet, but it would be very expensive today if you were going to build something like that. There are some older buildings that have units with 600- to 800-square-foot bays, but most buildings have larger units.

Rosen: If an investor is going to buy a 20,000-square-foot building, would it be good to have, let's say, 20 1,000-square-foot bays?

Waas: That would be excellent. If you have a 20,000-square-foot building with 5,000-square-foot bays and one tenant moves, you are 25 percent vacant. If one tenant in a 1,000-square-foot bay moves, you only have a 5 percent vacancy.

Rosen: How long a lease do you typically give tenants in small bay warehouses?

Waas: One year. Short-term leases are much better than long-term leases because they allow you to adjust the rent to meet market rates. We always want to buy a building where the leases are for not more than one year, without options to renew, and where rents are under the market rate. That puts us in the position of being able to raise the rents, which in turn will increase the cash flow and the value of the building.

Rosen: Are your leases gross or net leases?

Waas: They are generally industrial gross leases. It is one where the tenant pays the rent or CAM and their proportional share of any increases of taxes and insurance.

Rosen: What things comprise CAM?

Waas: Water, outdoor lighting, landscape maintenance, parking lot maintenance including cleaning. That's generally the bulk of the common area maintenance.

Rosen: When somebody moves in on a one-year lease, do you increase the rent after that?

Waas: Yes. No one's rent stays the same. Your expenses will probably go up every year.

Rosen: Do you quote the rent by the square foot to a prospective tenant?

Waas: No. The rent is quoted as a per-dollar amount plus CAM and sales tax. If I told a prospective tenant walking in the door that the rent was $1,000 a month, they would say, "Well that's a reasonable amount." But if I told them it was $12 a foot, they would say "Oh, that's a ridiculously high rent." In small bay warehouses, we never ever quote per square foot.

Rosen: What has been your relationship with tenants who have rented in your building for many years?

Waas: Sometimes having tenants for many, many years can be counterproductive to the owner's bottom line. You get to know them and their families on a personal level. As rents skyrocket, you have a difficult time raising their rents. You need to balance having a good-paying tenant with the turnover and expense of getting the unit ready to rent to another company. We came to a conclusion this year that we need to bring old tenants close to the market rents. We have had tenants that have been in 1,000-square-foot bays for many years paying several hundred dollars less in rent than what we are charging new companies.

Rosen: And so what did you do with those tenants?

Waas: This year we raised their rent to the market rate. Some of them squawked. And one person called me and said, "I knew you were going to do this. I couldn't believe that you waited this many years to raise my rent."

Rosen: In the overall marketplace, have rental rates increased over the past few years?

Waas: Yes. They have gone up drastically. My rents have increased by $3 to $4 per square foot in the last two years.

Rosen: What are your fees?

Waas: The management fees are usually 5 percent of the rents collected. The leasing fee is 6 percent for the initial lease amount and 2 percent on renewals. The management fees could change, depending on the size and scope of the project.

Rosen: Are there tenants in certain types of businesses that you will not rent to?

Waas: Yes. I could tell you that we could be full and never have a vacancy, but we turn away people everyday. We try to minimize the risk to the landlords and to our investors of any potential liabilities. For example, we do not rent to anyone in the car business, cabinet shop business, ornamental iron or welding shops, boat maintenance or repairs, and a long list of other businesses.

Rosen: What is the reason for this?

Waas: These types of businesses can cause fires and pollution. That's another reason that professional management is so important. If a new investor buys a 20,000-square-foot building with small bays, he or she is not going to have all that knowledge. I know a particular building where an owner has an 8,000-square-foot building with eight units and he's been managing it himself. He rarely goes out to the property, whereas we visit and inspect our properties on a daily basis. He comes to me every few months to ask me questions and I know eventually he will hire us to sell his building. He has been sued a couple of times. In one situation, somebody tripped on a piece of rebar and broke their hip. The injured person sued him for a substantial sum of money.

Rosen: What is your opinion of an owner self-managing rather than using a professional management company?

Waas: People do manage their own properties—they are either retired or semiretired, and it keeps them busy. They enjoy doing it. They enjoy talking to the tenants, they like that type of action. People manage their properties all the time.

Rosen: If an investor bought a very small building, let's say, 5,000 to 10,000 square feet, would you manage it?

Waas: In our particular case, it would have to be close to other properties we manage. I'm not going to spend two hours of my day driving because it is not cost efficient to do that. We manage two properties now that are around the corner from our offices. They are 8,200-square-foot buildings and there are five tenants in each building. When the investor bought it, his uncle managed it for about two years. The uncle was a retired army colonel and had the time to do it. Now I've been doing it for 10 to 12 years.

Rosen: How do you handle the maintenance of your buildings?

Waas: We have an outside maintenance company. We provide this company with about 98 percent of our work. They do any road calls for plumbing leaks, maintenance, and cleaning. They have been doing work for us for 21 years. They take care of 28 properties that we manage.

Rosen: That is part of your CAM?

Waas: Correct.

Rosen: How do you pay this maintenance company?

Waas: We do it job by job and not on an hourly basis.

Rosen: What portion of the market is flex space, warehouses that also contain offices?

Waas: A very small portion because most tenants don't need that much office space.

Managing Office Buildings

The management of office buildings is less like the management of the other properties we have been analyzing. Different owners will have different types of leases with regard to the structure of rents in their buildings. For example, within the same community or in any given area of the country, different buildings can have gross leases, modified gross leases, net leases, and triple net leases. It all depends on the objectives of individual landlords and what they think works best for them.

I spoke with Edmund Mazzei, the owner and president of Mazzei Realty Services, Inc., and Gina Anderhub, the company's commercial property manager, about their work. Mazzei Realty is a boutique firm that has served the South Florida commercial real estate market for the past 20 years. It specializes in sales, leasing, property management, and asset realization. Mazzei is active in the Coral Gables Chamber of Commerce; he serves on its International Affairs Committee and the Gables Property Advisory Board. He is a past president of the Building Owners and Managers Association (BOMA) in Miami and was selected as BOMA International Member of the Year in 1989.

Rosen: How long have you been a professional property manager?
Mazzei: Twenty-eight years.
Rosen: What is your specialty?
Mazzei: Commercial real estate services.
Rosen: What size office buildings have you managed?
Mazzei: The smallest one we have managed was 2,500 square feet, and the largest was 400,000 square feet.
Rosen: Does it pay for you to manage a building as small as 2,500 square feet?
Mazzei: It would depend on the circumstances. One general contractor from New York told me years ago: "We do peepholes." You know, there's no job too small, all things being equal.

Rosen: Under what circumstances would owners be better managing their own building than hiring a property manager?

Mazzei: I think it is fine for owners of small buildings who have the time, knowledge, and discipline to manage their own properties. I would recommend that these owners become members of a real estate association or trade association so they know what's happening in the market in order to protect and enhance their assets and get the best return on their investment.

Rosen: When an owner hires you to manage a building, what kind of contract do you enter into?

Mazzei: We typically seek a two-year contract. We provide for a termination clause, whereby either the owner or our firm can terminate the contract with a minimum of two months' notice. This allows for proper planning and an orderly transition.

Rosen: Do you handle both the management and leasing of a building?

Mazzei: We do both, and let me explain something that I think is important for owners and managers to understand. In this business, you don't make money managing property. If you break even, you're doing well. You make your profit and sometimes cover a significant part of the overhead from your leasing commissions, so management without leasing is a losing proposition over time.

Rosen: What is a gross lease?

Mazzei: Tenant pays the contract rental rate for the term of the lease, and the landlord pays all operating expenses. This is also referred to as a "full service" lease in some markets. However, in this type of lease, the tenant reimburses the landlord for all increases in operating expenses over the base year of the tenant's lease, which is typically the first year of the lease.

Rosen: What is a modified gross lease?

Mazzei: A modified gross lease is where the tenant pays a pro rata share of certain operating expenses.

Rosen: What is a net lease?

Mazzei: The tenant pays certain expenses. Usually, the rent is reduced by those expenses that the tenant pays directly. Some landlords will quote a rental rate "net of electricity costs" or "net of janitorial services."

Rosen: What is a triple-net lease?

Mazzei: Tenants assume responsibility for paying all operating expenses from the inception of their lease. Typically, the only expense that the landlord is responsible for is the maintenance of the roof as well as the exterior walls of the building.

Rosen: If an owner just hired you and the leases were on a gross basis but all of them expired within a year or two, which type of lease would you recommend to the owner?

Mazzei: It depends on a lot of factors. For a single tenant, triple net. High users of electricity and water, a modified gross. General office use would be gross or full service lease.

Rosen: Have you found landlords switching from gross leases to other types of leases?

Mazzei: In some markets in the United States, landlords have switched to triple-net leases or are quoting gross rent as a two-component rent [base rent and expenses]. This allows the landlord to create a budget for the new year and collect expenses monthly rather than waiting until year-end for recovery of expense increases. In this scenario, the landlord typically only pays leasing commissions on the base rent.

Rosen: What is the minimum size building you feel is necessary to have an on-site person to manage and lease space?

Mazzei: Generally, we will not want to have an on-site person managing a building less than approximately 50,000 square feet.

Rosen: Do you have a special accounting system for your operation?

Anderhub: Yes, it is homegrown and can be modified to meet each landlord's specific reporting and accounting criteria.

Rosen: Have you implemented any new techniques in the last year or two to increase the bottom line for your clients?

Anderhub: Yes, remeasuring buildings using laser technology; triple-net leases where appropriate, ongoing market studies are used to keep rental rates competitive; increased rates for on-site parking; sub-metering for tenants that use a lot of utilities, such as medical-related companies. We're always reevaluating and monitoring operating expenses to control costs without deferring or depriving the building of proper maintenance.

Rosen: How do you save an owner money?

Anderhub: By diligently managing the property to properly serve tenants so they remain and grow within the property. A satisfied tenant will not move from the building. This retention enables landlords to avoid vacancies, which assures cash flow, reduces tenant improvement costs, reduces leasing commissions, and enables the landlord to achieve the best rental rates.

Rosen: How much do you charge?

Mazzei: We typically charge 5 percent of rents collected. However, if a building is less than 25,000 square feet, the fee will be slightly higher.

Rosen: How much do you charge for your leasing fee?

Mazzei: Six percent of the total amount of the rent to be received by the landlord for the term of the lease on vacant space and 3 percent on renewals. We charge 4 percent on existing tenant expansions. Rent to be received includes fixed annual increases and parking charges.

Rosen: When is your management fee paid, and when is your leasing fee paid?

Mazzei: Management fees are paid at the end of the month for the month that was just completed. With regard to leasing commissions, we receive 50 percent of the total commission upon lease execution and the other 50 percent when the tenant occupies the space and begins paying rent.

Rosen: What kind of insurance do you require tenants to carry?

Anderhub: Commercial general liability, property damage, plate glass insurance.

Rosen: Do the tenants pay for parking in the buildings you manage? If so, what is the range?

Anderhub: They pay $65 a month for an uncovered space, $85 for a covered space.

Rosen: How do you screen a prospective tenant?

Anderhub: Is it a start-up business or a relocation? If start-up, what experience does the prospect have that shows they will succeed? If relocation, why, from where, how long were they there, can we see existing space where they are presently renting, can we talk to existing landlord to get a reference? We want to know what kind of tenant they have been and how timely rent is paid, and whether there have been bounced checks. We need to see at least two years' personal and business financials to determine financial ability. We need three business references, one of which must be their bank. A good source of information on the background of a tenant can be found in their credit report.

Rosen: When renting a vacant office, what is the term of the lease?

Mazzei: We typically seek five-year leases. Market conditions and an owner's policy may suggest doing some three- or four-year leases. We also analyze the rollover of leases to try and keep the rollover evenly distributed over each of the five years. In medical offices and health care, we will want 10-year leases because of the uniqueness of the tenant's use and the tenant improvement costs.

Rosen: Do you believe it is in the best interest of the owner to give tenants options to renew their leases?

Mazzei: No. A landlord needs to be in control.

Rosen: What is the longest lease that you recommend?

Mazzei: Ten years if it is a major deal with a national firm or a health care–related business. We would recommend to the owner to consider a 20-year term to a strong tenant occupying a freestanding building on a triple-net basis.

Rosen: Do you have your own customized lease form?

Mazzei: We have a basic lease form that is modified to meet owner needs and expectations. Certain properties have unique characteristics that need to be considered.

Rosen: Do you manage condominium office buildings? If so, what is your fee?

Anderhub: Typically, the same as general office buildings. Each assignment is analyzed based on its size, location, uniqueness, demands, and expectations.

Rosen: Do you believe that you generate more income for an owner than the cost of your management and leasing services?

Mazzei: Definitely. In addition, good management retains tenants, preserves the asset, and enhances the property value.

Rosen: Do you establish reserves in your budget for capital improvements and unknown contingencies?

Anderhub: Yes.

Rosen: Do you have a maintenance person on staff, or do you use outside contractors?

Mazzei: We have in-house maintenance personnel, and we contract with outside vendors and contractors for specialized work that is beyond the scope of our staff.

Rosen: Do you cooperate with other real estate brokers in leasing space? If so, how do you divide the leasing fee with them?

Mazzei: Typically it's a 50/50 split if both parties are working equally on the transaction.

Rosen: Are there tenants operating businesses that you believe have a negative impact on a building?

Anderhub: Yes. Call centers, criminal services–related companies, and certain entities that have a lot of visitors and a staff-to-space ratio below 175 square feet per staff member.

Rosen: Are there tenants who operate businesses that you believe have a positive impact on a building?

Anderhub: Professional services such as law offices, accounting firms, insurance agents, doctors, dentists, certain health care–related services, architects, engineers, selective retail, real estate brokers, mortgage companies, title companies, public relations, marketing, advertising, and technical services.

Rosen: What is the most important quality of a good property manager?

Anderhub: There are numerous qualities that a good property manager must have to represent an owner and do an outstanding job. But the one that I consider to be the most important is our tenant relations. The tenants can make or break the success of a building. We are proud to say that we keep our buildings more than 95 percent occupied because we respond to tenant issues promptly and with genuine concern. We create a comfortable, open-door environment for the tenants in our management office by providing amenities such as fresh flowers, coffee, Danish pastry, candy, and other goodies. You'd be surprised what an impression this makes on tenants.

The Bottom Line

The specter of managing and leasing property should not scare away would-be real estate investors. Organized investors who do their research and who have time to devote to the management duties may easily be able to manage their own small properties—or supervise an employee who can. But in general, property management is a job for experienced experts rather than well-intentioned amateurs.

An astute management company knows the markets and has the connections and expertise to oversee your investment properly. It not only takes care of everything from rent collection to maintenance but it *increases* the value of the property. In other words, not only will a good property management operation save you money, it will make you money. The fees paid will be more than offset by the overall gains seen by your property when it is well managed.

Strong property management is also a tool that will help investors weather ups and downs in the commercial real estate market. Experienced managers know strategies for maximizing a property's value. They also may recognize market shifts before the general population does, thus allowing property owners to be fast and flexible in making adjustments.

Real estate investment is a changing, challenging, and competitive business. You invest a great deal of time and energy into finding and acquiring Big Six properties. But it is just as important to nurture the properties—not only to enhance their value, but also to ensure the income stream that helps you live the life you've dreamed of.

"Businesses come and go, but income-producing properties are sound investments. Real estate lasts forever!" states Ted Pappas, chairman of the Keyes Company, one of the largest real estate firms in the country.

13

Condo Conversions

BIG MONEY IN SMALL APARTMENT BUILDINGS

The word condominium comes from Latin and means "ownership together." Condo buyers receive deeds to their units, pay real estate taxes on their units, and can mortgage and sell each unit just as they could if they owned a single-family home. The difference between a condo unit and a single-family home, however, is that the common areas of a condominium building—including the hallways, lobbies, elevators, roofs, storage areas, recreational buildings, swimming pools, and exterior amenities—as well as the land itself, are owned jointly by all the condo unit residents.

Condominiums are not a new concept. The Romans used the form of ownership typical of condominiums as early as the sixth century B.C. In Europe, individually owned property within a complex or on land that is owned in common by more than one person is something that has been available for many centuries. In South America, condominium-style ownership dates back at least two centuries.

The United States was one of the last industrialized countries to embrace the condominium concept. The initial attempt to develop condominiums in the United States or its territories came in 1948 with passage of the Horizontal Property Act of Puerto Rico, a model statute developed by the Federal Housing Authority. One of the first condominiums on the U.S. mainland was the Galt Ocean Club at 3800 Galt Ocean Mile Drive in Fort Lauderdale, Florida. The 218-unit, oceanfront high-rise was constructed in 1963, developed by Coral Ridge Properties. A prominent Miami attorney, Donald Rosenberg, set up the legal framework for this pioneer development.

Condos are appealing to people who live in apartments and want to shift from rental to ownership. They also are targeted toward people who want to own their residences but without the work and hassle of maintaining a yard. In a condominium, the grounds and exterior maintenance are handled by others, funded by the monthly condo fees that residents pay.

My Start in Condo Conversions

I got into the conversion of rental apartments to condos by accident. In 1975, one of my sales associates sold me a 2-story, 18-unit apartment building in an excellent location. His name was Benn Zack. He was the sales associate I referred to in Chapter 10, the colleague who helped me break my bad habit of seeing properties as overpriced simply because they had sold for less in the past. When Benn persuaded me to look at the 18-unit apartment complex, I liked it and signed a sales contract. During the 15-day due diligence period, everything checked out. I made a nonrefundable $20,000 deposit but then started to have second thoughts about the deal. I feared that I was paying too much for the property and that I had rushed into the deal too quickly. My panic was so extreme that I fretted about it for several sleepless nights. I was thinking about walking away and losing my deposit, but I decided to go back to the property to take a good, hard look and to do further number crunching.

I still felt uncomfortable. When I told Benn, he said, "Why don't you sell the units off as condos?" I had heard about condominium conversions, which had just begun to surface, but I knew nothing about them. Benn told me I'd need to convert the whole building from a rental to a condominium complex, then sell the units one by one. We projected what we could sell the units for and the expenses involved, and it looked like there would be a decent profit. My reaction began to shift from fear to confidence. I closed the deal and my attorney, Joe Reisman, drafted a Declaration of Condominium, which is an instrument for changing the legal form of ownership from a rental building to a condominium building. We obtained an engineering report and survey delineating the dimensions of each apartment unit and then registered the documents with the state. Within a few weeks, the rental apartment complex known as 47th Avenue Manor had been reborn as a legal condominium called Plaza Maria (see Figure 13.1).

I was in uncharted waters and there were no "how to" books on condo conversion. In fact, there was virtually no information on the subject at all, so I made numerous mistakes. My first conversion lost about $25,000, which was a fortune for me at the time. As time went on, I converted building after building. I still made mistakes, but by trial and error, I finally developed a strategy that worked.

Condo conversions at that time were unfamiliar to most of the public, and the process of conversion was complex. To bring in partners would have required endless time and energy explaining what I was doing—and I didn't know that much about it myself. Neither did I like the idea of having to get partners' approval for the experimental strategies and techniques I planned to use. Besides, if I were going to lose money, I'd rather lose my own money than see others

Figure 13.1 Plaza Maria Condominium

lose theirs. As a result, I ended up trailblazing a new phenomenon in real estate.

Even though I had some cash, I certainly knew that I didn't have enough money to buy buildings and pay all the costs connected with a conversion. Without partners, where was I to get the money? By then, I had established success in buying and selling small properties, and my relationship with some banks that financed my deals was good. I revisited those banks that were happy with the past business I gave them. I explained that what I was doing would become the wave of the future and, even though I had only begun the process, it was starting to catch on.

But they weren't yet convinced that conversions would fly, so I had to use what little money I had and to take out a second mortgage on my home in order to convert the first few buildings. I was able to sell out one building at a time and recoup my cash investment as well as see a small profit. I then invested that money into another building. After a few conversions, I accumulated a good amount of cash and felt I was ready to tackle bigger deals. Each conversion became more successful, and I was able to persuade a bank to loan me money, not based on my purchase price but on the projected sellout price. For example, if I bought a building for $1 million and expected to sell the units as condos for a total of $1.7 million, the bank would loan me 80 percent of $1.7 million— or $1.36 million. That covered my purchase price, while the balance was kept by the bank in a reserve account to pay for interest, improvements to the property, marketing, and other expenses.

I was able to cover closing costs, attorney's fees, and other professional fees with my own funds. That meant I had little or no cash tied up in most of my deals. The exception was the 1982 conversion of a 600-unit complex known as Kings Creek South, located in the Dadeland area of Miami, for which I paid $15.5 million. That required an outlay of more than $1 million cash. I had converted numerous buildings and was pretty flush with cash at the time, so I had sufficient down payment available. I obtained bank financing for the remaining $14.5 million. I finished selling the units 15 months later for $30 million. After all costs and expenses, I realized an eight-figure net profit. In addition, my sales agents made a barrel of money.

When that deal was concluded, I had converted 1,700 units in 22 buildings and had become the biggest condo converter in the state of Florida and one of the biggest in the country. I made many, many millions of dollars in the process. Not only were there big profits, but I felt good about creating affordable housing for people. At prices of $30,000 to $75,000 per apartment unit, many people with 5 percent or 10 percent down could get into these condo deals. Today, these units sell for five to six times their original prices.

In 1984, inflation was running rampant. The prime rate was 20 percent and fixed-rate mortgages of 30 years demanded an interest rate as high as 16 percent. The buying market dried up, and conversions came to an end.

Conversions came back with a vengeance after 2000, and through 2007 there were more than 1 million rental units converted to condos in the United States. In addition, a large number of new condominiums were built. Metropolitan areas experienced a frenzy of activity. Many of the buyers were speculators, both local and foreign, who bought condos thinking they could flip their contracts and make a ton of money without ever closing on the deals. Little did they know that this dream of "getting rich quick" would come to a screeching halt in 2007. The supply far exceeded the demand and, once again, condo conversions died.

Criteria for Converting Small Buildings

Although the conversion of large complexes has screeched to a halt in most parts of the country, there is still big money to be made converting small apartment buildings of 8 to 24 units. Let's look at the criteria for a successful conversion and the dynamics of the process.

Location

The complex should be situated in an "A" location (the first criteria of the Big Six) where property values have increased consistently over the years and will continue to increase. I have made all my condo money by buying and converting Class B buildings in "A" locations.

There are no absolute criteria with regard to age of the building under consideration for conversion. Each building structure must be evaluated on its own merits. A 2-year-old building or a 100-year-old building could be equally successful.

Architectural Design

When you drive down a street, it's easy to spot the buildings that have eye appeal and are classy looking. As with all other Big Six investments, condo conversions need "curb appeal." At the same time, good architecture and quality craftsmanship are essential.

Apartment Mix

There is no set rule as to the combination of efficiencies, apartments, one-bedroom, two-bedrooms, and three-bedroom apartments in an apartment complex earmarked for conversion. This will depend on the market in which you expect to sell and the age of potential buyers.

Privacy and Open Space

Again, we go back to proper architectural design. The building should not be jammed between two other buildings leaving poor views and giving a claustrophobic feel. The views from each apartment in the complex slated for condo conversion should be pleasant, not overlooking garbage in trashcans or other unappealing scenes. Attractive trees and landscaping help a lot. Depending on the parking ratio in a given community, the cars should be situated so as to be as inconspicuous as possible. In short, the exterior of the building should be one that is pleasing.

Low Maintenance

Small buildings need few frills. Unnecessary amenities only add to the cost of operating the complex, and we want to keep these costs at a minimum. Two-story walkup buildings eliminate the costs and maintenance connected with an elevator. Exterior entrances to the apartment units reduce maintenance costs because they eliminate the need to air condition or heat inside corridors leading to the units. The goal is to sell the converted units quickly by demonstrating that the carrying cost of buying a unit is approximately the same as rent. By keeping maintenance expenses low, you hold down the monthly payments for buyers, and that is one of the reasons that small apartment buildings can succeed in today's market.

Seclusion

Being on a main thoroughfare with good visibility is an advantage when you are converting large complexes. The reason for this is that potential buyers will see your sign in front of the building. This is known as having a good "window." A building off the beaten track will be less likely to attract potential buyers. In a small building with few frills, it is usually an advantage not to be on a main street. The residents in this type of condo prefer privacy and seclusion. A neighborhood with mature trees and foliage is ideal. You're looking for an area where the homes are approximately double the price that you expect to obtain for each condo unit.

Critiquing the Units

The traffic pattern of the apartment units should be such that the space is functional and not wasted. In the case of two-bedroom, two-bath units, we find that many buyers prefer that a bedroom be situated at each end of the unit (referred to as split bedrooms) to afford more privacy. Also, it is more desirable when entering a unit to walk into a foyer rather than directly into a living room. The more closets and the bigger the closets, the better your apartments are going to sell.

A kitchen should have many cabinets, plenty of counter space, enough room for tables and chairs so that it can be marketed as an eat-in kitchen, and, if possible, a window to let in sunlight and fresh air. A pantry closet is a plus. It is more important to have a large living room and a separate dining room or dining area than it is to have huge bedrooms but a small living room and no dining area.

Good soundproofing is also a desirable feature. One of the best ways to determine whether a building has good sound insulation is to play a radio loudly in an adjacent apartment to see if you can hear it. If the building is cheaply constructed, you will be able to hear the radio. If good sound insulating techniques have been used, normal noise and sound will be at a minimum.

Existing Tenant Profile

One factor contributing to success in converting small buildings is to sell as many units as possible to the existing tenants. This gives you immediate sales and faster closings than sales to outside buyers.

And since the bulk of the money from the closings will be used to pay down the mortgage on the property, your interest expense on the mortgage will keep decreasing. If certain factors are in place, the existing mortgage could well be paid off in full just from closings with the tenant purchasers. I was fortunate enough in my conversions that I was able to sell an average of 50 percent of the units to existing tenants. To determine the tenant profile, we need to first obtain the following information about the current tenants: age, marital status, occupation, income, length of time they have lived in the building, monthly rent, expiration date of their leases, and options to renew leases, if any.

The longer that tenants have lived in the building, the better the chance that they will buy their units. Most tenants who have lived happily in an apartment complex for a long time will be pleased that you have purchased their building for the purpose of conversion. They realize that this makes it possible for them to replace their lease with a deed and, thereby, have all the benefits of homeownership without the headaches.

If you have found the right building, in the right location, the tenant profile will usually reveal happy tenants who have lived in the building for a long time, consider it home, and really don't care to move. While a building such as this represents an ideal conversion, you can still be successful even if few of the existing tenants purchase their units. Why? It may be that the building had been mismanaged and/or the existing tenants cannot afford to buy their units. In the 22 complexes that I converted, about 30 to 70 percent of the existing tenants bought their units with the average being about 50 percent. On one conversion, the 54-unit Royal Caribbean Club apartment complex in Coral Gables, Florida, I sold 70 percent of the units to existing tenants and sold out the entire project within 90 days (see Figure 13.2).

Existing Leases

When analyzing the investment potential of an apartment complex, existing leases for one year without options to renew represent an ideal situation. Some leases are written for two or three years, but these are usually found in Class A luxury apartment complexes, not in the Class B buildings that are best to convert. The majority of leases in small complexes are written for one year. In those few

Figure 13.2   Royal Caribbean Club

instances where leases may have options to renew or are written for longer than one year, you may find some tenants balking at the idea of purchasing their units, especially if their rents are substantially under the market rate.

Purchase Price

Buying a rental apartment complex as a long-term investment is quite different from buying it for the purpose of converting to condos. When buying for conversion, you are, in effect, buying both a rental complex and a proposed conversion. In order to determine the price to pay for a building that we plan to convert, we need to project the sales prices of each unit, estimate how many units will be purchased by existing tenants, the expenses involved, and the cost of financing along with other factors.

And what happens if the conversion doesn't work? Although you wouldn't be buying the building if you didn't believe it would be a successful conversion, it is important to realize that the building must stand on its own as a rental complex if no conversion ever takes place or if the conversion is unsuccessful. This is a difficult balancing act. Nearly all of the buildings I have purchased for conversion cost more than what I would have paid if I were buying the buildings strictly as rentals. The reason for this is that individual apartments will sell for a greater price than the entire complex will as a single rental building. Having said that, I always look at the deal from the viewpoint that if I had to keep it as a rental investment, I would want to at least break even. There is some calculated risk to everything that we do. Luckly, in the 22 apartment complexes that I converted, I never had to fall back to a rental.

Doing your homework and research is paramount in any conversion. Look at every building that has been converted within three miles of the property under consideration. Talk with market experts to get their input. You must know the market inside and out. "Not preparing is preparing to fail," says Ken Weston, one of South Florida's most successful developers and condominium converters.

Announcing the Conversion

I had no idea on how to announce to the existing tenants what was planned at Plaza Maria, my first attempt at a condo conversion. So I sent out the following letter:

> December 10, 1975
> Dear Tenant,
>   We have purchased the eighteen-unit apartment building in which you are a tenant and plan to convert it to a condominium building immediately. The name of the building will now become Plaza Maria Condominium.
>   You will be able to buy your one-bedroom apartment for $16,990 and your two-bedroom apartment for $18,990 on an "as is" basis. Terms will be as low as 5 percent down payment and thirty-year financing at 8 percent interest. After tax benefits, your payments will be approximately the same as rent.
>   This is a great opportunity for you so stop by our office as soon as possible and sign a sales contract. Either Mr. Enrique Marin or Mr. Raul Alvarez in our office will be happy to answer all questions for you.
>   We thought you would want to get this news just before the holidays so that you'd be able to celebrate Christmas and

New Years knowing that you can become the owner of your
apartment rather than continue as a tenant.
Yours very truly,
Kenneth D. Rosen

All the tenants were renting on a month-to-month basis. After
receiving my letter, they all moved out except for one tenant, an
elderly gentleman who hadn't paid his rent in six months. Clearly,
the tenants had no conception of what benefits would accrue to
them as owners. It was not their fault, it was mine. But I still didn't
learn until my sixth condominium project that there was a better
way of announcing the conversion.

For the next four buildings, I invited all the tenants to a cocktail party and formally announced the conversions. This worked
fairly well on the first three complexes, but on the fourth, which
was a larger deal, many tenants used this as an opportunity air their
grievances about the building and the present landlord. It was like
a mob ganging up on me. I lost control of the situation, and very
few tenants ended up buying their units.

By my sixth conversion, I had an effective method that I used
for every conversion thereafter. I made no official announcements.
Rather, I called each tenant individually, introduced myself as the
new owner of the building, and made a personal appointment to
visit each tenant. At these personal visits, I disclosed my plan for the
conversion and presented them with a written summary of the sales
prices, the financing available, a list of the improvements I planned
to make, and the details of a Tenant Incentive Program (TIP).

How the Tenant Incentive Program (TIP) Works

If tenants bought their unit within 15 days from receipt of the TIP
offer, they would receive the following incentives:

- A 10 percent discount off the sales price of the unit.
- Seventy-five percent of their rent credited toward the sales
  price from the time they signed a formal contract to the date
  of closing (not to exceed ninety days) and 100 percent of
  their security deposit credited towards the sales price.
- A check for $5,000 to use as a decorating allowance or for
  any other purpose.

Tenants who bought their unit after 15 days but before 30 days would receive the following incentives:

- A 5 percent discount off of the sales price of the unit.
- Fifty percent of their rent credited toward the sales price from the time they signed a formal contract to the date of closing (not to exceed 90 days) and 100 percent of their security deposit credited towards the sales price.
- A check for $2,500 to use as a decorating allowance or for any other purpose.

In addition, I gave each tenant a simple, one-page analysis comparing the rent they were currently paying to what they would be paying as a unit owner.

This plan worked like dynamite, and virtually all the tenants who purchased did so within the first 15 days to take advantage of the full incentives. I used this same plan successfully on my next 16 conversions. The sooner you meet with the tenants, the better your chances of selling the units to them. Tenants who have rented for many years in the same building will resist the change until the benefits of ownership are pointed out to them and they feel comfortable with the transition. This is why the one-on-one meeting with each tenant is crucial. It allows an opportunity to explain how much better off a tenant will be as a unit owner rather than as a tenant.

Many times before I visited with the tenants individually, I did some research to find out if there were tenants who could be considered to be "centers of influence." In other words, were there tenants of such stature that if they bought, the other tenants might well follow suit. Tenants who were successful real estate lawyers, bankers, or brokers tended to be among the first to buy their units. I theorized that undecided tenants might be swayed by the fact that people they looked up to had already signed up to be unit owners.

Announcing the Improvement Program

In a conversion, the improvements begin as quickly as possible after we close on the transaction. The reason for this is psychological. Before we even visit with tenants, they are seeing that the property is being upgraded. The visit with the tenants needs to take place as soon as possible after the improvements begin—before rumors start flying and you have to dispel misleading ideas about what is going on.

Handling the Unsold Units

No matter how many incentives you offer, some tenants just won't buy. They enjoy the lifestyle of renting. That means there are always going to be unsold units to offer to the public. If certain tenants wish to continue renting their units, it might be a good idea for the converter to just keep these units for rental purposes. This is especially true if a large percentage of the tenants have already bought and you expect to recover most or all of our cash investment from those sales alone. In fact, once you see sufficient sales to recoup the cash investment, you will be positioned to receive an infinity rate of return. On my 600-unit Kings Creek South complex, I retained 100 units for rental purposes and sold them off later at substantially higher prices.

Over the years, as a converter, I have been sensitive to tenants who, for one reason or another, just find it very difficult to move— particularly elderly people who become fearful of any change at their stage of life. Because of my feelings for these people, I have been motivated to keep them on as tenants and simply charge a market-rate rent. This has been a winning proposition for both the tenants and myself. The tenants want the comfort of remaining where they have lived for many years, and I enjoy the tax benefits and the appreciation of the unit. If we prefer not to retain all or some of the unsold units, we offer them to the public.

I have found, regardless of the size of the conversion buildings or complexes, the most effective and least expensive way of selling units to the public is by erecting signs on the property. If a large complex is not easily visible from a main thoroughfare, I would put several signs on nearby streets that are heavily traveled. The fewer the words on a sign, the more effective it will be. On my conversion of Kings Creek South, I had exterior signs on the property with no phone number. The signs simply said "Please come to Sales Office, Unit 105." People poured into the complex, and we sold the majority of the units from these signs. We also managed to get good publicity in the local newspapers, and that also generated sales.

Another good way of selling unsold units is to contact a limited number of brokers who specialize in the sale of condos. There will be commissions as well as marketing costs, but your main objective is to sell out as quickly as possible and not let a few bucks stand in your way.

Legal Requirements

Each state in the country has its own condominium laws, rules, and regulations. States with numerous condominium projects have a separate government department to which the condo documents must be submitted and approved before recording them in the courthouse with jurisdiction over the property. In certain states, it may not be necessary to submit condo documents for small apartment buildings.

The condominium documents include the following:

1. The prospectus (offering circular or property report), which contains property information such as year built, unit mix, size of apartments, recreational facilities, personal property, type of construction, covenants and restrictions, parking, utilities, closing costs and expenses, and background information about the converter.
2. Declaration of condominium.
3. Articles of incorporation.
4. Bylaws.
5. Site plan and survey plat of each apartment.
6. Percentage of undivided interest of each apartment in the common property.
7. Engineer's report on the condition of building.
8. Proposed management contract.
9. Other service contracts such as waste removal, elevator, vending, security, swimming pool.
10. Annual estimated budget and applicable maintenance payments for each type of apartment.
11. Proposed improvements and changes contemplated by the developer.
12. Proposed price list.
13. Proposed agreement of sale and purchase contract.

The legal documents which are usually recorded are items 2, 3, 4, 5, and 6.

A condo conversion remains as a rental until the necessary documents have been recorded, which in usually done at the time of compliance with the lender's presale requirement.

Bradford Terrace: A Mini Case Study

Bradford Terrace is a 2 story, 12-unit building constructed 25 years ago. This fictitious complex is a Class B building in an "A" location three miles from downtown Seattle. The owners of the building are Don and Doris Duffy, and the prospective buyer is Saul Stone. (These are fictitious names.) The complex is in tiptop condition and there are beautiful mature trees on the property, which has exotic landscaping. The Duffys bought the building 15 years ago, manage it themselves, and take great pride in their property. They wish to sell it to move to northern California to be closer to their children and grandchildren.

There are eight two-bedroom, two-bath apartments consisting of 1,000 square feet each as well as four one-bedroom, one-bath apartments consisting of 750 square feet each, for a total of 11,000 square feet. The two-bedroom apartments rent for $1,300 per month, and the one-bedroom apartments rent for $800 per month, resulting in a gross annual income of $163,200. Based on market rates in the area, the rents at Bradford Terrace are 15 percent less than they should be. Thus if Stone raises the rents by 15 percent, the gross income will increase to $187,680. After a 5 percent vacancy factor, the adjusted gross income (AGI) will be $178,296. Stone estimates the operating expenses to be 42 percent of the AGI, or to $74,884, and the NOI at $103,412. Based on this NOI, Stone projects the value of Bradford Terrace as a rental complex, based on a 6 percent cap rate, to exceed $1.7 million—or $1,723,528 to be exact (see Table 13.1).

Stone has determined that 50 percent of the tenants are between 45 and 65 years old; another 25 percent are over 65. Their children are grown and married, meaning these tenants are unlikely to need to move into a bigger apartment or buy a single-family home. They are so-called empty nesters. Six of the tenants have lived in the building for more than 10 years, four have lived there for five years, and two moved in one year ago. Based on this tenant profile, Stone projects that eight of the 12 tenants will buy their units. He learned from the Duffys that one of these tenants,

Table 13.1 Bradford Terrace: Analysis of Value as a Rental Complex

Assumptions		
Eight 2/2 Apts @ $1,300 per month;		
Four 1/1 Apts @ $800 per month.		
Annual rent from 2/2s		$124,800
Annual rent from 1/1s		$38,400
Gross annual income		$163,200
Rent increase (15%)		$24,480
Gross annual income after rent increase		$187,680
Vacancy factor (5%)		$9,384
Adjusted gross income (AGI)		$178,296
Operating expenses (42% of AGI)		$74,884
Net operating income (NOI)		$103,412

NOI	Cap Rate	Value
$103,412	6%	$1,723,528

Nora Neiman, is president of a local bank who has lived in the complex for more than a decade. She once told the Duffys, "If this building ever goes condo, I want to be the first one to buy my unit."

The Duffys are in the real estate brokerage business, so they don't need to list their property with any brokers. They believe properties like Bradford Terrace are hard to come by and that it should sell quickly, especially to a converter. They have set a price of $2.2 million. Before Stone makes an offer, he does a comparable market analysis (CMA) and finds that condo units built 10 to 15 years ago in large complexes are reselling in the range of $250 to $275 per square foot. After an inspection of comparable units, he finds that they are less desirable than the units he plans to convert at Bradford Terrace. Stone knows that some people prefer living in small buildings without the glitz and glamour of big complexes, and these are the typical tenants at Bradford Terrace. At this point, Stone believes that he can sell the condo units at Bradford Terrace at an average of $265 per square foot. That would generate $2.915 million in gross sales.

Stone estimates total conversion costs at $382,900, which would leave him proceeds of $2,532,100. At the Duffys' asking price of

$2.2 million, there would be a net profit of only $332,100—too close for comfort. Stone, a shrewd negotiator, is willing to pay $2 million. He realizes, however, that if he makes an initial offer of $2 million, the Duffys might well propose splitting the difference at $2.1 million. To avoid this, he offers $1.85 million, although he's willing to compromise at $2 million. At $2 million, Stone's net profit would be a healthy $532,100 (see Table 13.2).

Table 13.2   Bradford Terrace: Analysis of Profit as a Condominium Conversion

Assumptions

Price per unit: $265 per sq. ft.

Six tenants buy their 2/2 apts within 15 days based on the TIP.

Two tenants buy their 1/1 apts within 15 days based on the TIP.

Four outside buyers purchase the remaining units at the retail price.

Project sold out in 3 months.

Gross Sales		$2,915,000
Conversion Costs		
Legal In & Out	$5,000	
Closing Costs (In)	$5,000	
Engineering	$5,000	
Improvements	$20,000	
Discounts to Tenants	$198,750	
Rent Credits to Tenants	$21,150	
Flat Allowance to Tenants	$40,000	
Marketing & Sales Commissions	$20,000	
First Mortgage Interest	$28,000	
Second Mortgage Interest	$5,000	
Closing Costs (Out)	$10,000	
Contingency Factor/Cushion	$25,000	
Total Costs		$382,900
Proceeds		$2,532,100
Purchase Price		$2,000,000
Net Profit		$532,100

Stone makes the $1.85 million offer, and the Duffys, somewhat perturbed, flatly refuse it. After back-and-forth negotiations, Stone increases the offer to $2 million, which the Duffys accept.

In all my conversions, I have had to stretch and pay a purchase price considerably more than what the property was worth as a rental property. My reasoning was that as long as I had the right property for conversion and could make a good profit, I had to be flexible on the price. If you want to succeed as a condo converter, you will have to do the same thing. As poet Robert Browning wrote, "A man's reach should exceed his grasp." But you should never pay such a high price that, if the conversion doesn't work out and it remains a rental property, you have a negative cash flow.

The Duffys want an all-cash deal but are willing to make the sale contingent upon a 30-day due diligence period and 60 days thereafter to obtain a bank loan for 80 percent of the purchase price, or $1.6 million. Best of all, Stone is able to negotiate with the Duffys to hold a second mortgage for $200,000 at 7 percent interest, payable interest-only monthly with the principal balance due at the end of three years. Thus, Stone will have to come up with only $200,000 cash as a down payment plus $25,000 in financing and closing costs, or a total cash investment of $225,000.

Everything checks out during the 30-day due diligence, and Stone is approved by the bank within 60 days for a loan worth 80 percent of the purchase price for a term of five years at 7 percent interest. This is based on an amortization period of 25 years with an additional five years at 8 percent interest. The bank agrees to release individual condo units as they are sold, based on Stone's paying the bank 90 percent of the sales price of each unit, which will be applied to the principal balance of the bank's mortgage. The bank will not release any units until 50 percent of the units have been sold under formal contracts with 10 percent deposits. The reason for this is that the bank wants to know that this deal will be successful and, just from the proceeds of the sale of 50 percent of the units, that the loan to the bank will be substantially reduced.

All contingencies of the deal have now been met, and the transaction is consummated. Stone has invested $225,000 cash in the deal. Shortly after closing, Stone begins making improvements to the property. Now it is time to quickly visit with each tenant before rumors start to take place among the tenants. Stone visits each tenant, beginning with Nora Neiman, who immediately puts up her deposit. Stone then meets individually with the remaining tenants and explains the benefits of owning versus renting, distributes the Tenant Incentive Program (TIP), and hands out a one-page analysis comparing the rent tenants were paying to what they would be paying as a unit owner (see Figure 13.3).

Stone sells the project out in 90 days and everybody comes out a winner. The bank has now been paid in full. The Duffys have received $2 million, including the payoff of their second mortgage and are on their way to northern California where they have bought a home closer to their children and grandchildren. Eight tenants and four outside buyers are now living in Bradford Terrace as condo owners and, with tax benefits, paying less than market-rate rent. In addition, they are building equity each month, and their units will probably appreciate substantially in value over time. Meanwhile, Stone's projections prove correct, and he is rewarded with net profit of $532,100 before taxes. Based on his initial cash investment of $225,000, Stone walks away from Bradford Terrace with a cash-on-cash return of 946 percent (see Table 13.3).

Stone now has a total of $757,100 ($225,000 initial cash investment plus $532,100 net profit). He has had his eye on a 20-unit apartment complex within a mile of Bradford Terrace and is now raring to go and preparing to make an offer on it. His goal is to net $5 million within three years by buying small apartment complexes to convert to condos. He is embracing the Big Six tenet: We make our money in buying!

Table 13.3   Bradford Terrace Condominium: Analysis of Cash-on-Cash return

Initial Cash Investment	$200,000
Closing Costs (including financing)	$25,000
Total Cash Investment	$225,000
Net Profit before Taxes	$532,100
Rate of Return (3 months)	236.5%
Rate of Return (annualized)	946.0%

March 21, 2008

Bradford Terrace Condominium
Comparison of Monthly Payment
Renting versus Owning

Unit No. 10	Purchase Price: $265,000 less 10% discount = $238,500

Unit Type: 2/2 (1,000 sq. ft.)	80% Mortgage @ 5.75% interest (30-year fixed): $190,800

Current Monthly Rent: $1,300 Market Monthly Rent: $1,500 Buyer's Tax Bracket: 25%	20% Cash Down: $47,700 plus closing costs: $6,300 Cash Investment: $54,000

A) ESTIMATED MONTHLY PAYMENT
Before Income Tax Savings and Amortization
(First Year Projection)

Mortgage Payment (Principal and 5.75% interest)	$1,113
Real Estate Taxes	$250
Maintenance	$250
TOTAL MONTHLY PAYMENT	$1,613

B) ESTIMATED MONTHLY PAYMENT
After Income Tax Savings and Amortization
(First Year Projection)

Total Monthly Payment as per Item A	$1,613

Less: Income Tax Savings
Mortgage Amount $190,800 @ 5.75% interest
equals $10,971 interest ÷ 12 equals $915
Monthly mortgage interest of $915 × 25% tax bracket
equals tax savings of... $229

Monthly Real Estate Taxes of $250 × 25% tax bracket
equals tax savings of... $63

Total Monthly Income Tax Savings	$292
Total Payment After Income Tax Savings	$1,321
Less: Average Monthly Mortgage Amortization	$204
NET EFFECTIVE MONTHLY PAYMENT	$1,117
Market Rent	$1,500
Net Monthly Savings as a Condo Owner	$383

Prepared by: Saul Stone

Figure 13.3 Bradford Terrace Condominium: Comparison of Monthly Payment (Renting versus Owning)

The Bottom Line

In the 1990s, Faith Popcorn was a bit of a phenomenon. The so-called "futurist," who started her careers as an advertising agency director, began to make money by predicting long-term trends. Her success underscored the importance of being able to anticipate what will be the next big thing with lasting impact. That's what happened with condominium conversions.

Real estate investors who spotted the potential of condominiums made money. But the joy is that people continue to make money in condo conversions, which are the quintessential example of a real estate investment that benefits everyone. In a well-executed conversion, the converter can generate generous cash-on-cash returns in a short period of time. The trend also lets tenants become homeowners, usually at about the same cost, more or less, as to continue as renters—and without the need to take home ownership responsibilities like yardwork and maintenance. In addition, conversions frequently create more affordable housing options in good neighborhoods.

Although conversions can be a tremendous investment vehicle, conversions must be approached carefully—just like any other Big Six purchase. You must carefully weigh your costs and expenses against your projected profit from the investment. You must do thorough number crunching when it comes to how much you should pay for the building you buy for conversion. And you must weigh in the possibility of an unsuccessful conversion, which leaves you with rental property to manage. But, if you do your homework, condo conversion remains a powerful instrument for making big profits in a relatively short period of time.

CHAPTER

14

One Good Investment Is Worth a Lifetime of Labor

Investing in commercial real estate can change your life. You can achieve greater wealth than you dreamed possible. But it's not going to happen overnight. Nor will it happen because of fate or luck or simply by being in the right place at the right time. It will happen because of your motivation, your knowledge, and your determination to succeed. If you understand and put into action the Big Six formula, adhering to the criteria and addressing each component step by step, your journey to attain financial independence is within reach.

This chapter spotlights the personal stories of six individuals, myself among them. One is an artist. The others are real estate brokers who discovered that the big money is in buying and selling, not in working for commissions; most of them spend their time today as investors. Each of these investors began the process by acquiring small properties, which was all they could afford. As time went on, they took part in bigger and bigger deals. Today they own several properties. In this chapter, each one tells their story.

The common factor? Each of them invested in one outstanding property that became valuable. Today they need not spend a lifetime working. Instead, they can use their time to do the things they enjoy and to take a more active role in community affairs.

You may be thinking that because five of the six stories involve people who are brokers, they have an advantage over those who are not brokers. This is not the case. Out of a total of two million real estate brokers and agents in the United States, it is estimated that only 5 percent have invested in real estate except for their own homes. Most real estate investors in the country are not brokers and, in many cases, have a better overview and feel for the market than brokers. These investors have no concern about the prices that properties have sold for in the past, whereas brokers do have this tendency.

Now let's read the six success stories.

The Shift
by Jeffrey Cohen

The shift from only brokering deals to principally being an investor was the best move in my real estate career.
—Jeffrey Cohen

Figure 14.1   Jeffrey Cohen's Building

Jeffrey Cohen is a successful real estate investor, developer, and broker as well as a real estate columnist and frequent real estate speaker. He heads up the commercial division at EWM, which is one of the largest real estate firms in South Florida, employing more than 150 real estate agents. During his career, Jeffrey has bought and sold more than $20 million worth of commercial properties for himself. As a broker, he has been involved in the sale and purchase of more than $300 million in real estate.

Growing up in Miami Beach in the late 1950s and early 1960s, I hung out with my dad, a general contractor who built, owned, and operated industrial properties. I learned a lot about the construction business and, after graduating from college, I worked for my dad for 15 years on the development of industrial properties.

In the early 1980s, I became a real estate broker and opened my own office focused on Miami Beach. Then I decided to shift my concentration to an area then known as Overtown (and now called Park West) surrounding the core of the city of Miami. In the early 1920s, this was a prestigious location with elegant high-quality structures, buildings with tall ceilings and many amenities. These buildings were clustered between Biscayne Bay and the railroad tracks within Shippers' Row, so called because businesses in the area supplied ships coming into the Port of Miami.

Over time, this elegant area deteriorated and many buildings were vacant and neglected. Still, there was something about Overtown that intrigued me. I had a strong feeling about the neighborhood's potential and believed it would get livelier and turn around.

In 1988, the $52.5 million Miami Arena, home to the new NBA franchise, the Miami Heat, had just gone up at the fringe of Overtown. The arena sat across from a Metrorail public transit stop, making it easily accessible for county residents. There were also rumblings about the development of a performing arts center just around the corner. Overtown's potential seemed clearer and clearer to me. That's when I came across two contiguous warehouse buildings that looked ideal for one of my clients. One was a two-story corner building with 12,000 square feet on the first floor and 3,500 square feet on the second floor. It was designed so trucks could pull right up. At this time, the building was being used to store merchandise for dollar stores. The look and feel of the space was spectacular. The other was a one-story structure with 6,500 square feet, also at truck level. The buildings had the same user-owner, and both were for sale.

When I showed these buildings to my client, I probably oversold the deal because of my tremendous enthusiasm and my sincere belief that this area was on the upswing and the properties would be worth a fortune one day. "If you don't buy this property, I will," I declared. I had never said that to any client. It was a little scary, but I meant it.

This marked the beginning of my shift from brokering deals to becoming an investor. My rationale was that if I could broker good deals and make others rich, why shouldn't I do it for myself?

It was at this point that I made a disclosure: I told the buildings' owner that I, personally, wanted to buy the properties directly from him. My offer of $565,000 for the two buildings included a 6 percent commission. The commission would help with the cash to close and was treated as a credit. Meanwhile, I was able to persuade the owner to hold a mortgage for $415,000 at 9 percent interest. Funds I had earned on a previous commission and credit from the commission on this property made the transaction possible.

We signed a sales contract and closed the deal on Oct. 16, 1998.

At the time, the City of Miami was trying to figure out how to stimulate activity in Overtown, and there was talk of turning it into a 24-hour nightclub district. My buildings were smack in the middle of the area that would be open around the clock.

Speculators started searching for buildings they could buy or lease and then convert into nightclubs. The action started to get more intense, and I became familiar with every property in the area. Soon after closing my deal, I got an offer for the smaller of my two buildings: $250,000 plus closing costs. I then arranged to refinance the remaining building for $500,000. I paid off the mortgage from the original owner of $415,000. That left me with the corner building and $335,000 in cash. I used this money to carry the building and make some necessary improvements, including a new roof and hurricane windows. I did the refinancing at an interest rate 0.5 percent over prime, to be adjusted in three years. My new payments were about $5,000 a month. These were later reduced when the interest was adjusted down to 4.5 percent.

As the city trumpeted its plan for nightclubs in the 24-hour district and the newspaper started reporting on the area, more and more interested parties came looking. The first nightclub to open was Space, just a few doors down from my building. It operated around the clock and attracted big crowds, prompting other entrepreneurs to get in on the action. Nightclubs started to spring up all over the neighborhood.

I leased my property to a nightclub operator who spent close to $1 million rehabilitating the building. The tenant paid me $12,000 a month in rent, more than enough to pay the mortgage. I had an excellent tenant who had made substantial improvements to my property; my instincts had led me correctly from the city of South Beach to downtown Miami. Meanwhile, a large developer was acquiring every parcel of Overtown real estate he could find. In 2005, I was offered $3.6 million for my building, an offer I couldn't refuse. I sold the building and did a 1031 tax-free exchange whereby I acquired an 80,000-square-foot multitenant industrial property for $3.8 million. After the acquisition, I did a bit of rehabilitation, changing the windows to impact-resistant glass, painting the building, and doing some renovations. Recently I turned down a purchase offer of $6.5 million for the property. This single building generates a substantial six-figure cash flow, which provides well for my family and allows me to be active in the community and to support worthy causes—something I was never able to do before.

I Came to New York
by Christine Marie

I am not a mogul, but real estate has been very good to me and has made it possible for me to have a prosperous and secure life.

—Christine Marie

Figure 14.2 Christine Marie's Building

Artist Christine Marie, born in Le Puy, France, moved to the United States in 1968. She studied at Pratt Graphics Center in New York. She exhibits and sells her art, which embraces surrealistic humor, in the United States, Europe, Japan, and South America. She has traveled throughout the world and resides in New York's Chelsea district.

I came to New York from Paris on August 1, 1968. I did not speak English, but I always wanted to know what America was really like. A friend of mine, an artist as am I, convinced me that the art world was waiting for us in New York. We came with just enough money to last three months. After two difficult years of little jobs as a coatroom attendant, babysitter, and private French teacher, I began to see some income from my work as an artist, and I rented a nice apartment near Washington Square.

In the early 1970s, small factories began moving out of Manhattan, looking for lower taxes, which left whole buildings empty. Many of these were huge lofts. Some investors bought these buildings and began selling them by units. I got one floor, approximately 1,900 square feet, at University Place in Greenwich Village for $8,000 cash, plus a $10,000 mortgage held by the owner because no bank was willing to give such a loan to an artist.

The building consisted of 10 floors. The one I bought was an old T-shirt silk-screen factory. The place was in terrible shape. Everything had to be cleaned up and scraped to the bone before the repairs could be done. All these buildings had a commercial status. To get a certificate of occupancy, which was a permit to reside there, everything had to be upgraded to the New York City residential code. The whole process took about four years, during which time I had to constantly pay assessments to repair the entire building, which was in bad shape. I think I spent another $25,000 for general repairs and fixing my own floor. I would say that the whole operation cost me around $60,000.

During the 1980s, lofts were very much in fashion, and a new crowd, the young Wall Street executives, began buying artists' lofts. I was selling mostly prints (etchings), and the print market was not strong. I realized that I had to find a new way to get extra income. Because prices in the loft market were high, I looked around to see how I could replace my loft with a property that could provide me with an income. By that time, my original mortgage of $10,000 had been paid off.

I started to look for a building where I could live and have one or two units to rent. It was difficult to find a building without rent control for under a million dollars. After visiting at least 35 buildings, I found one in Chelsea, an area that was not very fashionable then. In 1989, I sold the loft for $650,000 clear and then bought a building in Chelsea for $750,000. I took out a mortgage of $100,000 which, for an artist with no fixed income, was difficult to get.

The building was in good condition. Since 1989, I have done normal repair work on it and installed a new roof, new water heater, and new boiler (changing from oil to gas). I have painted the outside walls and done the usual maintenance and repairs.

The building is brick construction with four floors, two of which are rented. I occupy the first two floors with access to a beautiful garden. The upstairs consists of my bedroom and bath, and I have a beautifully lit studio with a fireplace. The ground floor has a sitting room, kitchen, another full bath, and a guest room. There is a full basement for storage. I get $5,000 monthly in rent and I spend about $1,500 a month to operate the building. I paid my mortgage in full about 10 years ago with money from my job and the rental income I collected.

Chelsea is now booming, and I can probably sell the building for around $3 million in today's market. Construction of new buildings and conversion of industrial property into apartments is everywhere. The neighborhood is better than ever. Whole Foods, Chelsea Market, and Garden of Eden are within walking distance. There is easy access to the promenade along the Hudson River, to 360 art galleries, and to the High Line elevated park, which is in a safe environment. In addition, there is almost no noise. In my garden, I feel like I'm in the country. The flowers burst in the spring; birds, squirrels, and other wildlife constantly amuse me. In the winter, the garden is often draped in pristine snow drifts. If I wanted to rent my own two-story apartment, I could get at least $5,500 a month for it. But I am so happy living here that, for now, I will stay.

I have had an apartment in Paris since 1960. I sold one and bought another, then sold that and bought yet another. Eventually I found one I really liked in a terrific neighborhood off the Rue de Rivoli. Sometimes I rent it, but I try to have it vacant for the summer months, which I spend in France. The monthly rent income is equivalent to about $1,500.

Since my move from France, I have become a U.S. citizen, and my English has improved dramatically. Although my friends have a little trouble distinguishing whether I am "hungry" or "angry," I can understand even the subtlest jokes. I am not a mogul, but real estate has made it possible for me to have a prosperous and secure life.

Love at First Sight
by Tony DeRosa

This building definitely put our company on the map. It has been a great investment and the building itself inspires us.

—Tony DeRosa

Figure 14.3 Tony DeRosa's Building

Tony DeRosa is the founder and president of WestVest Associates. Opened in 1993, WestVest Associates is one of the leading independently owned real estate firms in South Florida. It specializes in industrial and commercial real estate. Tony is an active investor, having acquired more than $40 million in commercial properties since 1990. His firm has been instrumental in the landscape of the Miami Airport West Industrial area with commercial real estate production in excess of over $500 million.

My story reads like a love story. It has similar joys and agonies. For 15 years, I had my eye on a building that was then called Overseas Tower. I refer to it as "she."

She was in a great location and had approximately 41,000 square feet, including 35,900 square feet of rentable space, on one-and-a-half acres with 116 parking spaces. She was designed by Arquitectonica, a cutting-edge Miami firm, in an area known as Airport West (but now part of the bustling newly incorporated city of Doral). I dreamed about putting my office there before I even had an office, before I ever had any money. Over the years, I called no less than 30 times to inquire about buying her. She was not for sale.

She was built in 1982 and was owned free and clear by an absentee owner, a Venezuelan. The main occupant was a bank with 18 percent of the space, complemented by many small suites ranging in size from 350 square feet to 1,500 square feet. That was a good configuration because it spread the risk. The building was managed—or, rather, mismanaged—by a family friend who was also the caretaker of the owner's wife, who lived in the United States. This friend rarely answered the phone; I can't imagine that she was there more than three days a week.

About seven or eight years ago, I intensified the calls. No dice. Then in November 2003, I got a phone call: The owner had died and his son wanted to sell off the assets. I vowed to make this deal no matter what.

The location was good, the building and design were great, and it was a buyer's dream in the upside department. It was only 30 percent occupied and the leases were short—at maximum, six months—or even nonexistent, with tenants renting month to month. The penthouse where I envisioned my office was still the original shell space. In 20 years, it had never been built out.

The asking price was $3 million. An attorney represented the offshore trust. I asked for a 30-day inspection with a 60-day closing. The attorney countered by insisting on a nonrefundable $350,000 deposit, a 3-day inspection period, and a 21-day closing. That's right: a three-day inspection! I had three days to go hard with no loan. In addition, I had to pay a commission to the manager. It made no sense to give her a commission, but I didn't care because the building was rented below the market with short leases. So I paid her $100,000.

I kept my eye on the ball. I stopped thinking how I could get a better deal, knowing that even $1 million *more* would have been good. I believed so strongly in the deal that I knew I'd find the money.

My immediate plan was to rent the spaces cheaply, from $16 to $22 per square foot, just to fill the building. This reflected an increase of $6 per square foot (times 35,900 total square feet) or an immediate annual increase of $215,400 in income. Not until recently did I realize that with just these increases, the building immediately became worth $6 million.

The big problem was getting the money for a mortgage. I went to International Bank of Miami, which was astute and realized the value of the deal. The bankers saw that the building was losing money, but they also saw my passion and realized the deal made business sense. I would take a floor there myself. The bank would work with me.

Originally, I had partners, but during the 20 days leading to the closing, I ended up doing the deal alone. I also worked with only one bank, and it gave me a tremendous deal: a fixed interest rate of 4.25 percent for the first year with an 80 percent loan-to-value ratio. That translated to a $2.4 million loan. In addition to the 80 percent loan-to-value, the bank agreed to a line of credit earn-out provision. Under that, once I reached a certain percent of occupancy, I would have a $400,000 secured line of credit against the building. This was amazing considering that it was a loan on a building with substantial negative cash flow.

The financing worked. We moved our company from a dingy windowless cave to the 5,400-square-foot penthouse with views of the whole city. We are so proud that the building is identified with us. For the past several years, we have hosted Christmas parties for more than 500 people under tents in the parking lot.

The rents keep increasing because the location is great. The money on this deal was made on the buy—the minute the ink was dry on the contract. She is the home of my company. The potential for upside has been realized.

I think of this building as a great romance. I dreamed about her for years. She is gorgeous and gets more beautiful with age as we continue to improve the building and the grounds. She's a keeper. I know she will take care of me in my old age. I am able to have peace of mind with steady income. She embodies everything in the Big Six.

If I Never Made Another Deal
by Cliff Suchman

The income on the investment is well over $1 million per year and has provided me and my extended family not only financial security but an exciting way of life.

—Cliff Suchman

Figure 14.4   Cliff Suchman's Building

Cliff Suchman has been a real estate broker and developer in South Florida since 1957. At one time, he and a partner operated the largest brokerage business in the area. For the past 25 years, he has been working primarily with his son, Larry, doing commercial brokerage, acquisition, and development of shopping centers. He is also active in Suchman Retail Group, specializing in land acquisition, sales, leasing, managing, and consulting.

If you pass the corner of U.S. 1 and SW 67th Avenue in south Dade County, Florida, you'll see a Tony Roma Restaurant. You'll also be at the intersection where I made my best real estate investment.

In 1969, I was 38 years old and struggling to buy a new house in a Miami-area neighborhood now known as Pinecrest. We needed a place for me, my wife, and four children, a mother-in-law, a niece, a collie, and a gerbil. It was that year when two major events took place. One was the birth of my daughter, Pam. The other was that a piece of property came to my attention through a friend.

That property was the old Palms Motel with 72 tired rooms, two swimming pools, a restaurant, and a cocktail lounge all spread across seven acres of land along the two-lane gravel road that would eventually be renamed as SW 67th Avenue. When I looked at the property, all I could see was its potential as an amazing location for an office building, shopping center, major hotel, or maybe even high-rise apartments. But that would be in the future. First I had to purchase it.

All of the property was zoned for commercial, motel, and/or apartment use. The owner was asking $675,000. Immediately, I felt that the land alone was worth more than that; I would be buying it for less than $100,000 per acre. This was an operating motel with a restaurant and cocktail lounge, and I could run the complex as a business, which would generate income to help me carry the mortgage I'd need. I met the asking price by borrowing $500,000 from a commercial bank with the help of several partners, although I owned about 36 percent of the deal and was the principal partner. I borrowed an additional $100,000 to spruce up the old motel, add four tennis courts in the rear, and start a tennis club. The Dadeland Inn was born.

In the meantime I got word that SW 67th Avenue was to be paved past our property. I met with the authorities and negotiated a $65,000 price for the additional right-of-way that they would need to extend the road to bridge Snapper Creek Canal at the end of the road, with other points south. I put in the Stage Door Deli, a 24-hour restaurant on U.S. 1 and unveiled the Checkmate Lounge, a popular jazz spot with name entertainers including Joe Williams and Ahmad Jamal. One partner ran the cocktail lounge and another, my jack-of-all-trades brother-in-law Marty Shane, managed the restaurant. He was proud of his eggs Benedict and his tuna salad. His nephew was assistant manager. We were having a ball, and we were paying the mortgage.

One of the greatest assets that I inherited with this property was Pete Roberts, the manager of the motel. Pete came to be my comptroller and trusted employee for the next 38 years. He retired at the end of 2007.

This rhythm went on for about five years, when it became apparent that the motel was obsolete and it was time to change course. I borrowed $750,000 and built the Dadeland North Shopping Center. Tony Roma (the old man himself) came along and wanted a long-term lease on corner where the Checkmate Lounge sat to build only the second restaurant in what would become his huge national chain. He offered us $40,000 per year. Ten years later, he exercised an option to purchase the half-acre corner for $600,000. We also sold off the back two acres, where a mini storage facility now stands, for $1.25 million. Our entire investment had been returned to us.

Canton Chinese Restaurant was our first tenant in the shopping center, and it is still there more than 30 years later. Owners Alan and Betty Ng are good friends of the Suchman Family, and we have done very well together.

About 17 years ago, I sold a parcel of property near the Florida Turnpike. Some of the cash from that sale could be reinvested in a tax-free exchange, so I offered $1.5 million to buy out a 36 percent partner in the shopping center project. He quickly accepted and later called it the best deal he ever made. It was the second best deal I ever made. The first was the original purchase of this gem of a property.

I now had 72 percent ownership in one of the area's best shopping centers. A good mix of tenants combined with a prime location and good management has increased the rent roll from $6 per square foot to more than $35 per square foot over the years.

We have been offered many millions of dollars for this center, but it is the golden goose that keeps on giving. I am not in any particular hurry to sell this special piece of real estate, which has given my family the ability to live a very comfortable way of life and the opportunity to give back to the community.

You Can Never Know Too Much

by Anthony Dilweg and Andy Roberts

*We are information junkies who diligently watch neighborhood
shifts and trends. That's how we found The Power Building.*
—Anthony Dilweg and Andy Roberts

Figure 14.5 Dilweg and Roberts's Building

Anthony Dilweg is CEO of the Dilweg Companies, LLC, one of the most respected
commercial real estate firms in the Southeast. Anthony founded the firm in 1999,
and it now has a portfolio worth nearly $300 million. In December 1999, Andy
Roberts joined the company as a leasing agent. He rose to the position of director
of office acquisition. His expertise and keen sense for value is demonstrated by the
success realized in the acquisition of The Power Building.

In 2002, The Power Building was a 500,000-square-foot office complex occupying five-and-a-quarter acres—an entire city block—in the Central Business District of Charlotte, NC. The property was occupied entirely by Duke Power Company, which had built it in 1925 and was a mainstay of the Charlotte economy. Duke Power sold the building to State Farm Insurance in 1978, but remained in the complex as a tenant. The building sits adjacent to Duke's corporate headquarters.

In late 2002, State Farm made a strategic corporate decision to divest all its commercial real estate holdings in the country. That included The Power Building. State Farm and its brokerage company, CB Richard Ellis, agreed to let the market dictate the sale price, but there was a general belief that the building could sell in the $18 million to $20 million range.

We look for properties with three characteristics: They are available below replacement cost, they are in "A" locations, and their sellers are motivated. The Power Building was certainly available below replacement cost. And since State Farm wanted to divest its real estate assets by year-end, the seller was motivated. But there were still challenges connected to the acquisition.

Three or four years earlier it had become obvious that the area where the building sat was on the verge of significant change. Our goal was to act quickly to pick up properties ahead of the change. But there was no certainty that it would be as massive and complete as it ended up being. In fact, there were rumors of corporate relocations *out* of the center city, doubts about continued residential growth, and widespread derision of proposed public projects, including light rail, a park, and a baseball stadium.

We began researching scores of old articles in *The Charlotte Observer*, *The Charlotte Business Journal*, even *Creative Loafing*, and other local publications. We looked at what the city's movers and shakers were saying about the area, to whom the messages were addressed, and who would benefit. Then we delved into neighborhood minutiae.

We mapped every parcel of land within a nine-block radius of The Power Building, building a dossier that included the properties' ownership, acquisition date and price, zoning, and building setback requirements. We studied Charlotte zoning codes to see what could be built near The Power Building, recorded all construction—residential, commercial, and governmental—and the profile of the prospective tenants for those projects. We met with architects, contractors, city planners, and civic booster groups to measure the likelihood of these proposed projects coming to fruition.

We also contacted the owners of all parcels adjacent to The Power Building to see what their plans were and, specifically, to find out if they were thinking about selling. We spoke with the Charlotte Transit Authority to understand the funding schedule for the proposed light-rail station earmarked for the business district. We checked the big employers in the neighborhood and researched the remaining lease terms on their buildings. And we met with the Johnson & Wales University Culinary School to estimate growth of the student population and sites suitable for new student housing.

We concluded that the business district was going to continue its transformation. We moved quickly to buy the building with an eye on quickly reselling it at significant profit. But there was still an important unknown. Would Duke Power remain a tenant in the building, or would it vacate the property when its lease came up for renewal? Each possibility had completely divergent upside potential.

Duke's rents were the lowest in the entire neighborhood, and it had a lease that called for five-year renewal periods with rental rates about 80 percent below market. We weren't interested in having Duke renew the lease under those terms. But it would be costly for the utility to move its operations.

It turns out that even though Duke's rent was low, it also paid all operating expenses and all repair and replacement costs for maintenance in the old building. And Duke could manage with 60 or 70 percent *less* space if moved to a newer, more efficient building.

We went forward with our plan to buy The Power Building in hopes that Duke would vacate the property and we could sell it to the developer of an entire city block. That's when we discovered that the 75-year-old office complex came with environmental contamination. No one had taken any extraordinary efforts to quantify the extent of the contamination and the cost of its remediation. We called for core drilling of soils to test for possible groundwater contamination, a complete inspection of all built structures to search and test for asbestos and other contaminants, and two separate estimates for removing contaminants, dismantling or demolishing the building, and sending all contaminated components to an acceptable landfill.

Demolition and remediation costs turned out to be at least triple those originally anticipated. But, after discussion, the seller agreed to cut the sales price. We bought The Power Building for $7.9 million in April 2004. Duke's lease expired two years later and we sold the building to a high-rise condo developer, Novare in Atlanta, for $17 million.

I Made It in Buying
by Kenneth D. Rosen

The Kendar building has weathered several downturns since I bought it, leading me to believe that Class B buildings in "A" locations are recession-proof.

—Kenneth D. Rosen

Figure 14.6   The Kendar Building

For many years, I was obsessed with a stately building on a triangular island of land surrounded by tree-lined streets. I wanted to own it. But by the time I learned that it had gone on sale for $3.3 million, the owners had changed their minds and withdrawn it from the market.

So I tracked down the broker and asked: "Would the owners still sell the building?" The owners said they would, but now the price was $3.7 million! Still, I wanted it. I planned to move my company, Kendar Realty, Inc., into the building, and I could envision a beautiful sign with the name "Kendar" on its facade.

The owners were very rigid with the price of $3.7 million and adamantly stated that they would not take a penny less—a statement that I had often heard and paid no attention to. After back-and-forth negotiations, we settled on a price of $3.6 million, or $300,000 more than the original price. Even though I thought it was too much money, I knew deep down that this building would become a winner, so I signed a contract to buy the property.

One of the redeeming features of the deal was that I could close the deal with less than 15 percent down ($500,000) and assume an existing $2.7 million mortgage held by an insurance company. The owners agreed to hold the remaining $400,000 in the form of a second mortgage at 8 percent interest, payable interest-only monthly, with a balloon payment due at the end of five years. My contract provided a contingency for a 30-day due diligence, during which time I thoroughly checked the property and assembled all the pertinent information.

Without knowing it, I was instinctively following the formula of the Big Six, which I didn't develop until years later. It was in an "A" location just two miles from Dadeland Mall, one of the five highest-grossing shopping malls per square foot in the country. The median income of residents in that neighborhood was very high, and there were many good services, including a public transit high-speed elevated train system within walking distance. The building was well constructed by an established contracting firm, and its architecture was striking. It was a strong Class B building in good condition.

The mix of tenants was excellent and consisted of attorneys, CPAs, mortgage brokers, real estate brokers, insurance agents, and therapists. The offices ran from 300 rentable square feet (RSF) to 2,500 RSF, with the average rent at $11 per RSF, which was substantially under the market rate. Most of the leases ran for three years with options to renew at the then-market rate. That meant there was upside. I projected the rate in three years to be $15 per RSF, which would increase the bottom line by $174,400 (43,600 RSF × $4 per RSF increase equals $174,400). Based on a 10 percent return, which was the norm at the time, the value of the building would increase by $1.744 million.

The financing terms were excellent, because I was going into the deal with less than 15 percent cash down and an assumable mortgage. If I'd had to obtain a new mortgage, it would have cost me about $75,000, including financing fees and closing costs. Still, the price I had to pay was a thorny point. But after I got into the due diligence and found out that the rents were below the market rates, I began to change my mind.

I closed the deal thirty days after my due diligence, and moved my firm into the new Kendar Office Building. It had about a 95 percent occupancy rate, which was the norm at that time.

Five years later, in 1986, the value of the building was $4.5 million and I was able, under the future advance clause, to increase the first mortgage held by the insurance company from its existing balance of $2.5 million to $3.4 million. I used the $900,000 cash proceeds to pay off the balloon second mortgage of $400,000, which had become due at this time, and I used the remaining money to pay myself back my initial cash investment of $500,000. That meant that I now had only one mortgage (held by the insurance company) in the amount of $3.4 million and I had no cash in the deal. Every penny of cash flow from that point on represented an infinity return. Furthermore, the $900,000 proceeds from refinancing were tax free since refinancing proceeds are not taxable until such time that the building is sold.

Fast forward to 1996 when I had to obtain a new $1.6 million second mortgage from a private party at 10 percent interest, payable interest-only, in order to pay off some debts incurred in connection with a previous investment. When I added that to the existing first mortgage, which had now been reduced to $2.3 million, my total mortgage debt on the Kendar building was around $3.9 million. In 1998, the balance of the insurance company mortgage was down to $2 million, but the private-party second mortgage was still $1.6 million. I refinanced again with a local bank for $3.975 million at 8 percent interest, which was the market rate at the time. The mortgage was based on a 25-year amortization period with a 10-year balloon maturing in December 2008. It provided for prepayment at any time without penalty.

The total cost to get this mortgage was $100,000, including paying the bank points, attorney's fees, appraisal and engineering fees, and other closing costs. After I paid off the existing first and second mortgages, I was left with $275,000. I put this money in the bank for future capital improvements.

In 2000, interest rates fell into the 6 to 7 percent range. I called the senior loan officer at the bank and asked that my rate be reduced from 8 percent to 6.5 percent. Never before had a lender ever reduced my interest rate, but the bank surprised me: It cut the rate to 7.25 percent. A year later, I asked for a rate reduction to 6 percent and, again, the bank shocked me by agreeing to cut it to 6.75 percent. That brought my mortgage payments down by $47,000 per year, which meant that my cash flow increased $47,000 per year. That raised the value of the property by $550,000. The amazing thing is that for each reduction, it cost me only $5,000. So I was able to recoup my $10,000 investment in a little over two and a half months.

As this was happening, new retail establishments—including the Shoppes at Sunset Place, featuring an AMC24 movie theater; the 12-story Plaza San Remo office condominium with a 42,000-square-foot Whole Foods supermarket on the first floor; and the Village of Merrick Park, a collection of high-end stores including Neiman Marcus, Nordstrom, and Tiffany & Co.—appeared nearby.

There is no vacant land left in the area and, since 1981, there has been only one rental office building constructed in the vicinity of the Kendar building. As a result, the demand for office rentals far exceeds the supply, and the Kendar building has been virtually 100 percent occupied during the past five years. I had employed several managers who worked under my supervision but, a year ago, I hired a professional management firm, Mazzei Realty Services, Inc., to manage and handle leasing of the Kendar building on-site. Mazzei has reduced the expenses and increased the income, more than offsetting the fees and commissions it charges. Tenant satisfaction has never been higher and, even though I am in the office every day and involved in the major decisions of the building, it has freed me to pursue other interests, including writing this book.

This building has paid off handsomely. Today it is worth about $13 million. The principal balance of my mortgage is $3.4 million, so I have a very good equity in the property. My annual cash flow is in the substantial six-figure range and increasing each year.

In December 2008, the mortgage will become due and payable in full to the bank. I'm in the process of extending and modifying this loan with the bank for an additional 10 years and reducing the interest rate from 6.75 percent to 5.75 percent. This represents a savings of $34,000 per year in interest—once again increasing the value of the property.

Right from the start, the Kendar building had all the elements of the Big Six. The building is part of my very fabric and soul. Like a good marriage, it continues to get better and better.

The Bottom Line

Prior to 1981, I had had a successful career in the Miami area buying and selling small residential properties, then by buying and selling commercial properties, and then as a condo converter. That's when, with a truckload of cash from conversions, I bought three choice properties.

One was the Nichols Apartments, a 40-year-old oceanfront apartment building in the upscale Bal Harbour neighborhood, which I later sold at a substantial seven-figure net profit to developers who demolished the building and constructed a high-rise condominium complex. The next property I bought was Kings Bay Yacht and Country Club, built in the 1940s, which we renamed Deering Bay. It was a sexy and enticing property that appealed to my ego. This prestigious landmark had 10,000 feet of frontage on Biscayne Bay and was situated in a top location in the southern section of Dade County. It comprised 209 acres with spectacular views of Biscayne Bay including an 18-hole golf course (later redesigned by Arnold Palmer), a clubhouse, and a hotel. The plan was to build a 186-unit condominium community on the property.

My only involvement in condominiums had been the conversion of existing buildings, so I knew nothing about development and construction. Because I knew I couldn't handle a deal of the scope of Deering Bay, I brought in well-known partners with a good deal of experience in developing residential communities. For a number of reasons, the project was not successful, and it was sold to a large development company at a substantial loss in the mid-1990s. This turned out to be the worst investment of my career. But I learned two lessons: Never let my ego override my business sense, and never stray from my area of expertise, which was buying existing income properties. They were expensive lessons to learn, but they proved valuable to me in the future.

The success of the Kendar building has brought me financial independence and permits me to continue looking for good real estate deals. It has also given me more time to spend with my wife and family as well as do more sailing, study Spanish, and travel. And this one special investment has given me the opportunity to involve myself in community activities. I was a volunteer guardian ad litem for abused, neglected, and abandoned children for seven years. For the past 10 years I have been a volunteer skipper for Shake-A-Leg of Miami, an organization that teaches disabled children how to sail and helps them learn about marine biology and environmental sciences. I was one of the founders of the Jerome Bain Real Estate Institute at Florida International University and serve on its advisory board.

Besides my volunteer work, I have been able to make financial contributions to these wonderful organizations. The sense of gratification from being able to help those less fortunate than myself has been one of the highlights of my life.

When people ask me how I made my money, I tell them: "Follow the Big Six. And remember, you make your money in buying!"

Glossary

A

Abstract of title – A historical summary of all official records and recorded documents related to the title of a parcel of real estate.

Adjustable-rate mortgage (ARM) – A mortgage loan that allows the interest rate to be changed at specific intervals over the maturity of the loan.

Ad valorem tax – Real estate taxes on the assessed value of a property.

Amortization – A gradual paying off of a debt by periodic installments.

Amortized loan – Any loan with at least some payments to principal.

Anchor tenant – The main tenant in a shopping center.

Appraisal – A professional estimate of the value of a property.

Appreciation – The increase in the value of a property.

Assumable mortgage loan – A mortgage loan that allows a new purchaser to take on the loan obligation with no change in loan terms.

B

Balloon mortgage – A mortgage with monthly payments that amortize over a stated term but that provides for a lump-sum payment to be due at the end of an earlier specified term.

Base (expense) year – A lease condition whereby the landlord agrees to pay all expenses based on the expenses for a base year, typically the first year of the lease. The tenants pay their proportionate share of the increases in expenses for the subsequent years.

Blanket mortgage – A single mortgage that covers more than one parcel of real estate.

BOMA – Building Owners and Managers Association.

Bridge loan – Short-term financing between the termination of the one loan and the beginning of another loan.

C

Capitalization rate – A rate of return used to determine the value of an income stream. The net operating income divided by the capitalization rate equals the value.

Cash flow – The sum of money remaining after deducting the operating expenses and debt service from gross income.

Cash-on-cash return – That return calculated by dividing the cash flow by the cash investment.

Cash purchase – The same as "all cash," meaning that the real estate investor buys the property without getting outside financing.

Closing – The legal act of transferring the ownership of a property from a seller to a buyer in accordance with a purchase and sale agreement.

Closing costs – The fees associated with the sale of a property. These include commissions, title insurance fees, appraisal fees, attorney's fees, documentary stamps, recording costs, and points and bank closing costs if new financing is obtained.

Condominium conversion – The change in the legal form of ownership from a rental building property with a single ownership entity to a condominium where units are individually owned.

Condominium reversion – A rental building that was converted to a condominium building and then converted back to a rental building. This generally happens when few or no condominium units are sold.

Conduit loan – A loan that is pooled with other loans and serves as collateral for bonds sold to investors.

Consumer price index (CPI) – A government measurement of how inflation affects consumer buying power.

Counselor of Real Estate (CRE) – A member of the American Society of Real Estate Counselors (ASREC). Membership is based on competence, experience, and professional conduct.

D

Debt service coverage ratio (DSC) – The relationship between net operating income (NOI) and annual debt service (ADS).

Deed – A legal document conveying title to a property.

Deed of trust – An instrument used in many states in lieu of a mortgage. Legal title to the property is vested in one or more trustees to secure the repayment of the loan.

Depreciation – Allocating the cost of an asset over its estimated useful life.

Due-on-sale clause – A provision in a mortgage that states the loan is due on the sale of the property.

Due diligence contingency – A clause contained in a sales contract giving the buyer the opportunity to evaluate all aspects of a property. If the buyer is dissatisfied with anything, the buyer can cancel the contract, and he or she is entitled to a refund of all deposits made.

E

Earnest money – A deposit made by a purchaser of real estate to evidence good faith.

Easement – The right, privilege, or interest that one party has in the land of another.

Eminent domain – The right of the government or a public utility to acquire property for necessary public use by condemnation; the owner must be fairly compensated.

Environmental audit – A study of the property and its area to determine whether there are any hazards.

Equity buildup – The gradual increase in a mortgagor's equity in a property caused by amortization of loan principal.

Exclusive right of sale – A contract given to only one broker to sell a property, with the right to collect a commission if the property is sold by anyone, including the owner, during the term of the contract.

Exculpatory clause – A provision in a mortgage allowing the borrower to surrender the property to the lender without personal liability for the loan.

F

Finder's fee – Money paid to someone other than a broker who locates suitable property or a purchaser. It is prohibited or restricted in most states.

Fixed-rate mortgage – A real estate loan featuring an interest rate that is constant for the term of the loan.

Flex space – Space in industrial building that can be apportioned in variable amounts to offices, research laboratories, or industrial purposes.

Floor rate – The minimum rate of interest charged on an adjustable-rate mortgage.

FSBO – Pronounced "fizz-bo." It stands for "for sale by owner" and means a real estate broker does not list the property.

G

General warranty deed – A deed in which the grantor agrees to protect the grantee against any other claim to title of the property and provides other promises.

Gift deed – A deed for which consideration is love and affection. No material consideration is involved.

Good and marketable title – Title to a piece of real estate that can be shown, usually by title search of an abstract of title, to be vested in the owner of record and free of any claims or liens.

Grandfather clause – A provision in a law that ensures that the law is not retroactive; what was legal under the previous law remains legal.

Gross lease – A property on which the landlord pays all operating expenses.

H

Home equity loan – A mortgage loan, which is usually in a subordinate position, that allows the borrower to obtain multiple advances of the loan proceeds at his or her own discretion, up to an amount that represents a specified percentage of the borrower's equity in a property.

Hybrid mortgage – A mortgage with elements of both a fixed-rate mortgage and an adjustable-rate mortgage.

I

Indexed loan – A loan in which the term, payment, interest rate, or principal amount may be adjusted periodically according to a specific index. The index and the manner of adjustment are generally stated in the loan contract.

Infinity return – A rate of return that is so great that it is immeasurable.

Installment sale – When a seller accepts a mortgage for part of the sale, the tax on the gain is paid as the mortgage principal is collected.

Institutional lenders – Prime sources of real estate loans such as banks, life insurance companies, pension funds, corporations, and investment banks as opposed to private party lenders.

Interest-only mortgage – A loan in which interest is payable at regular intervals until loan maturity, when the full loan balance is due. It does not require amortization.

J

Joint venture – An agreement between two or more parties who invest in a property.

L

Land banking – The activity of purchasing land that is not presently needed for a use.

Leasehold mortgage – A lien on the tenant's interest in real estate.

Leasehold value – The value of a tenant's interest in a lease, especially when the rent is below market and the lease has a long remaining term.

Lease with option to purchase – A lease that gives the tenant the right to purchase the property at an agreed-on price under certain conditions.

Letter of credit – An arrangement, with specified conditions, whereby a bank agrees to substitute its credit for a customer's credit.

Letter of intent – The expression of a desire to enter into a contract without actually doing so.

Leverage – Use of borrowed funds to increase purchasing power and, ideally, to increase the profitability of an investment.

Libor – London InterBank Offered Rate. Banks often use this as an index for adjustable rate mortgages.

Limited liability company (LLC) – An entity recognized in many states that may be treated as a partnership for federal tax purposes and whose members (partners) have no personal liability.

Listing broker – One who has been authorized by a principal to sell or lease a property.

Loan-to-value (LTV) ratio – The portion of the amount borrowed compared to the cost or value of the property purchased. It is equivalent to mortgage debt divided by the value of the property.

Lock-in period – The period during which a loan cannot be prepaid.

Long-term capital gain – For income tax purposes, the gain on a capital asset held long enough to qualify for special tax considerations.

M

Member of the Appraisal Institute (MAI) – A professional designation conferred by the Appraisal Institute to someone who has passed several written proficiency examinations and has performed acceptable appraisal work for a specific period of time.

Mezzanine financing – A loan that is below the first mortgage in priority and has other liens subordinate to it. It has the same priority as if it were called a second mortgage.

Mortgage commitment fee – A deposit made to a lender towards the fees charged by a lender at closing.

Mortgagee – One who holds a lien on property or title to property as security for a debt.

Mortgagor – The owner of real estate financed with a mortgage; someone who pledges property as security for a loan.

Multiple Listing Service (MLS) – A single network through which real estate brokers share property listings with each other.

N

National Association of Realtors (NAR) – An organization of Realtors devoted to encouraging professionalism in real estate activities.

Negative amortization mortgage – An increase in the outstanding balance of a loan resulting from the failure of periodic debt service payments to cover required interest charged on the loan.

Negative cash flow – Situation in which a property owner must make an outlay of funds to operate a property.

Net income – The amount of money remaining after subtracting operating expenses from the gross rental income.

Net lease – A lease whereby, in addition to the rent stipulated, the lessees (tenants) pay their pro rata share of operating expenses of the property.

Net operating income (NOI) – Income from property after operating expenses have been deducted, but before deducting mortgage payments.

Net worth – Total assets less total liabilities.

Nonrecourse – No personal liability. Lenders may take the property pledged as collateral to satisfy a debt, but have no recourse to other assets of the borrower.

O

Open-end mortgage – A mortgage under which the borrower may secure additional funds from the lender, usually stipulating a ceiling amount that can be borrowed. Also known as a future advance clause in a mortgage.

Operating expenses – The costs to operate a property, such as property taxes, utilities, insurance, janitorial, repairs and maintenance, and the like. Mortgage payments and depreciation are not operating expenses.

Optionee – One who receives or purchases an option.

Optionor – One who gives or sells an option.

Option to purchase – A contract that gives one the right (but *not* the obligation) to buy a property within a certain time, for a specified amount, and subject to specified conditions.

P

Phase I environmental site assessment – A preliminary examination of a site to determine the potential for a contamination. The assessment includes a review of present and historical land uses and preliminary tests of suspect areas. A Phase I study is required to support a claim to be an innocent purchaser.

Phase II environmental site assessment – A field investigation, undertaken when results of a Phase I reflect a possible hazardous substance, to confirm the presence of contamination and estimate the cost of remediation.

Phase III environmental site assessment – A study that enumerates the steps in remediation and followup procedures.

Points – Fees paid to induce lenders to make a mortgage loan. Each point equals 1 percent of the loan principal. Points have the effect of reducing the amount of money advanced by the lender, thereby increasing the lender's effective interest rate.

Prepayment penalty – Fees paid by borrowers for the privilege of retiring a loan early.

Pretax income – The net income before deducting income taxes.

Prime rate – The lowest commercial interest rate charged by banks on short-term loans to their most creditworthy customers.

Purchase money mortgage – Mortgage given by a buyer to a seller in partial payment of the purchase price of real estate.

R

Rate of return – Ratio of net operating income (net income) to purchase price as if the property were purchased for all cash; if the purchase is financed, it is the ratio of cash flow to cash invested.

Real estate investment trust (REIT) – A real estate mutual fund created through income tax laws in order to circumvent corporate income taxes. A REIT sells shares of ownership and is required to invest in real estate or mortgages.

Realtor – A real estate professional who subscribes to a strict code of ethics as a member of the local and state associations and of the National Association of Realtors.

Release clause – A clause in a mortgage that gives the owner the privilege of paying off a portion of the mortgage, thus freeing a portion of the property from the mortgage.

Rentable square feet (RSF) – A method of calculation usually applied to suites in an office building. It is the measurement of the interior space of an office suite (usable square feet) plus the tenant's pro rata share of the total common area square footage. (Common area square footage does not include stairwells and elevator shafts.)

Reverse leverage – A situation in which financial benefits from ownership accrue at a lower rate than the mortgage interest rate.

Right of first refusal – The opportunity of a party to match the price and terms of a proposed purchase and sales agreement before the agreement is executed.

S

Sale leaseback – A technique whereby an owner sells a building and then leases it back as a tenant from the new owner.

Section 1031 exchange – The section of the internal revenue code that deals with tax-deferred exchanges of certain property.

Segregated cost depreciation – A method that identifies and reclassifies personal property assets to shorten the depreciation time for taxation purposes. It has the impact of reducing current income tax obligations.

Self-amortizing mortgage – A mortgage that will retire itself through regular principal and interest payments.

Seller financing – A sale where the seller holds a mortgage for part of the purchase price.

Selling broker – The broker that sells the property to a buyer.

Special-purpose property – A building with limited uses and marketability, such as a church, theater, school, or public utility.

Stagflation – A term coined in the 1970s to describe a sluggish economic condition accompanied by inflation.

Subordination clause – A clause that allows a mortgage recorded in the future to take priority over an existing mortgage.

Subprime loan – A loan with onerous terms made to a borrower with a poor credit history.

T

Taking – Acquisition of real estate through condemnation.

Tax roll – The list of all properties subject to a tax in a county or other property taxing jurisdiction. It identifies all properties and indicates their assessed values.

Tax shelter – An investment that produces after-tax income that is greater than before-tax income.

Time value of money – A concept that money available today is worth more than the same amount in the future because of its potential earning capacity.

Title insurance – An insurance policy that protects the holder from loss sustained by defects in the title.

Treasury bill rate – The rate of interest paid by the U.S. Government on a debt obligation and backed by its full faith and credit with a maturity date of one year or less.

U

Unimproved property – Vacant land.

Unsecured loan – A loan that is made by a lender to a borrower without collateral.

W

Wraparound mortgage – A mortgage that includes in its balance a preexisting mortgage.

About the Author

Kenneth D. Rosen is a successful real estate investor, a condo conversion pioneer, a prominent member of the South Florida real estate industry, and a civic activist.

During the past 30 years, Ken, who is the founder and president of Kendar Realty, Inc., has bought and sold $300 million worth of investment property, including office buildings, apartment complexes, industrial buildings, and land.

From the mid-1970s through the mid-1980s, he stepped into what then was uncharted territory: the conversion of rental apartments to condominiums. He converted 1,700 units in 22 apartment complexes to become the state of Florida's leader in that area. He is the author of *Condominium Conversions: Ken Rosen's Success Formula for Big Profits.*

Ken served two terms as president of the Realtor Association of Greater Miami and the Beaches and is the recipient of several awards, including "Realtor of the Year." In 2003, the Florida Association of Realtors named him a "Hometown Hero" for his volunteer work as a guardian ad litem for neglected, abused, and abandoned children. He was the driving force behind the formation of the Jerome Bain Real Estate Institute at Florida International University.

In his spare time, Ken sails and is a volunteer skipper with Shake-a Leg of Miami, an organization through which children with disabilities can learn to sail on Biscayne Bay.

He is a graduate of Boston University, a 32nd degree Mason, past master of his Masonic Lodge, and a Shriner. He is a member of Temple Israel and serves on its advisory board. Ken is married to Ellen Kempler and has seven children and five grandchildren.

Index